READER'S DIGEST

**all-season guide
to gardening**

early spring

READER'S DIGEST

all-season guide to gardening

early spring

PUBLISHED BY
THE READER'S DIGEST ASSOCIATION LIMITED
LONDON • NEW YORK • SYDNEY • MONTREAL

contents

foreword

The *All-Season Guide to Gardening* provides a complete practical and inspirational guide to making the most of your garden season-by-season, with year-round detailed information to help you plan, plant and enjoy the garden of your dreams. Each of the volumes is presented in four key sections:

inspirations offers a source of design and planting ideas taken from contemporary and traditional gardens photographed during the season. The plants featured have been identified to enable you to re-create or adapt the ideas to your own garden scheme.

practical diary is a guide to the most important tasks to be done in the garden at this time of year. The information is divided into subject areas – such as Perennials, Climbers, or Patios & Containers – that reflect particular gardening interests. The headings appear in the same order in every volume in the series, so you can easily find the information you need. Under each heading is a list of the season's main tasks. The most important jobs are then explained in more detail, with step-by-step photographs and expert tips. The Healthy Garden, at the end of the section, is a full checklist of priority seasonal tasks for the whole garden. Since many jobs require follow-up attention in a later season, a 'Looking

useful terms

alpine Although this strictly refers to a mountain plant that grows naturally in free-draining soil at high altitude, the term is used by gardeners to mean any plant suitable for growing in a rock garden.

annual A plant that grows, flowers, sets seed and dies in one growing season.

anther The part of the flower that produces pollen.

aquatic plant In its widest sense, this can mean any water plant, but usually refers to plants such as water lilies that grow in deeper water, rooted in the bottom of the pond or in special baskets.

bareroot This refers to plants, usually trees and shrubs, that have been dug up and supplied to the customer without any soil on their roots. Roses are often supplied in this way.

bedding (plant) A plant used outdoors for temporary or seasonal display, often as part of a planned 'bedding scheme'.

biennial A plant that completes its life cycle in two growing seasons.

biological control The treatment or prevention of pests, diseases or weeds by natural, rather than chemical, methods, usually involving a naturally occurring parasite or predator.

cloche A glass or plastic cover used to shelter plants from cold or windy weather. Cloches are available as separate units or in tunnel form, often called 'continuous cloches'.

coldframe A low, unheated structure with a transparent top, in which plants can be grown in protected conditions.

cordon A plant restricted by pruning and training to a single, unbranching stem. Examples include apples, tomatoes and sweet peas grown on canes.

corm The swollen stem base of plants like crocuses and gladioli, where food is stored during winter. A new corm forms each year on top of the shrivelled remains of last year's.

cultivar A distinct, named plant variety that has originated in cultivation, rather than in the wild. Cultivars are often simply (but incorrectly) called 'varieties'.

deadhead To cut off the spent flowers.

die-back The result of attack by a fungal disease, which causes shoots or branches to die back from their tips.

direct sow To sow seeds in the ground where the plants are to grow, rather than starting them indoors or in a temporary seedbed for later transplanting.

drill A furrow or channel made in the soil at the correct depth for sowing seeds.

ericaceous Any plant belonging to the erica or heather family, for example pieris and rhododendrons. Also refers to the acid conditions these plants like and the special lime-free compost in which they are potted.

espalier A tree such as an apple or cotoneaster that is pruned and trained as a single upright trunk, with side branches extending horizontally to form symmetrical layers or 'tiers'.

foliar feed Liquid fertiliser sprayed or watered on the leaves of plants, usually applied for rapid results or when plants are not actively absorbing nutrients through their roots (after injury or in cold weather, for example).

glyphosate A chemical weedkiller that is absorbed through leaves and moves through the plant so that all parts, including roots, are killed (see systemic).

habitat The natural home of a plant growing in the wild. Not to be confused with habit, which is the typical form or shape of a plant.

harden off To gradually acclimatise a plant previously grown indoors to unprotected conditions outside in the garden.

hardwood cutting A piece of this year's shoot taken for propagation from a shrub, tree or climber during the autumn, when their stems are hard and ripe.

heel A small strip of bark torn from the main stem when a sideshoot is pulled off to make a (heel) cutting.

heel in To bury the roots of a plant in a temporary hole or trench when it is not to be planted immediately.

humus The dark, water-retentive component of soil that results from the decay of organic material.

in situ Literally, in position, or where plants are to grow permanently.

internodal cutting A cutting that is trimmed midway between two leaf-joints, rather than immediately below the leaves.

layering A method of propagation in which a shoot is rooted while still attached to the

ahead' feature indicates when you will find details of follow-up action in another volume.

plant selector is a directory of the plants which are at their best at this time of year, as selected by our gardening experts. Within each subject grouping the plants are arranged by colour, and within each colour sequence they are generally listed alphabetically by botanical name. Each plant is shown in a photograph, with information supplied including the plant's common name, size, site and soil preferences, best uses, general care and suggestions for good companions. Each plant is also given a 'hardiness' rating:

● 'Hardy' plants can be grown outdoors in all parts of the British Isles.

● Plants rated 'not fully hardy' can be grown outdoors in milder parts of the British Isles but elsewhere will need some protection in winter.

● 'Half-hardy' plants can withstand temperatures down to 0°C (32°F). They are often grown outdoors in summer displays, but propagated and kept under glass between autumn and late spring.

● 'Tender' plants require protection under glass for all or part of the year.

At the end of the section, there are lists of the plants best suited to different garden conditions and soil types.

garden projects offers ideas and instructions for garden improvements, ranging from building a patio, pergola or raised bed to designing and planting up a new border or pond. Major DIY projects are illustrated with step-by-step photographs and all the projects are within the capabilities of a fit, practical person. Although some projects are specific to a season, many of them can also be undertaken at other times of year.

---

parent plant. Rooting a branch where it touches the ground is called simple layering, while serpentine layering involves rooting a long flexible stem in several places; long stems can be tip layered by burying their growing tips.

loam A type of soil that contains a balanced mixture of sand, clay and organic material.

marginal plant A waterside plant that is grown at the edge of the pond, either in shallow water or on the bank.

mulch Any material used to cover and protect the soil surface. Organic mulches include straw, manure and lawn mowings, while polythene sheet and stones are examples of inorganic mulches.

naturalise To deliberately plant, or allow plants to grow and spread, as in the wild.

node The place on a plant's stem where a leaf forms.

nursery bed A piece of ground specially reserved for raising young plants.

organic This literally refers to any material derived from decomposed animal or plant remains. It is also used to describe a gardening approach that uses little or no obviously chemical substances such as fertilisers and pesticides.

perlite A granular, absorbent soil or compost additive made from expanded volcanic rock.

perennial (correctly herbaceous perennial) A durable non-woody plant whose soft, leafy growth dies down in winter, but grows again the following year.

pinch out To remove a growing tip, using finger and thumb.

pot on To move a potted plant into a larger container.

pot (up) To transfer a plant from a seed tray or open ground into a pot.

prick out To transplant seedlings from where they have been sown to a container or piece of ground where they will have more space to grow.

rhizome An underground root (strictly, a stem) that behaves like a bulb by storing food from one season to the next. Also used to describe the buried creeping shoots by which some plants, especially grasses, spread underground.

rootballed This describes plants packaged for delivery by wrapping their mass of roots and soil or compost in a net bag.

rootstock (or stock) The rooted portion of a grafted tree. This usually influences the habit and ultimate size of the selected variety joined onto it (the scion).

seedbed A piece of ground for raising seeds, specially prepared by removing all weeds, stones and large lumps of soil.

semi-ripe cutting A section of this year's stem cut off for propagation, usually during summer while the tip is still soft but the base has become firm and woody.

softwood cutting A cutting prepared from a portion of a young new shoot that has not started to harden.

spit A measurement of depth equal to the length of a spade-blade (about 25cm/10in).

standard A trained form of woody plant with a single upright stem that is clear of all leaves and shoots. Full standard trees have trunks about 2m (6ft) high, half-standards 1.2m (4ft). Standard roses are about 1m (3ft) high, while half-standards have 75cm (2ft 6in) stems.

subsoil The lower layer of ground below the topsoil (see below). Often paler and relatively infertile, this is usually coarser in texture and hard to cultivate.

sucker A shoot growing from below ground and away from the main stem of a plant, sometimes from its rootstock.

systemic A type of pesticide, fungicide or weedkiller sprayed onto leaves and absorbed into all plant parts in its sap.

tender perennial A plant that can live for several years but cannot tolerate frost or very cold conditions.

thin out To reduce the number of plants, buds or fruit so that those remaining have enough room to develop fully.

tip cuttings Softwood cuttings (see above) formed from the outer ends of young shoots.

top-dressing An application of fertiliser, organic material or potting compost spread on the surface. Also refers to replacing the top layer of compost in a large container with a fresh supply.

topgrowth The upper, visible part of a plant above ground level.

topsoil The upper layer of soil, usually darker and more fertile than the layers below (see subsoil), and where plants develop most of their feeding roots.

tuber A fat, underground root (in dahlias, for example) or stem (begonias), constructed differently from a bulb or corm but used in the same way for storing food from one season to the next.

variety Botanically, a distinctly different variation of a plant that has developed in the wild, but commonly used to mean the same as cultivar (see left).

By early spring, we are all looking forward to better weather, longer days and fresh colour in the garden. The weather remains beyond our control, but by planning ahead, gardeners can bring spring forward a little. Deciduous trees may still be bare, but who will notice when the ground beneath is studded with snowdrops, winter aconites and early crocus? These bulbs bridge the gap between winter and spring with a wonderful freshness of form and colour, and there are many flowering trees, shrubs and wall plants whose blooms open early in the year. Even last-minute gardeners can add colour in the space of an afternoon by filling an arrangement of pots and troughs with an uplifting mixture of seasonal flowers.

inspirations

early signs of spring

Leave winter behind and give spring a head start by planting generous drifts of the most gem-like early flowering bulbs. While most of the garden still sleeps, the onset of spring is announced by early narcissi, wood anemones and bright blue chionodoxas.

The dainty, milk-white flowers of *Narcissus* 'Thalia' (above) are a welcome sight – their fresh colours seem to define the season. Make sure of generous displays in years to come by deadheading as the blossoms fade.

With its starry blue spring flowers, *Ipheion uniflorum* deserves to be more widely grown. Plant bulbs during autumn into humus-rich, well-drained soil where they will build into reliable clumps (left).

When sunny celandines (*Ranunculus ficaria* subsp. *ficariiformis*) open their shiny-petalled flowers, spring is in the air. In wild grassy spots and hedge bottoms they associate well with *Anemone blanda*, thriving in semi-shade where the soil is moist (right).

The wild primrose (*Primula vulgaris*) is a true sign of spring. Here clumps have been allowed to stud the turf in a wild area of the garden (left).

Chionodoxa luciliae

Narcissus and blue-flowered *Chionodoxa forbesii* bring fresh colour to an early spring border (below). Their foliage will have died back by the time summer plants are coming into flower, but should not be removed until the leaves have turned yellow.

A sunny border of well-drained soil is a good spot for naturalising star of bethlehem (*Ornithogalum fimbriatum*). Green-striped buds open early in the season and flatten into white stars (above). Their foliage dies away neatly before late spring and summer plants begin to grow.

a season of surprises

As the gradual increase in daylight hours and spells of warm weather wake plants from their winter rest, buds burst into new life. The thrusting growth and sudden explosion of colour can take even the seasoned gardener by surprise.

A far cry from its cousin the weeping willow, *Salix hastata* 'Wehrhahnii' makes a small, slow-growing shrub whose bare twigs come alive with a fine display of soft silvery catkins in spring (above). These mature to show yellow pollen as bright green leaves burst from their buds.

Lenten roses (*Helleborus hybridus*) are a promiscuous bunch, capable of seeding around and producing some beautiful hybrids. This ruby-flowered plant pierces a ground covering of hardy *Cyclamen coum* (right). Both enjoy well-drained, humus-rich soil in partial shade.

Early spring is when drifts of purple *Crocus tommasinianus* and clumps of naturalised snowdrops coincide with the flowering of hellebores (above). For the best show, remove shabby hellebore leaves as flower buds form, and divide large clumps after flowering.

A young shuttlecock fern (*Matteuccia struthiopteris*) unfurls perfect new fronds, breaking through the leaf litter in a woodland situation (below).

The early, fragrant blooms of *Hyacinthus* 'Amethyst' make an ideal accompaniment to emerging peony stems (right). As spring progresses, a ground cover of forget-me-nots will rise up to mask the dying hyacinths and continue the display through into summer.

Thrusting their way through bare earth after a long winter, these daffodil shoots are full of promise (below). The bulbs are well adapted to withstand even wet winters and, from their early autumn planting, should emerge to flower in spring year after year.

carpeting the ground

Many plants flower on the woodland floor before deciduous trees break into leaf, while others stud the short, springy turf of sunny meadows with their jewel-like early blooms. The same plants make brilliant swathes of flower and leaf in our spring gardens.

Primroses and grape hyacinths (*Muscari*), backed by the heart-shaped leaves of *Brunnera macrophylla* (left), encapsulate early spring, and summer-flowering plants can grow through them later.

Squills (*Scilla bithynica*) are often planted as ground cover in woodland glades, where they will spread and seed themselves over a large area (below). The star-shaped blue flowers complement all daffodils in either sun or semi-shade.

Mixed hellebores grow well together and will spread to form an established group under a tree (right). These plants give a long season of interest, as their beautiful flowers die gracefully, enclosing the developing seed capsules.

Time the mowing of grassy areas carefully, and turf can be richly embellished by wild and naturalised flowers (left). Late mowing allows the wildflowers to set seed. Native primroses are joined here by mauve *Anemone blanda* and dainty pink *Cyclamen coum*.

One of the first surprises of the year is provided by the winter aconite (*Eranthis hyemalis*), seen here with golden crocus (above). Each yellow aconite flower sits on a collar of green, and an initial sprinkling of tubers will eventually spread into a brilliant carpet.

Crocus etruscus 'Zwanenburg'

Sturdy dutch crocuses often provide the first sign of spring (below left). Standing proud against closely mown grass, they naturalise well. Plant corms in early autumn, in sun.

The colour range of wood anemones (*Anemone blanda*) runs from white to deep mauve. Their pretty flowers will enliven a wild lawn, the individual plants spreading into impressive clumps (below). Leaves die back after flowering, enabling the grass to thicken up again.

early spring blossom

The grey and brown winter landscape is transformed by the white, pale pink and cheerful yellow of early flowering shrubs and trees. Furry magnolia buds crack open to reveal their exotic petals, and gardens are wreathed in dainty blossom.

Cheerful yellow-flowered forsythia lights up the spring garden (above). These are easy shrubs to grow, but regular pruning immediately after flowering encourages the best displays.

In full bloom, *Magnolia* x *soulangeana* is a breathtaking sight (right). The goblet-shaped flowers open *en masse* in warm sunshine and have a sweet, lemony perfume. Give plants room to grow properly, as they neither need nor want pruning.

Flowering here above a carpet of daffodils, *Viburnum grandiflorum* 'Snow White' is one of a tribe of easy-going deciduous viburnums whose fragrant blossom shows clearly against bare stems (left). Pink-flushed white flowers open from clusters of dark pink buds.

Fresh spring foliage is always delightful, but some shrubs excel by producing very colourful new growth. *Pieris* (above) are known for their shiny, pink-red young leaves. They need acid soil, but can be grown in pots of ericaceous compost.

One of the most beautiful of the japanese cherries, *Prunus* 'Taihaku' is known as the great white cherry (below). It enhances any garden with room to accommodate its spreading canopy.

Cherry blossom is fleeting, but it is more than worthwhile and trees often have more to offer than their flowers. *Prunus sargentii* (above) is a top performer, with chestnut bark and bright, bronze-red new foliage in spring, plus stunning autumn colour.

The waxy flowers of ornamental quince (*Chaenomeles*) often cluster on bare branches over a long period and will withstand a dusting of frost (right).

colourful containers

Give spirits a lift by making sure vibrant spring flowers are in full view. Containers of fragrant hyacinths, crocuses and hellebores planted in early autumn, or assembled in season, can be set near the house for all to enjoy.

Purple-red hellebore flowers (*Helleborus hybridus* Ballard's seedling) bring depth to the cheerful yellow of spring polyanthus and dwarf narcissus planted with it in a glazed container (above).

Fresh early spring crocus and *Iris reticulata* flowers add colour to a frosted landscape (right). Either plant the bulbs in early autumn, or buy plants budded and showing colour from the garden centre, and arrange in a contemporary container for instant effect.

Containers planted to withstand wet winters and early springs need good drainage above all else. This smart pot of *Euphorbia* x *martinii*, pansies and white primulas is raised off the ground by pot feet to allow excess water to drain away easily (above).

The idea is simplicity itself. In early autumn, take a few packets of sturdy little *Narcissus* 'Jetfire' bulbs, a selection of terracotta containers, some crocks and good compost. Then plant up to enjoy a lively and cheerful display in early spring (above). Bulbs can remain in their containers from one year to the next, or be planted in the garden.

This studied set piece makes a beautiful still life, the components grown separately and arranged at the last minute (below). The gold-laced primulas and double-flowered *Primula* 'Miss Indigo' are complemented by the heuchera leaves, while the pot of hyacinths adds height.

Hyacinthus 'Pink Pearl'

Heathers have a long season of interest as their buds open during winter and spring. Here, a heather is teamed with the acid-loving shrub *Pieris* (left) so an ericaceous compost is essential, but grown alone, winter-flowering heathers will tolerate any well-drained compost.

brightening boundaries

The vertical surfaces of the garden can be home to some of the most desirable early spring plants. As this is usually a cool season, the flowers of alpine clematis, ornamental quince, camellia and garrya stay fresh and hold well for a long period.

In the shelter of old walls, venerable rhododendrons flower earlier than usual (above left). Apart from an annual mulch of leaf-mould, there is little more to do on this display than to control the odd strand of over-enthusiastic ivy or periwinkle.

The unfussy ornamental quinces (*Chaenomeles*) are good for covering large or small walls and fences (left). Train their stems flat against a fence and prune back outward-facing shoots to about four leaves directly after flowering. They bloom well even in the shadiest sites.

Bringing jewel-like colours of pink, purple or blue to the spring garden, *Clematis alpina* are easy to grow against a wall, fence or pergola. Here, *C. alpina* 'Ruby' clothes a wall with a dense curtain of dusky pink flowers against green foliage (above).

With its vanilla perfume and generous clusters of white flowers, *Clematis armandii* 'Snowdrift' (above) lights up large areas of wall or fence in sheltered areas. This evergreen climber is vigorous, but can be cut back hard in late spring.

It is easy to see why *Garrya elliptica* is known as the silk tassel bush (left). This classy evergreen lends itself well to wall training, where adequate support and pruning straight after flowering ensure a flat backdrop of grey-green foliage to show off the pale catkins.

Flamboyant camellias do well on a lightly shaded wall, away from early morning sun and in acid to neutral soil enriched with leaf-mould. They are easy to train, and will reward you with sumptuous blooms (below).

The first stirrings of spring rekindle our enthusiasm for gardening. An early start puts the gardener ahead for the whole season, making work more leisurely and enjoyable. When soil conditions allow, digging and forking the kitchen garden beds prepares the ground for later sowings and plantings. Owners of a greenhouse can start sowing seeds indoors. Several shrubs can be pruned early in the year, including roses and those like lavatera and caryopteris, which flower later on this year's wood; winter jasmine can be cut back immediately after flowering. And a few minutes spent tidying containers planted in autumn, or cutting away dead and damaged leaves of hellebores, will make you feel that the new season has begun.

practical diary

perennials

The earliest perennials are already gracing the garden with colourful blooms, while clumps of fresh green foliage herald the show to come. Early spring is an excellent time to plant and propagate many more plants by seed, cuttings or division, to fill your garden with flowers for very little outlay.

now is the season to . . .

■ **weed, feed and mulch** established plants. Cut off any remaining dead growth, and tidy up evergreens (see opposite).
■ **lift, divide and replant** established clumps of ornamental grasses and those perennials that flower from mid to late summer onwards (see Autumn and below).
■ **plan new planting schemes,** then buy and plant new perennials and grasses while weather conditions are cool and moist. Well-established plants in large pots are a good buy as you can divide them immediately into several smaller clumps.

■ **divide and repot container-grown** perennials and grasses that have become congested, and top-dress those remaining in their pots with fertiliser and fresh compost (see page 36).
■ **harden off plants** you have raised or overwintered under cover before planting them out.
■ **pot up young plants** that have developed from root cuttings taken in autumn or winter.
■ **protect new shoots** from slugs and snails, particularly on delphiniums, lupins, peonies, hostas and other susceptible plants (see Late Spring).
■ **remove winter protection** once weather conditions improve, although in cold areas vulnerable plants may need protecting throughout early spring.
■ **take basal cuttings** of suitable perennials (see opposite).
■ **sow seeds** of many perennial species, either bought or those you collected the previous year (see opposite).

Emergent peony shoots are a cheering sight, but must be protected from slugs and snails.

■ **pot on tender perennials** overwintering under cover into fresh compost and water well to encourage new growth. Soft-tip cuttings can be taken from the young shoots (see Late Spring).

and if you have time . . .

■ **take root cuttings** early in the season (see Winter).

maintaining established perennial borders

You need to prepare established perennials and grasses for the coming year, before they start to grow rapidly and form new shoots that could be damaged by the work.

● **first lift,** divide and replant young, vigorous portions of older perennials that have formed congested clumps.
● **then lightly fork** over the bare soil between plants, mixing in a dressing of slow-release fertiliser at the same time.

Pulmonarias enjoy shady conditions and are one of the earliest perennials to flower. *Pulmonaria officinalis,* with spotted leaves and long-lasting funnel-shaped pink-and-blue flowers, makes good ground cover.

tidying a perennial border

Dig out all perennial weeds, such as tap-rooted dandelions and thistles.

Cut dead and untidy stems from grasses and perennials to make way for fresh new growth.

The young foliage of *Alchemilla mollis* pushes through dead leaves.

● **remove all weeds,** particularly the roots of perennial ones, and closely inspect each clump of plants for weeds that may have taken root within the plant itself.

● **cut out to ground level any dead stems** that were not removed previously.

● **remove dead foliage** from evergreen grasses by combing carefully through the clump with your fingers, and cut off tatty leaves from evergreen perennials such as bergenias.

● **finally, mulch the bare soil** with a 5cm (2in) thick layer of organic matter, such as well-rotted manure, garden compost or chipped bark.

propagation

As new growth appears, it is time to take basal cuttings of a number of perennials including achillea, anthemis, chrysanthemums, delphiniums, gypsophila and lupins. Sever the new shoots when they are 8–10cm (3–4in) high and insert them in a pot of cuttings compost; keep covered until they root (see Late Spring).

sowing seed

This is the time to sow many perennials and grasses, which is an economical way of stocking a new garden or border. Certain varieties will even bloom this year if you sow them early and under cover (see below). A few perennials need a period of cold in order to germinate, which you can achieve by putting the seed in a polythene bag with a little damp sand, and placing it in the refrigerator for several weeks before sowing in the following way:

● Sow seed in pots or trays of moist seed compost, or direct into the soil in a coldframe or protected by a cloche.

● If sowing direct, draw out shallow drills with a hoe and mix a little potting compost into the drill bottom to help retain moisture. Water the drill before sowing.

● Sow sparingly, then cover seeds with a thin layer of compost. Keep moist at all times.

● Once the seedlings are big enough to handle, prick out into modular trays, so each plant develops a compact root system.

looking ahead . . .

☑ LATE SPRING Put in supports for tall-growing perennials such as delphiniums and phlox.

☑ Continue taking basal cuttings and pot up when rooted.

☑ Continue to prick out seedlings and pot on young plants.

DIVIDING TIP Newly purchased grasses provide more value for money if you divide them into several smaller clumps which can then be planted separately. Once established, they will spread out in the bed.

some perennials that flower in their first year

● *Achillea* Summer Pastels Group ● *Agastache cana*
● *Anaphalis margaritacea* ● *Chrysanthemum* varieties
● *Coreopsis grandiflora* 'Early Sunrise' ● *Helenium* 'Autumn Lollipop' ● *Malva moschata* ● *Papaver orientale* 'Checkers'
● *Rudbeckia* Satellite Mixed ● *Tanacetum coccineum* Robinson's Mixed Single ● *Verbascum* Sunset Shades

annuals & biennials

Most summer annuals and bedding plants are sown now, indoors in the warmth of the greenhouse, or outside in a prepared nursery bed. Meanwhile, spring bedding transplanted in autumn will be coming into flower as the days lengthen.

now is the season to . . .

■ **sow tender bedding plants** and other half-hardy annuals under glass in early March (see pages 28 and 68). Include plants such as nemesias, impatiens, petunias, nicotianas, gazanias and mesembryanthemums.

■ **sow annual climbers** to make a good size by planting time. Cobaea, rhodochiton, thunbergia, morning glory, canary creeper and nasturtiums can all be started in small pots indoors in warmth (see page 37).

■ **buy seedlings and plug plants** from garden centres, and pot up to grow indoors until planting time (see page 28).

■ **prick out seedlings sown** earlier, to give them more space to develop (see page 29).

■ **protect all indoor sowings** and seedlings against damping-off disease (see page 72).

■ **repot overwintered** tender perennials, such as pelargoniums and fuchsias, and water more freely to start into growth (see page 67). Take cuttings when new growth is long enough.

■ **plant out autumn-sown** sweet peas with suitable supports (see right). Move spring-sown plants to a coldframe, and sow a final batch in warmed soil where they are to flower.

■ **remove cloches** and other frost protection from autumn-sown annuals, and thin seedlings if necessary. Lift thinnings carefully, without damaging the roots, using an old kitchen fork or seed label, and transplant elsewhere. Protect seedlings from slugs and snails (see Late Spring).

■ **dig or fork sites** for new flower beds. Ground dug in autumn can now be raked and levelled, ready to prepare seedbeds for outdoor sowing (see right).

■ **late in the season, begin transplanting** hardy annuals from their winter quarters to flowering positions; check seed packets for the correct spacing.

■ **at the end of March, start sowing** hardy annuals outdoors (see right) or under glass if conditions are unsuitable for direct sowing.

■ **protect newly planted** seedlings from wind.

and if you have time . . .

■ **weed among spring bedding** when the ground is dry, and hoe lightly to loosen the surface.

planting out sweet peas

1 Space 2.5m (8ft) long canes 30–45cm (12–18in) apart in rows or as wigwams, and make sure they are firm.

2 Using a trowel or dibber, plant one potful or paper tube of sweet peas next to each cane; water in well.

3 Secure young shoots to the cane with a loop of string or special sweet pea rings. Once plants start growing, tie in new growth every two or three days.

planting out sweet peas

Before planting out autumn-sown sweet peas still in pots or paper tubes, you need to harden them off gradually by leaving them outside during the day to accustom them to outdoor conditions. After a week of this they should be ready to plant.

sowing annuals direct

Many hardy annuals make the strongest bushy plants if sown under glass (see page 68). For large displays this is laborious, and it is often better to sow direct in late March or April.

Prepare the ground as soon as it is workable by forking the soil one spade blade deep where it has not been cultivated since last autumn. Sites that have already been dug over should need only light forking to break up the surface and any

Protect a seedbed from heavy rain or prolonged dry weather with a portable coldframe.

Lavatera 'Mont Blanc'

annuals to grow for cut flowers

- annual chrysanthemums • annual grasses • calendula
- candytuft • china asters • clarkia • clary • cornflowers
- eschscholzia • flax (*Linum*) • godetia • gypsophila
- honeywort (*Cerinthe*) • larkspur • lavatera • malope
- nigella • poppies • red orache (*Atriplex*) • scabious
- sunflowers • woodruff (*Asperula*) • zinnia

Double daisies (*Bellis perennis*) make colourful and long-lasting spring bedding if sown the previous spring or early summer.

large clods. Then rake to level and to leave a fine tilth, ready for sowing. You can protect this seedbed from heavy rain or prolonged dry weather by covering it with a plastic sheet, weighted down with bricks, or a portable coldframe. This will also warm the soil, and after two to three weeks you can sow seeds you have bought or saved last year with a good chance of rapid germination.

hardy annuals for cutting

Many annuals make long-lasting cut flowers. Surplus plants at bedding time can be lined out in the vegetable garden or beside paths, or you can sow direct in rows solely for this purpose. Water plants regularly, and mulch and support them to ensure long, straight stems.

thinning outdoor seedlings

Thin autumn-sown outdoor seedlings in stages to 8cm (3in) apart while they are still small and the soil is damp.

thinning outdoor seedlings

1 **Pull up and discard** surplus seedlings while pressing firmly with your fingers around seedlings to be retained, so they are not disturbed. Alternatively, chop out spare seedlings with a narrow onion hoe.

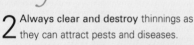

2 **Always clear and destroy** thinnings as they can attract pests and diseases.

3 **Thin outdoor annuals** again when they touch each other, this time spacing them at their recommended distance apart. Intermediate seedlings will be large enough to lift carefully with a kitchen fork or a seed label for transplanting elsewhere. Water well after thinning.

annuals & biennials/2

raising annuals under glass

Half-hardy annuals cannot stand frost. They are always sown under glass because if you wait until conditions are warm enough to sow outdoors, the plants will flower very late. Most can be sown now, but some need a long growing season, and antirrhinums, pelargoniums and *Begonia semperflorens* are best sown in late winter if they are to make substantial plants in time for bedding out (see Winter).

For successful germination you need to provide an ambient temperature of about 18°C (64°F) in a greenhouse or propagator. If this is not possible, wait until March, when artificial heating to 10°C (50°F), combined with increased sunlight, should still ensure success.

Where an unheated greenhouse or coldframe is the only aid available, buy temperature-sensitive plants like begonias, lobelia and petunias as seedlings or plugs, and concentrate on sowing more robust, faster-growing tender annuals like china asters, dahlias, nemesia, tagetes and zinnias in April.

Lack of heat is no handicap with hardy annuals. These are normally sown direct outdoors (see page 26), but may also be started indoors without artificial heat in early March to provide strong, branching plants for transplanting outdoors in late April or May. Use this method to raise superior plants of calendulas, clary, dimorphotheca, lavatera, nasturtiums and larkspur for containers and greenhouse pot plants, and for filling gaps in borders.

These ready-made sowing disks come in a plastic tray. The seeds start to germinate when water is added.

potting on plug plants

Small plug plants need to be potted on into 8cm (3in) containers as soon as possible after buying, so that their roots can develop and the plants grow on to a suitable size for planting out.

Early spring is a busy time for sowing. Seeds of half-hardy annuals should be sown under glass; those of hardy annuals can also be sown direct outdoors.

pricking out seedlings

1 **Make sure seedlings** are moist before you ease a cluster out, using the forked end of a dibber or the point of a seed label. Gently separate the seedlings and spread them on a board.

2 **Fill a seed tray** with compost and make holes about 5cm (2in) apart; four rows of six is a useful plan. Handle seedlings by their leaves (the fragile stems are easily crushed) and insert each into a hole, then gently firm.

3 **Once the tray is full,** water with a fine rose and label the tray. Keep in a well-lit place, but shade the seedlings from hot, bright sunlight for a few days, and plant out when the leaves are touching each other.

the importance of thinning

Most annuals germinate very quickly if sown in the right conditions, and tagetes, annual chrysanthemums and zinnias emerge less than a week after sowing. They soon develop into dense clusters of seedlings, all struggling for light and becoming spindly, conditions that often encourage the spread of damping-off disease.

To avoid early overcrowding, sow seeds as sparingly as possible. Prick out or thin seedlings as soon as they are ready, to ensure that they have space to grow strongly and avoid the soft, leggy growth and matted roots that result from overcrowding.

pricking out

By the end of February, some of the earliest seedlings should have one or two true leaves above the initial pair of seed leaves, and will be large enough to handle comfortably. Prick them out into trays, preferably modular ones of 6, 9 or 12 compartments, which gives them room to develop individually, or space them out in plain seed trays (see above). Pot up larger seedlings individually in 6–8cm (2½–3in) pots.

annual grasses

Most annual grasses are very easy to grow and produce graceful, airy plants for garden display and also for drying. They tend to mature quickly, rather than last the whole season, but you can avoid an untidy appearance in late summer by cutting off the dry seed heads for indoor use, clearing plants and replacing them with late flowering annuals or more grasses from a later sowing made in June.

- Sow and keep indoors in 8cm (3in) pots during March, because seedling grasses are hard to distinguish from weed grasses.
- Grow a few seeds in each pot, and thin if necessary to leave several evenly spaced seedlings.
- Harden off and plant out in late May, or early June for tender species such as sorghum.
- Plant in bold groups, or thread the grasses between other bedding for maximum effect.
- Cut for drying just before seeds are ripe, as they shed easily, and hang up in a warm, airy place.

there is still time to . . .

- **order seeds, seedlings and plug plants** from catalogues, but make haste before order books close.
- **transplant biennials** for spring bedding to their flowering positions from early March, and fill gaps in autumn-planted displays.
- **sow slow-maturing** tender bedding such as pelargoniums and begonias in a warm greenhouse.
- **direct sow** sweet peas in soil warmed by cloches.

looking ahead . . .

☑ LATE SPRING Buy and harden off summer bedding plants.
☑ Sow biennials.
☑ SUMMER Clear spring displays.
☑ Plant out summer bedding.
☑ Transplant biennials.
☑ LATE SUMMER: Take cuttings of tender perennials, which are treated as annuals.

hardy **annual grasses**
- foxtail millet (*Setaria italica*) 60cm (2ft) • greater quaking grass (*Briza maxima*) 45cm (18in) • hare's tail (*Lagurus ovatus*) 45cm (18in) • purple millet (*Panicum miliaceum* 'Violaceum') 60cm (2ft) • squirrel tail grass (*Hordeum jubatum*) 45cm (18in)

bulbs & tubers

Early spring is the time when you really appreciate bulbs and the colour they bring to the garden. With a minimum of effort now you can ensure this colour year after year – and with a little more you can enjoy bulb displays into the summer months.

now is the season to . . .

■ **check bulbs in winter store,** to ensure they are still in good condition, and make plans for planting them in batches for extended summer flowering.

■ **bring indoors the last potted spring bulbs** and keep in a cool, well-lit place until buds show colour (see Autumn).

■ **move or divide clumps** of snowdrops and winter aconites while they are still in leaf (see opposite).

■ **plant lilies outdoors in borders** or pots. You can transplant lilies by digging them up with large, undisturbed rootballs while the stems are still short.

■ **feed bulbs naturalised in grass** in March, and those in pots and borders after flowering (see right).

The cheerful yellow trumpets of daffodils are one of the most welcome sights of spring.

■ **sprout gladioli corms under glass.** Press them into a tray of compost and keep them moist and warm, then plant them out in March, together with some dormant corms that will bloom two to three weeks later.

■ **take dahlia cuttings from tubers** sprouted in winter, and start more tubers into growth (see opposite).

■ **mark the position of outdoor bulbs** that might need moving.

■ **plant summer-flowering bulbs** in mild gardens (see opposite).

■ **pot up begonias, ranunculus and other bulbs** in coldframes and unheated greenhouses for flowering indoors.

and if you have time . . .

■ **pot or repot tender bulbs,** such as vallotas and clivias, together with a last batch of amaryllis (see Winter).

after flowering

● **deadhead outdoor bulbs** by pinching off large heads such as daffodils and stripping off the faded flowers of hyacinths, but leave the stalks and leaves intact to die down naturally.

● **when indoor bulbs finish flowering,** cut off the dead heads and stand them, in their pots or bowls, in an unheated room or a coldframe. Continue to water and feed them with a high-potash liquid fertiliser. In March, harden them off for a few days, then plant the contents intact in the ground, where the foliage can die down naturally. Let the bulbs flower normally next year, but lift them again for forcing the year after.

Deadhead daffodils singly, as their flowers fade and die.

For hyacinths, strip off the small blooms individually because the stem continues to manufacture food in the same way as the leaves.

the importance of leaving bulb foliage

Leaves are a plant's food factory, so their early removal can weaken a bulb and prevent it from flowering the following year. Over several years, bulbs can die out altogether if the foliage is tidied excessively. Never knot or cut off bulb foliage until it starts to yellow naturally – usually six weeks after flowering. If dying foliage spoils the appearance of a border, sprinkle seeds of a fast-growing annual such as nigella around the leaves to disguise them.

bulbs in lawns

Naturalised bulbs such as narcissi, crocuses and fritillaries can compete comfortably with the grass in a lawn, provided you do not feed that area with a lawn fertiliser, as the high nitrogen content will boost the growth of the grass more than that of the bulbs. Instead, feed the bulbs as they appear in early spring with a light watering of high-potash liquid fertiliser or a sprinkling of bone meal, which will benefit the bulbs without stimulating grass growth.

starting dahlias for soft-tip cuttings

One of the easiest ways to propagate dahlias is to take soft-tip cuttings in spring and root them in gentle heat. Start in early spring by checking the tubers and cleanly cutting off any withered sections, before burying them in trays of moist compost.

Bury dahlia tubers to half their depth in a tray of moist compost to encourage them to shoot.

● Space the tubers so that they sit on a shallow layer of compost in the trays and heap more compost around them until the lower half is buried; water once thoroughly.
● Keep in a warm, well-lit position as the buds break and develop into new shoots.
● Sever the shoots just below the lowest leaf when about 5–8cm (2–3in) long, and root in a propagator.

● Let the parent plant continue to grow until late spring, when it can be planted outdoors, or potted up in a deep, 10–13cm (4–5in) container.

summer bulbs

Most summer bulbs are planted from late April onwards (see Late Spring), but it is worth starting a few earlier in mild gardens and warm, sheltered positions. Suitable bulbs include brodiaea, eucomis, galtonia, sparaxis, tigridia and tritonia. Make sure the site gets full sun and drains freely; in heavy soils, bed the bulbs on a 5cm (2in) layer of grit and plant 8–10cm (3–4in) deep.

dividing aconites

Like snowdrops, winter aconites are best divided and transplanted 'in the green', before their leaves die down.

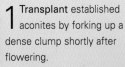

looking ahead . . .
☑ LATE SPRING Continue to feed bulbs outdoors.
☑ Plant out well-rooted dahlias and begonias.
☑ SUMMER Lift and dry spring bulbs.

dividing winter aconites

1 **Transplant** established aconites by forking up a dense clump shortly after flowering.

2 **Tease the clump apart** to separate individual tubers or small clusters, according to the number of plants you require.

3 **Use a narrow trowel** to open up small holes in fresh ground or part of the lawn, spaced 15cm (6in) apart. Replant a tuber in each hole, making sure it is deep enough to bury the white portion of stem; gently tread firm all round.

roses

This is the main pruning season for all except rambler roses. A little care now will ensure shapely bushes, strong, youthful growth and masses of blooms later in the year. As you prune, watch for early signs of pests and diseases, and clear up the debris afterwards.

now is the season to . . .

■ **refirm roses** if frost has lifted their roots.

■ **finish planting bare-rooted roses** and tidying rose beds, clearing away fallen leaves and other winter debris.

■ **trim and tidy ground cover** and edging plants growing in rose beds and borders.

On climbing roses growing up supports, loosen or replace any ties that are too tight and tie in new growth as it appears.

■ **check climbers and ramblers**, making sure the supports are in good repair, and that ties are secure and not too tight.

■ **mist roses in pots under glass** with water occasionally to stimulate new growth and deter red spider mite. Keep the plants at about 10–15°C (50–60°F) for early flowers; watch out for pests and diseases, and feed at every other watering once new growth appears.

■ **cut out dead and damaged wood** from all roses early on, in preparation for pruning.

■ **sow rose seeds** that have been exposed to cold over winter (see Winter and opposite).

■ **remove winter protection** from young and newly planted roses.

■ **start pruning roses**, beginning with climbers, if not done in late winter. Then move on to shrub roses (see page 34), before pruning hedges and other kinds.

■ **protect bushes** with wire guards where rabbits are a problem; keep in place until buds have opened into strong new shoots.

■ **in a mild season, feed pruned roses** in late March with a balanced dry fertiliser or special rose feed (see Late Spring), and hoe or rake into the soil surface.

■ **watch out for the first signs** of pests and diseases; these can appear as early as February in warm weather (see opposite).

and if you have time . . .

■ **start weeding between roses** during mild spells.

The red-tinged early shoots on rose bushes and climbers are a sign of healthy new growth but also a magnet for greenfly, so keep an eye open.

good companions for roses

SMALL BULBS • chionodoxa • crocus • dwarf narcissi • snowdrops • *Tulipa turkestanica*

SPRING FLOWERS • aubrieta • primroses • violas

SHORT ANNUALS • ageratum • candytuft • nasturtiums

PERENNIALS • *Alchemilla mollis* • hardy geraniums • stachys

EVERGREEN SHRUBS • cotton lavender • dwarf lavender • rosemary • sage • thyme

Tulipa turkestanica

underplanting roses

Opinions are divided about the merits of growing other kinds of plants between roses. They can impede access for pruning and other maintenance work, you need to take more care when mulching the roses, and cultivation can take longer because you may have to hand weed rather than hoe. On the other hand, suitable companion plants can complement and enhance the display, shroud bare stems and supply colour when the roses are not in leaf or bloom. As a compromise, you might prefer to limit planting to a perennial or annual edging.

Choose plants with short, compact growth and shallow roots to avoid competing with the roses, and be prepared to feed and water a little more often in a dry season so there are adequate resources for all plants. Make sure that none of the companion plants obscure or clash with the roses; if you wish, select softer, more pastel coloured flowers or confine your choice to plants with variegated foliage.

sowing roses

Seeds extracted from rose hips and exposed to cold (see Winter) can now be sown in pots or trays of soil-based compost. Space them 2–3cm (1in) apart, cover with a thin layer of compost and keep in gentle heat, no higher than 15°C (60°F). Seedlings emerge erratically over several months. Prick them out individually into 8cm (3in) pots and stand in a coldframe or a cool, well-lit place. Pot on as they grow and plant out next spring.

pests and diseases

Some roses are prone to more than their fair share of ailments, especially where they are growing in less than ideal situations. A few simple precautions can stop a minor outbreak developing into a serious problem.

● **choose disease-resistant varieties,** some of which have remarkably good health under normal garden conditions.
● **buy healthy plants** and plant them in well-prepared sites.
● **inspect plants regularly,** in particular shrub roses, which often begin growing first and offer an early bridgehead for aphids and diseases.

disease-resistant varieties
• 'Albéric Barbier' • Bonica • 'Buff Beauty' • 'Cécile Brünner'
• 'Charles de Mills' • 'Félicité Perpétue' • 'Fritz Nobis'
• Gertrude Jekyll • Just Joey • 'Maigold' • 'Paul's Himalayan
Musk' • 'Penelope' • Remembrance • 'Roseraie de l'Haÿ'
• Winchester Cathedral

common rose pests and diseases

1 black spot
2 mildew
3 greenfly

Many roses are prone to particular ailments. It is important to recognise the symptoms so that you can deal with them promptly, but, better still, try to prevent them taking hold (see below).

● **feed plants at the right time;** avoid over-feeding or the excessive use of high-nitrogen fertilisers, which can cause roses to develop soft, vulnerable growth.
● **clear up all leaves,** dead material and prunings promptly, especially where diseases like black spot have occurred before.
● **treat problems straight away,** choosing the right product and measuring out and applying it exactly according to the instructions.
● **if you grow a lot of roses,** consider starting a regular spraying plan early in the season to prevent outbreaks (see Late Spring).
● **disperse roses** in a mixed border to reduce the incidence of diseases.

Take preventative measures by spraying new growth against common rose problems.

roses/2

pruning

To prevent your roses turning into shapeless, tangled shrubs with few flowers, it is necessary to prune them annually. In an average year this should be done in mid-March in the south and west of the British Isles, and in late March in central areas, but in northern gardens and those on high or exposed ground, delay the job until April. The danger of pruning too early is that buds are stimulated into life and may then be injured by hard frosts. Pruning too late, when the sap is rising, means you cut off growing shoots, wasting the plant's energy and exposing open wounds to disease.

identifying rose types

It is important to know a rose's type, so you can prune it to achieve the best results.

● **hybrid teas** have long, sturdy stems with flushes of large shapely blooms borne singly or in small groups at the ends of a few sideshoots.

PRUNING Limit the main stems to about five per bush, and shorten these to four or five buds from the base, or just two buds for extra vigour and fewer, superior flowers.

You may need to use a pruning saw or long-handled pruners to cut through old, woody stems on roses that are too thick for secateurs.

differences between climbers and ramblers

CLIMBERS Stiff, thick stems with large flowers, held singly or in small trusses on thin, twiggy sideshoots
prune in late winter to retain a framework of mature branches.
examples ● Compassion ● Golden Showers ● 'Pink Perpétue' ● 'Zéphirine Drouhin'
RAMBLERS Vigorous, pliable stems with small flowers in huge trusses borne on new shoots, often in a single summer display
prune after blooming by cutting out much of the flowered growth for replacement by young stems.
examples ● 'Albertine' ● 'Dorothy Perkins' ● 'New Dawn' ● 'The Garland' ● 'Wedding Day'

Rambler *Rosa* 'The Garland'

● **floribundas** bear smaller flowers in clusters or sprays almost continuously throughout the season on freely branching bushes. Patio roses are compact, bushy floribundas that seldom exceed 60cm (2ft) in height, with trusses of proportionately smaller flowers.

PRUNING Keep five or six stems on each plant, and prune older stems to five or seven buds long; lightly trim young new shoots or leave them unpruned.

● **climbers** have stiff stems pruned in winter to retain a framework of mature branches (see Winter). The large flowers often come in flushes or are borne continuously throughout summer.

● **ramblers** have long, flexible stems with smaller flowers in large trusses, usually borne in a single spectacular display.

PRUNING In late August or September, prune to replace flowered stems with young shoots (see Late Summer).

● **shrub roses** are a varied group. Some old roses, like rugosas and centifolias, may only bloom once a year, whereas others, sometimes classed as modern shrub roses, are repeat flowering and vary from dainty bushes to virtual climbers.

PRUNING Lightly prune to shape, thin any overcrowded shoots, and cut one or two of the oldest branches to ground level or a low sideshoot to stimulate new growth.

● **ground-cover roses** are a kind of shrub rose with low, dense, spreading growth that can cover large areas.

PRUNING Treat like shrub roses, but also cut out any vigorous upright stems that disturb the low profile of the plant.

● **miniature roses** are no more than about 45cm (18in) high, usually bushy, sometimes with a slightly tender constitution.

PRUNING Prune lightly to maintain size, or fairly hard for improved flower quality, cutting all stems back to four or five buds.

● **standard roses** These are hybrid tea or floribunda roses grafted on a tall stem.
PRUNING They should be pruned according to their type. Weeping standards are mostly grafted forms of rambler roses, and are pruned in the same way as ramblers.

looking ahead . . .
☑ LATE SPRING Finish pruning roses.
☑ Feed outdoor roses.
☑ LATE SUMMER Collect rose hips for seed.
☑ Start pruning ramblers.

between flowers and new growth.

● **hard pruning** Reduce main stems to two or three buds from the base. This is used for most shrub roses immediately after planting, but is otherwise reserved for hybrid teas intended for exhibition and for rejuvenating overgrown shrub roses.

the three degrees of pruning

The basic pruning routine (see below) can be adapted for all kinds of rose. The severity of your pruning will affect the size, vigour and flowering of a rose, and needs to be adjusted according to the type and variety, and also the amount of growth it makes in your soil.

● **light pruning** Shorten older stems by no more than a third and remove the tips from young shoots. This restrains very vigorous varieties, which would produce even stronger stems if they were hard pruned, and maintains size, especially on poor or dry soils.

● **moderate pruning** Cut the main stems to half their length, and shorten weaker shoots to two or three buds. This suits general garden purposes, ensuring a healthy balance

shearing roses

Trials have shown that simply shearing off excess growth is just as effective as the traditional rose pruning methods; plants are equally healthy and vigorous afterwards, provided they are fed and well-tended. Some gardeners prefer this less time-consuming approach to rose pruning. Prune at the normal time, using garden shears, secateurs or a hedge trimmer to cut bushes down to about half their height, leaving the weaker, twiggy growth unthinned but removing all dead stems at their base.

there is still time to . . .

● **plant bare-rooted roses,** provided you complete this by early April.
● **prepare planting sites** for container-grown roses.

basic moderate pruning of shrub roses

1 **Cut out all dead stems** and trim parts that are damaged or diseased back to healthy wood, which will show a white cut surface.

2 **Remove thin, spindly** shoots, and any that cross one another or that are growing into the centre of the plant. Also cut out or pull off any suckers.

3 **Shorten the remaining** strong, healthy branches by half to an outward-facing bud or shoot. Compost or dispose of the prunings.

4 **Prune out** one or two of the oldest branches to ground level using long-handled pruners, to stimulate strong new growth.

climbers

This is an excellent time to prune, put in new plants, particularly evergreens, and sow some annual climbers to enjoy their colourful, if short-lived, contribution to summer. After pruning, make a habit of tying in new growth regularly to prevent it from becoming tangled.

now is the season to . . .

■ **plant new climbers early,** before the weather becomes warm and dry. Spring is the best time to plant evergreen climbers and wall shrubs, and any plants on the borderline of hardiness (see Late Spring).

■ **prune winter jasmine** (*Jasminum nudiflorum*) if you have not already done so (see Winter), as well as overgrown deciduous climbers like common jasmine (*Jasminum officinale*) and honeysuckle.

■ **prune clematis** that flower in summer and autumn (see opposite).

■ **repair or replace supports** before climbers grow strongly.

■ **remove winter frost protection** as soon as weather conditions permit.

■ **protect blooms of early flowering climbers** such as *Akebia quinata* and *Clematis* 'Early Sensation' from late hard frosts. Cover whole plants with fleece overnight, but remove it during the day.

■ **mulch all climbers** and apply a slow-release fertiliser.

■ **sow annual climbers** under cover (see opposite).

■ **trim back self-clinging climbers,** such as ivy, climbing hydrangea and parthenocissus, to keep them well away from woodwork, roofs and guttering.

■ **tie new shoots** into wires on walls and fences.

■ **pot up semi-ripe cuttings** taken in late summer, if rooted.

■ **check layers** prepared the previous year.

■ **top-dress, feed and water** container-grown climbers (see right).

■ **prune out frost-damaged shoots** in April, cutting them back to healthy growth.

and if you have time . . .

■ **propagate climbers** by layering (see Winter, Late Spring).

Carefully check to see whether layers started last year are well rooted, disturbing them as little as possible.

Tie in the new growth of herbaceous climbers to their wires, using soft string or sweet pea rings.

upkeep of climbers in containers

Climbers that have been in the same pot for more than two years should be replanted into a larger container. If the plant is already in a large pot, or if repotting is difficult because climbers are entwined with trellis or wires, top-dressing will keep the plant growing strongly. This involves gently scraping off the top few centimetres of old compost and replacing it with fresh soil-based potting compost mixed with controlled-release fertiliser. Water regularly and do not allow the compost to dry out.

The chocolate vine (*Akebia quinata*) flowers early, but may need to be protected if spring frosts threaten.

Brightening a fence in spring, *Clematis* 'Early Sensation' is one of the first clematis to flower. Protect its blooms in the event of late frosts.

pruning and training

After pruning, get into the habit of tying in new growth regularly to prevent it from becoming tangled and messy.

pruning clematis

The severity of pruning will vary according to the flowering time of the variety.

- **large-flowered clematis** that bloom in early to midsummer, such as 'Lasurstern', 'Nelly Moser' and 'The President': first remove all dead, damaged or weak shoots, then cut back healthy stems to a strong pair of buds. Hard prune some shoots and lightly prune others for a plant that flowers from top to bottom.

- **species and large-flowered hybrids** that bloom in late summer, such as 'Ernest Markham', 'Gipsy Queen', 'Jackmanii', *Clematis tangutica* and *C. viticella* and its hybrids: cut back all stems to 30–60cm (1–2ft), just above a strong pair of buds.

- **if you are not sure** of the variety, then treat as for the first group mentioned above to be sure of a good crop of flowers and to encourage strong, healthy shoots.

annual climbers to sow now

HARDY ANNUALS • canary creeper (*Tropaeolum peregrinum*) • climbing nasturtiums • rhodochiton • sweet peas (sow a few now for late blooms)
HALF-HARDY ANNUALS • *Cobaea scandens* • morning glory (*Ipomoea*) • thunbergia

overgrown climbers

Take the opportunity now to prune overgrown specimens of campsis, common jasmine (*Jasminum officinale*) and honeysuckle (*Lonicera periclymenum*) so that they have time to produce new flowering stems for the coming year.

Take out any crossing stems that may rub together, and shorten long, straggly stems.

sowing annual climbers

Annual climbers are splendid for summer colour. They grow rapidly from seed and may reach 2.5m (8ft) by the end of summer, smothered in colourful blooms. You can direct sow hardy annuals outside, but the best results come from seeds sown in pots or modular trays of moist potting compost (see below). Half-hardy annuals must be raised under cover and planted out once frosts are past.

Sweet peas do best in paper tubes or root trainers to develop their deep root system (see Autumn). Transfer hardy annuals to a cool, frost-free coldframe or greenhouse; half-hardy annuals need a warmer environment.

looking ahead . . .
☑ LATE SPRING Plant out annual climbers.
☑ Propagate late flowering clematis.

sowing seeds of morning glory

2 Move to a well-lit spot as soon as the seedlings appear, a week or so later. Transplant to one plant per 8cm (3in) pot and stake them as growth develops.

1 Sow two or three seeds to a cell in a six-cell tray. Stand the tray in a warm place or propagator.

shrubs & trees

Spring is the season for trimming evergreens into shape and there is plenty of pruning and propagation to do, but take time to enjoy the froth of blossom on early flowering shrubs and trees.

now is the season to . . .

■ **continue planting deciduous species,** but try to get all bare-rooted plants in the ground by the end of March.

■ **refirm recent plantings** if their roots have been lifted by wind or frost. In a dry season, water and mulch to keep the roots moist.

■ **inspect all supports** and tree ties, and repair or adjust where necessary.

■ **cover vulnerable plants** such as cistus and hydrangeas if frost threatens.

Where a shrub has succumbed to frost damage, or 'scorch', prune out the affected shoots before new growth gets started.

■ **shelter recently planted evergreens** from wind and frost by erecting a temporary windbreak of hurdles or netting (see page 152).

■ **watch out for** early signs of pests and diseases, and take prompt action to prevent them spreading; some evergreen diseases, such as mahonia rust, are present or visible all the year round (see page 40).

■ **prune late flowering shrubs** such as buddleia, perovskia and caryopteris, together with frost-shy shrubs like hardy fuchsias and hydrangeas (see page 41 and Late Spring).

■ **trim winter-flowering heaths** to remove dead blooms and keep plants compact (see page 40).

■ **start pruning early flowering shrubs** such as forsythia and winter jasmine (see Winter) as their display finishes.

■ **prune mahonias** to prevent leggy growth (see page 40).

■ **hard prune shrubs with coloured stems,** such as cornus and salix, to encourage vivid young growth, and cut back canes of white-stemmed brambles (*Rubus*) to the ground (see Winter).

■ **renovate overgrown evergreens** and evergreen hedges by pruning them hard in late March (see opposite).

■ **move misplaced evergreen shrubs** growing on heavy soil (see Winter).

■ **pull up or cut off suckers** from shrubs such as lilac and sumach, or mow them off if they are growing in a lawn.

■ **layer shrubs and trees** that are difficult to propagate from cuttings. Plants with low pliable branches can be layered in the ground (see Late Spring), while those with stiffer upright stems are better air layered (see page 43).

■ **sow tree and shrub seeds** that have been stored over winter.

■ **pot up seedlings and cuttings** started last autumn, and grow on ready for planting in a nursery bed in early summer.

■ **take root cuttings** of shrubs such as sumach, aralia and ceanothus, and root them in a coldframe or indoors in warmth (see page 42).

■ **trim or start training topiary** plants towards the end of March (see page 44).

■ **trim rose hedges** in late March; use shears or a hedge trimmer to clip them to size, then prune out any dead and diseased wood. Feed after pruning.

■ **water plants in containers** if prolonged drought or winds have dried out the compost.

and if you have time . . .

■ **paint tree trunks** and branches of deciduous plants with an antiseptic winter wash if pests and diseases have been a problem. Do this as early as possible and before buds start to open. Cover all plants beneath to prevent injury from splashes.

avoiding the dangers of late frost

Spring frosts are unpredictable and potentially lethal to flower buds, young growth and plants that originated in warm climates. Injury can be serious after a sequence of warm weather, followed by a sharp frost and then another mild spell. Use fleece or a similar temporary cover to protect vulnerable plants when frost threatens. The young shoots of hydrangeas and fuchsias are also vulnerable, together with plants of borderline hardiness, such as forms of rosemary and lavender (see below).

plants vulnerable to spring frost

• camellia • grey and silver-leaved shrubs (especially cistus and halimium) • hydrangeas • lavenders (*Lavandula lanata* and *L. latifolia*) • *Magnolia stellata* • romneya • rosemary (*R.* 'Prostratus')

Camellia japonica 'Akashigata'

hard pruning overgrown evergreens

Laurel, holly and rhododendrons are typical of evergreen shrubs that require little annual pruning, but eventually become too straggly or outgrow their allotted space. You can cut them back radically between late March and early June, to stumps about 45–60cm (18–24in) high. Remove damaged or diseased wood and weak growth, leaving only the strongest stumps to regrow.

Renovating an overgrown laurel hedge by pruning in late March will ensure plenty of healthy new growth.

Overgrown evergreen hedges, such as box, holly and yew, are treated similarly (see below), but the work is better spread over a few years to ensure regrowth all over the hedge.

● **start by cutting** the top to the required height, then trim all the branches on one side almost back to the main stems. Feed and mulch the hedge; water well in dry weather.

● **when new shoots are growing well** on the cut face, which may be two or three years later, the second side may be hard pruned in the same way.

HEDGE SHAPING TIP Where a hedge acts as a windbreak, you can sculpt the top in free-form undulations or castellate it like battlements. This helps to filter the wind, whereas a level top makes a barrier rather like a solid wall or fence, causing wind turbulence.

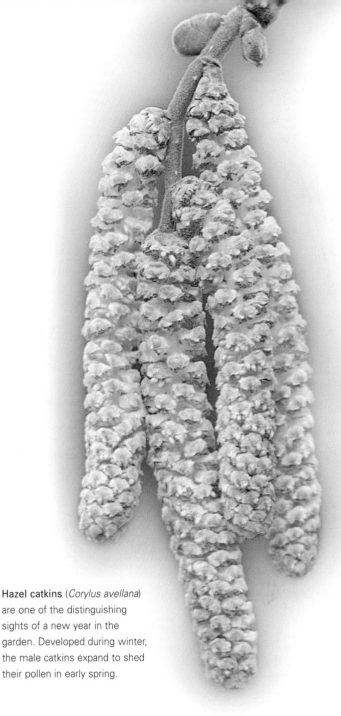

Hazel catkins (*Corylus avellana*) are one of the distinguishing sights of a new year in the garden. Developed during winter, the male catkins expand to shed their pollen in early spring.

hard pruning a box hedge

1 **Set up a string line** at the desired height and cut the top of the hedge to this height using hedging shears.

2 **Clear away** clippings before tackling one face of the hedge. Trim branches almost back to the main stems (see above).

regenerating overgrown shrubs

If neglected or only lightly pruned over a number of years, shrubs such as cornus, *Buddleja davidii* and many hydrangeas become tall and leggy, with a bare base and fewer, small flowers. You can often rejuvenate them by cutting them hard back in early spring, leaving a series of healthy stumps to regrow. Small shrubs can be cut back in one go, but larger specimens, such as mature hydrangeas, are better tackled in stages, spreading the work over two or three years by cutting back a third or half of the stems each year. Feed after pruning and leave the new growth unpruned for a year to become established. Always check when you buy a shrub that it withstands hard pruning, because some kinds, such as brooms (*Cytisus*), do not regenerate well from old stems.

shrubs & trees/2

early spring pruning

This is pruning time for shrubs that bloomed late last year and those that have just finished flowering. By doing this annually you will keep the plants shapely and encourage plenty of flowers for next year. Some early blossom and new growth is particularly vulnerable to frost, but a combination of late pruning and protection will keep damage to a minimum.

trimming heathers

If left unpruned, heathers and heaths often become tall, leggy and straggly, with a lot of dead growth that can shorten their lives. Do not prune so hard that you cut into the old, tough wood, which often cannot regenerate.

One-handed shears or large scissors are the best tools for clipping off all the dead flowerheads and some of the young growth of heathers, to leave a neat, compact finish.

● **prune winter-flowering heaths** (mainly *Erica* x *darleyensis* and cultivars), now, as flowers fade and new growth appears.

● **you can prune summer and autumn-flowering heathers** such as *Calluna vulgaris*, *Daboecia cantabrica*, *Erica cinerea*, *E. ciliaris* and *E. tetralix* and their varieties after flowering, but as the dead flowerheads of many varieties remain attractive over winter, you may prefer to leave pruning until March.

● **check variegated heathers** for all-green reversions, and cut these out at their base.

pruning mahonia

1 As soon as flowering finishes, trim off the end rosettes of foliage, cutting just above the next set of leaves down the stem.

2 If you want a more compact bush, use long-handled loppers to prune the stems harder, down to a low sideshoot.

mahonias

Tall mahonias such as *M. japonica* develop long bare stems unless pruned annually (see above). You can prune shorter-growing *Mahonia aquifolium* in the same way, unless it is grown as a hedge or ground cover, in which case shear off all the stems, almost to ground level, to keep growth young and leafy. You can use the prunings to propagate (see page 43).

● **mahonia rust** is present all the year round and causes deep reddish purple patches on older leaves, with powdery brown pustules on the undersides. Prune and burn diseased foliage, and spray young growth with copper-based fungicide at monthly intervals during the growing season.

winter and early flowering shrubs

Shrubs such as winter-flowering *Viburnum* x *bodnantense* and *V.* x *burkwoodii*, which flower early on stems produced the previous year, are pruned as soon as their blooms fade. New stems grow freely from the base of these shrubs, so cut out about a third of the oldest branches, and trim the rest to shape; in this way the plants are constantly rejuvenated, with enhanced flowering.

On ornamental quince (*Chaenomeles* x *superba* 'Nicoline'), clusters of waxy cups open on bare stems. Prune after flowering, cutting back flowered shoots on wall-trained specimens to within three or four buds of the permanent framework.

late flowering shrubs

Most late flowering shrubs, including *Buddleja davidii*, caryopteris, lavatera, leycesteria, perovskia and santolina, produce their blooms on growth made in the current year, and these stems need pruning now, just before or as their new leaves begin to open.

● Shorten all the shoots that flowered last year to within one or two buds from their base.

● Thin congested growth by removing or shortening some of the older stems.

pruning hydrangeas

This is the best time to prune hydrangeas such as *H. paniculata*, *H. arborescens* and *H. macrophylla* hybrids, both lacecap and mophead (Hortensia) types. The dead flowers are usually left untouched over winter, because they are considered to provide a degree of frost protection.

● Cut old flowering stems to two or three buds from the base.

● Remove any weak or old exhausted shoots.

● Mulch plants with a deep layer of rotted manure.

pruning hardy fuchsias

Fuchsias are also often left until spring before pruning, especially in colder gardens, for the sake of the frost protection given by the old growth. Now all this must be cut back hard, almost to ground level.

In milder areas you can prune more lightly, allowing a framework of permanent older branches to develop. You then simply remove any framework branches that are exhausted, shorten the sideshoots to their base, and lightly trim the remaining stems to shape.

pruning cotinus

Prune smokebush (*Cotinus*) now, according to the effect you require (see below). Cutting back large bushes hard will restore their shape and vigour, stimulating more handsome and colourful foliage, whereas light pruning maintains size and allows the bush to flower more lavishly.

Shear off the dead and untidy stems of potentillas to neaten their growth before summer flowering.

pruning cotinus

1 An overgrown cotinus can be hard pruned in early spring to a more manageable shape, resulting in vigorous new growth with improved leaf size and colour.

2 Use loppers or a saw to remove complete branches, cutting back to a main stump or the junction with another, better placed branch.

3 Thinner growth can be left unpruned to maintain a leafy, although reduced canopy, or it can be trimmed off to leave a clean cut.

4 Alternatively, shorten the younger shoots by half for a compromise between total renewal and retaining some of the flowering wood.

shrubs & trees/3

With its attractive rounded leaves and pink, bell-shaped blooms, *Rhododendron* Temple Belle Group brings long-lasting colour to the early spring garden.

propagation

Shrubs and trees can be propagated in several ways at this time of year. Air layering is a traditional method that is particularly satisfying, as you get a sizable plant that needs less cosseting than one raised from cuttings. Also, being above ground it is less likely to suffer accidental damage than layers in the soil.

The advantages of taking root cuttings are simplicity and reliability. No elaborate equipment is necessary unless you choose to take the cuttings under glass, and you will often have 100 per cent success.

Besides the more conventional cuttings taken from shoots or leaf buds, some evergreen shrubs can be propagated from stem cuttings taken when pruning the plant (see opposite).

taking root cuttings

Root cuttings from shrubs and trees are treated like those taken from fleshy rooted perennials (see Winter).

- In late winter and early spring, while the plants are still dormant, scrape away some of the soil until part of the root system is exposed.
- Cut off a few roots at least 5mm (¼in) thick and close to the stem. Keep them moist until preparation.
- Trim the cuttings to about 15cm (6in) long and remove any fine side roots. Make a flat cut at the top (the end that was nearer the stem) and a sloping cut at the base.
- Plant the cuttings in a coldframe, outdoors in a well-drained spot and covered with a cloche, or in deep pots of cuttings compost in the greenhouse. Insert them upright with the flat cut at the top, spacing them 5–8cm (2–3in) apart. Cover the tops with a thin layer of soil or compost.
- Rooting takes about six weeks under glass or two to three months outdoors. Pot up growing cuttings individually or transplant 15cm (6in) apart in a nursery bed.

shrubs to grow from root cuttings

- ailanthus • aralia • ceanothus • clerodendron • embothrium • gymnocladus • koelreuteria • myrica • paulownia • rhus • robinia • sassafras • sorbaria • zanthoxylum

Rhus typhina

propagating mahonia from stem cuttings

1 **Use mahonia prunings** as propagating material by selecting a firm green (not brown) stem and cutting this just above a leaf joint and about 4cm (1½in) below it.

2 **To save space** under glass and reduce water loss, trim the stem back to just beyond two or three pairs of leaflets.

3 **With a sharp knife,** trim off the rough edges round the bottom of the cutting and peel a strip of bark from one side to increase the rooting area.

4 **Insert an upright cutting** to the base of its first leaf in a 10–13cm (4–5in) potful of cuttings compost. Firm and water in well, then keep warm in a propagator.

air layering

Some shrubs and trees are reluctant to root as cuttings, while simple layering in the ground is impossible because of the lack of suitable low, flexible branches. Air layering is the solution. You can air layer stems any time from early spring to late summer; it takes about a year to ensure a good supply of roots (see right). When you can see roots appearing at the surface of the moss, remove the plastic carefully and cut off the stem just below the rooted area. Plant the layer outside in a nursery bed and leave for a year or pot up the cutting in a 10–13cm (4–5in) pot of soil-based compost.

shrubs and trees to air layer

- citrus • hawthorn (*Crataegus*) • quince (*Cydonia*) • davidia
- ginkgo • witch hazel (*Hamamelis*) • kalmia • liquidambar
- magnolia • medlar • rhododendron • styrax

Ginkgo biloba

air layering a rhododendron

1 **Choose a young,** straight branch. About 30cm (12in) from its tip, make an angled cut half way through the branch to form a tongue about 5cm (2in) long. Dust the cut surfaces with hormone rooting powder (inset).

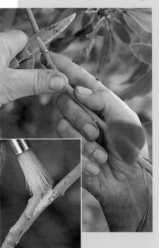

2 **Wedge the tongue** open with a fragment of moist sphagnum moss, then wrap more moss round the cut like a fat bandage.

3 **Hold the moss** in place with a square of clear plastic sheeting, tightly sealed with waterproof tape at top and bottom, and along the overlapping edge.

shrubs & trees/4

training and topiary

When creating a large shape from an established shrub, such as this yew teddy bear, you may have to shorten some thicker branches with a saw or loppers. New growth will soon appear to cover the bare patch.

It takes about five to ten years to train and clip evergreen shrubs into simple geometric shapes such as balls, cubes and pyramids, and a little longer to sculpt more complex representational figures like birds and small animals. Box and yew are the classic plants for this traditional art form, although some larger-leaved species such as holly, bay and portugal laurel (*Prunus lusitanica*) can also be used. Deciduous plants like hawthorn (*Crataegus*) and golden privet (*Ligustrum*) also clip well into simple shapes.

topiary training techniques

Start with an existing bushy specimen, larger than the finished shape, and carve it freehand with secateurs or one-handed shears. Alternatively, plant a smaller container-grown bush inside a wire former and use this as a template to guide your cutting (see opposite). The bush will eventually cover the former completely.

A standard bay (*Laurus nobilis*) makes an immaculate and traditional centrepiece for a herb garden, or two can be planted in a pair of matching large containers to flank a doorway. You can buy fully formed specimens, but it is not difficult to train your own from a single-stemmed plant, a rooted offshoot or a strong cutting (see below).

Most topiary figures need clipping at least twice a year, in April and late summer. More frequent trimming maintains a precise outline and bushy growth; fast-growing species like privet may need four or five trims a year. Feed topiary in early spring with a general fertiliser to sustain replacement growth. FROST-PROTECTION TIP Standard plants such as bay, yew or box kept in containers are vulnerable to temperatures below -4°C (25°F), so insulate both tree and container, or move them under cover when hard frost is forecast.

training a standard bay

1 Pot up a straight-stemmed rooted cutting or offshoot in a 10cm (4in) container of potting compost mixed with extra grit. This may take a year or more to start growing well, during which time keep it in a warm greenhouse and occasionally mist to keep humidity high.

2 As the plant grows, pot it on into a larger container and trim off the lower leaves and sideshoots to start developing the clear trunk. Support the stem with a cane and tie it in several places to keep it straight. Continue potting on and tying in as necessary.

3 When the young tree is a little taller than the required height, prune off the growing tip. Remove shoots forming on the trunk, and cut or pinch out the tips of sideshoots in the head when about 15cm (6in) long. Shorten sideshoots growing from these in the same way.

4 Keep pinching out the tips of sideshoots to encourage a dense, shapely ball of leafy growth. Repot or topdress annually in spring, and trim the head with secateurs twice a year.

using a ready-made frame

2 **As the plant grows,** trim its foliage with scissors or small shears at least once a year wherever it protrudes beyond the wire former.

1 **For small topiary** items, plant the shrub centrally in the pot, then anchor the frame's 'legs' firmly in the compost. Choose a bushy, small-leaved species like box.

using a self-assembly frame

1 **Topiary frame kits** are easy to construct. Stand the base in the bottom of a pot and half-fill with soil-based compost. Assemble the components, securing them with wire twists; here, they form a sphere.

2 **Plant the young shrub** in the centre, then fill with more compost. Trim off any foliage extending beyond the frame, or tie the flexible shoots of a plant like this *Cotoneaster horizontalis* to the wires for faster coverage.

Well-established ivy against a wall has been trimmed with shears into an ornamental 'house', while the impact of a dominating conifer has been cleverly reduced by exposing part of the stem to admit light and cutting the base to create the effect of a standard growing in a pot.

making decorative stems

While trees are young you can sculpt their flexible stems by training them round formers, such as spirals of wire, or plait them for a 'barleysugar' twist that is retained even when the trunk has firmed up. Start while stems are young and pliable and can be bent without cracking. Twist or ply multiple stems evenly (see below), holding them in place with ties. When the tree reaches the desired height, allow the sideshoots to develop into a head. Shorten these top branches by half to encourage dense busy growth.

Pot up the young plant and, if it has several stems, gently plait these together, then secure them to a strong cane with string or wire twists. Trim all shoots, buds and leaves from the lower part of the stems to reveal their decorative arrangement.

there is still time to . . .
● **move shrubs and trees** to new positions, but complete this work by early March (see Winter).

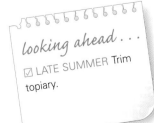

looking ahead . . .
☑ LATE SUMMER Trim topiary.

alpine gardens

Many alpines will be coming into flower at this time, and those with silvery leaves, especially, still need their roots and foliage kept dry if they are to survive a wet spring. As the growing season gets under way, prepare troughs, sinks or raised beds for planting.

now is the season to . . .

- **prepare beds** and other areas for planting alpines.
- **protect vulnerable plants** from slugs and snails (see opposite) before they can eat new shoots.
- **protect plants** against wet spring weather to prevent basal rot from developing, especially on plants with silver or hairy leaves, by covering them with a pane of glass balanced on pots or bricks (see Winter).

Trim the growth of untidy alpines by cutting back long straggly shoots.

- **trim any straggly plants,** and those that have encroached on their neighbours, by cutting back the long growth to 8–10cm (3–4in) above the ground.
- **control weeds** by carefully hoeing between plants to take out annual weeds before they can produce seed. Treat perennial weeds as they emerge by spot treating them with a weed pen or paint-on gel to avoid disturbing the soil.

- **replenish gravel mulches** over alpine beds and borders to a depth of at least 2–3cm (1in). This will improve drainage, prevent weed seeds from germinating and deter slugs and snails.
- **divide oversized plants** in the same way as border perennials, but leave those coming into flower until early summer or autumn.
- **check root cuttings** taken in autumn; if they have rooted, plant them out in April or pot up individually.
- **propagate new alpines** from seeds and cuttings (see opposite).
- **visit shows** and Internet sites, and scrutinise catalogues in search of new plants to add to the alpine garden.

Tidy individual alpines by removing any dead or dying leaves before replenishing the gravel mulch.

Cushion-forming *Draba rigida* (below) is a hardy evergreen perennial, bringing spring colour to rock gardens, troughs and raised beds. It is vulnerable to excessive damp; protect with a pane of glass if needed.

preparing an alpine bed

Good drainage is essential to the success of alpines, together with an open, sunny site clear of trees. Whether you plan to grow alpines in a raised bed (see page 143), or in the open garden, you need to prepare the site thoroughly by breaking up the lower levels and incorporating plenty of drainage material to keep the growing medium open and free draining. Fill the bottom third of a raised bed with pea shingle, top up with a mix of soil-based compost or good quality garden soil and grit, then leave it to settle for two to three weeks before you plant. It is worth making up a fresh compost mix when you are replenishing a tired alpine sink or trough (see below).

replenishing an alpine sink

2 **Take the plants** carefully out of the sink and trim any straggly ones, then remove the upper third of compost and replace with the fresh mix.

1 **In a bucket,** mix a quantity of sterilised loam-based compost, such as John Innes No. 2, with equal parts of horticultural sand or grit. Use washed sand or grit to ensure that it is free of clay particles.

3 **After replacing** the old plants, and adding any new ones, mulch with a layer of gravel or coarse grit to a depth of 2–3cm (1in).

slug control

Young plants and new shoots need protection from foraging slugs and snails. Biological control in the form of parasitic nematodes is of no use at this time of year as the soil will be too cold for them to survive, but there are other measures you can take.

- **use citrus peel** as a bait and dispose of the slugs and snails while they are feeding.
- **lay extra grit** around the base of plants to act as a barrier.
- **apply slug bait** as granules or pellets at about 10 per m² (9 per sq yd).

propagating

Keep a close watch on seed trays in the coldframe, as many alpine seeds sown in winter will start to germinate (see Winter). Carefully prick out individually those that have germinated and replace trays in the coldframe in case more seeds germinate later.

You can also sow seeds outdoors now, including any you have collected and stored over winter in a refrigerator (see Autumn). Sow seeds thinly in a clay pot or pan filled with equal parts of John Innes seed compost and grit, cover with a layer of grit and label; the grit helps the stems to elongate, making the tiny seedlings easier to prick out. Place the pots in a cool, exposed position before watering thoroughly.

taking cuttings

Many alpines can be increased from cuttings at this time, but the method will vary according to the growth habit of the particular plant.

- **take advantage of new shoots** to take basal cuttings, and trim them to about 2–3cm (1in).
- **detach individual rosettes** from saxifrages and pot up (see Winter).
- **root branching succulents** from sideshoots, and sedums from individual leaves.
- **insert all these cuttings** into pots or pans of cuttings compost, mixed with an equal amount of extra grit or perlite. Water them from below by standing the container in a dish of water until the compost surface is moist, then cover the surface with 5mm (¼in) of grit; label the cuttings.

water gardens

As temperatures rise it is time to remove ice protection and reintroduce the pump as the pond starts into life.

Any cleaning that is necessary should be done early, before plants develop and pond creatures begin to breed.

In milder areas you can start planting and can divide overgrown plants.

now is the season to . . .

■ **order new aquatic plants** from mail-order or Internet suppliers. Start planting new pond plants in mild areas, or leave it until late spring in colder ones (see Late Spring).

■ **remove, clean and store** pond heaters or other ice-guard devices.

■ **replace a submersible pump** that has been stored over winter after checking that it works properly. Stand it on a brick or a block of wood to avoid drawing in sediment from the base of the pond.

■ **test external pumps** after removing winter insulation.

■ **refill barrel and other container ponds** towards the end of the season and reintroduce plants or fish that have been kept under cover for the winter (see Autumn).

■ **start to feed fish** as the weather warms up. Feed daily but take care to give only as much food as the fish will eat in about half an hour, as uneaten food is a major cause of green algae in ponds. Net the pond to protect fish from herons if not already done (see Autumn).

■ **divide established clumps** of early flowering marginals such as kingcup (*Caltha palustris*) as soon as possible (see Late Spring). There is less urgency for marginal grasses and plants that flower later, although they should also be divided during spring – except irises, which are divided in summer after flowering.

■ **divide bog garden plants** in the same way as perennials once they have formed established clumps (see Autumn). If you plan a new, large bog garden, growing from seed is an economical way of raising new plants, including cuckoo flower (*Cardamine pratensis*), many moisture-loving primulas and purple loosestrife (*Lythrum salicaria*).

■ **protect frog and toad spawn** from birds by netting that area of the pond. Do not transfer spawn from other ponds as this can spread disease.

■ **clean out ponds** if necessary (see opposite).

■ **set up a water butt** to collect rainwater for topping up the pond, which will be much better for pond life than nutrient-rich tap water.

The unfurling leathery leaves and spiny stems of a dramatic *Gunnera manicata* erupt into growth in early spring, emerging from a protective winter covering of straw.

cleaning out the pond

All ponds tend to turn green in spring. This is caused by algae that feed on the nutrients that proliferate in the water at this time of year. The water usually clears once the pond plants begin growing strongly, taking up the nutrients and starving out the algae (see Summer).

A total clean out is a major job that is only necessary every five years or so for small ponds and double that for larger ones. The exception is if the water is black, smelly and obviously polluted, such as occurs when leaves and debris have been left to rot in the pond.

Choose a time in early spring, before fish and other creatures start breeding, to empty your pond if it needs a total clean out, so that it has time to settle down before winter. Take the opportunity to check the liner and make any necessary repairs, and to divide and replant any plants that are overgrown. Inspect pond snails and dispose of those with spiral shells (great pond snails), as they eat plants.

spring cleaning a pond

1 **Remove all pond plants** and place them on a plastic sheet if they will be out of the water for a few hours only; if longer, stand them in buckets part-filled with water. Get ready three large bowls of clean water. Scoop out fish and other wildlife, and keep fish, spawn and snails in separate bowls (fish need wide containers for plenty of oxygen). Put some plants in with the fish for shelter and food.

3 **After baling out** the last few centimetres of water with a container, scoop out the mud from the bottom using a net or sieve – don't worry about removing every last bit. Pile the mud on a plastic sheet next to the pond and leave it there for a couple of days so that any creatures can crawl back into the water.

2 **To siphon out the water,** take a 1.5m (5ft) length of hose and place in the pond so it fills with water. Holding one end under water with your thumb sealing it, quickly bring the other end out of the pond to a lower point than the one in the pond, releasing your thumb at the same time. The pull of gravity should start the flow of water, which can be caught in a bucket. If there is a lot of debris in the pond, place an old sieve on the pond end of the hose to stop it from getting blocked. If you cannot find a lower point, you will have to bale or pump out all the water.

4 **Scrub inside the pond** with a stiff brush and clean water; do not use detergents. Bale out the resulting dirty water. Refill the pond, using rainwater first and topping up with tap water, then replace the plants. Allow temperatures to stabilise for a day or so before replacing fish, spawn and snails.

patios & containers

It is a good idea to get a head start on the year and take care of as many jobs as possible on fine early spring days. Start planning and planting now so you can enjoy colourful containers right through the summer.

now is the season to . . .

■ **clean patios and decking** before the space is filled with container displays.

■ **remove winter protection** and return pots to their original positions as soon as the weather permits. However, keep some fleece handy to protect susceptible young growth and flowers if late frosts threaten.

■ **brighten up your containers** and patio borders with spring bedding plants that are tough, colourful and long flowering. There is plenty of choice in garden centres or nurseries, including double daisies (*Bellis perennis*), forget-me-nots, primulas and wallflowers, plus ready-grown bulbs.

■ **water regularly** as the weather warms up, particularly on breezy days when containers dry out rapidly.

■ **order young tender perennials** and bedding plants from mail order or Internet suppliers.

■ **protect the blooms of spring-flowering shrubs** like camellias, rhododendrons and azaleas by placing containers in a sheltered spot away from the early morning sun.

■ **mulch rhododendrons** with chipped bark to protect their shallow roots from extremes of temperature.

■ **feed spring bulbs in containers** while they are in flower and until the leaves start to yellow and die, so they will make a superb display next spring. Label each container so that you can identify the bulbs when dormant.

■ **deadhead winter pansies** to encourage new flowers.

■ **plant lily bulbs** to twice their depth in soil-based potting compost. Put three bulbs in a 25–30cm (10–12in) deep pot and stand in an unheated greenhouse or coldframe or a sheltered spot outside.

■ **plant up containers** of tender plants in a heated

Deadheading winter pansies will prolong their flowering display into early summer.

greenhouse or conservatory; small plug plants are very useful for hanging baskets and flower pouches (see below). By growing the displays under cover through spring, you will have well-established containers to put out after the frosts.

■ **plant perennials**, ornamental grasses and ferns. Many of them make low-maintenance container plants; they will establish quickly if planted now. Good-looking foliage and early flowering perennials are particularly useful during spring when there is little else around. Some tolerate shade and so are perfect for brightening gloomy corners (see opposite).

■ **prune patio roses**, removing all dead, weak and damaged shoots and shortening sideshoots.

■ **pot up roses and shrubs** (see Late Spring).

■ **top-dress permanent plants** by replacing the top few centimetres of compost with an appropriate compost mixed with controlled-release fertiliser (see page 36).

■ **in April, start to harden off** shrubs of borderline hardiness that overwintered under cover (see Late Spring), so that they acclimatise to outside conditions before being returned to the patio in late spring.

■ **control weeds in paving cracks** at an early stage, by hand or with a weedkiller or garden flame gun. Once the cracks are clear, and if you like an informal garden, sow seed of plants that thrive in crevices such as mexican daisy (*Erigeron karvinskianus*) and yellow fumitory (*Corydalis lutea*).

■ **bring garden furniture out of store** and clean or treat if necessary. Resin furniture only requires washing with hot water and a mild detergent. Wooden furniture usually needs treating with stain or preservative every other year; choose the right product for hardwood or softwood furniture.

Plug plants can be ordered by mail. They should be potted on into 8cm (3in) pots as soon as they arrive, to grow on to a larger size.

cleaning patios and decking

Patios, decks and paths look much better for a thorough cleaning at the end of winter, and are much safer to walk on, as algae can make surfaces dangerously slippery. Shady areas are the worst affected by moss and algae, as the surface tends to stay damp for long periods. The best method of cleaning is to use a pressure washer, but first make sure that the water can drain away freely.

When using a pressure hose on brick paving, take care not to wash the sand out of the joints.

You can use the washer alone or in conjunction with a proprietary cleaner, in which case choose an environmentally friendly product to avoid harming living things. Apply cleaner before using the washer and carefully follow the manufacturer's instructions. Bear in mind the following points:

● **paviors and some types of slab** may be damaged if water is applied at high pressure. On these surfaces, use moderate pressure of around 1000 psi, or hold the applicator high above the surface of the paving to lessen the force of the water.

● **when cleaning concrete,** do not concentrate pressure on a single area for more than a few seconds, or it could begin to damage the surface.

● **patios should slope gently** to allow water to drain readily, so start at the highest point and work downhill.

● **for decking,** use low pressure of around 750 psi, as water applied at high pressure can drive dirt into the wood. After cleaning, allow decking to dry, then apply a sealer to the surface, according to the manufacturer's instructions.

perennial plants for containers

FOLIAGE PLANTS ● grasses, such as *Hakonechloa macra* 'Aureola' (sun or part shade) and *Festuca glauca* (sun)
● hardy ferns, such as *Athyrium filix-femina* and *Asplenium scolopendrium* (shade) ● heucheras (sun or part shade)
● hostas (part or full shade) ● dead-nettles, *Lamium maculatum* varieties (part or full shade)
SPRING FLOWERS ● lily-of-the-valley, *Convallaria majalis* (shade)
● *Dicentra formosa* 'Alba', *D.* 'Langtrees', *D.* 'Luxuriant' (sun or part shade) ● *Erysimum* 'John Codrington' (sun)
● *Primula* 'Wanda' (sun or shade) ● *Viola sororia* 'Freckles' (sun or part shade)

looking ahead . . .
☑ LATE SPRING Harden off containers of tender plants.
☑ Move container shrubs of borderline hardiness outside.

In a large galvanised planter, spring bulbs (*Narcissus*) and *Helleborus foetidus* make colourful companions for permanent pieris and ivy.

lawns

Often early spring is catch-up time for doing any maintenance and repair jobs that were missed in autumn, especially if the grass was wet under foot. Now that the lawn is coming to life and starting to grow again, this is also the time to get it into good condition to cope with the stresses of the year ahead.

now is the season to . . .

■ **keep off the lawn** if it is frosted or very wet.

■ **brush off worm casts** regularly (see right).

■ **trim the edge** of your lawn (see opposite) and repair any broken edges if necessary (see Autumn).

■ **level any humps or hollows** that have developed in the lawn over the winter months (see Autumn).

■ **aerate the lawn** with a hollow-tiner, spiked roller or garden fork to improve drainage and ease surface compaction. Then apply a top-dressing of equal parts loam, sand and peat substitute at a rate of 1.5kg m² (3lb per sq yd). For heavier soils with high clay content, use a mix of four parts horticultural sand to one part loam or garden compost.

■ **start mowing the grass** if it begins to grow (see opposite).

■ **re-seed** any bare patches (see opposite).

■ **start feeding lawns** with a spring fertiliser.

■ **control weeds** and moss (see right).

■ **prepare the site for a new lawn** (see Late Spring). Thorough cultivation is essential for a good quality lawn, and problems created by taking short cuts are difficult to rectify later. Cultivate down to at least 30cm (12in), as the roots of many grasses can penetrate to this depth.

and if you have time . . .

■ **brush the lawn** to knock off any heavy dew. If it is left, the humid conditions can encourage the spread of fungal disease.

controlling weeds and moss

The most effective way of controlling lawn weeds is through a combination of chemical and cultivation practices, which involves weedkiller use in conjunction with frequent mowing.

● **use a fan-shaped rake** to lift low-spreading weeds, such as speedwell and yarrow, before mowing, so that the blades slice off their topgrowth.

● **kill tap-rooted weeds** like dandelion and dock by digging down and cutting them off about 8cm (3in) below soil level.

● **control larger areas** of spreading weeds by applying a spray or granular lawn weedkiller, which will kill broad-leaved weeds without harming the grass.

● **brush off worm casts** as these contain weed seeds brought up from below ground, which will germinate when exposed to daylight. Always brush the lawn before mowing, using a stiff brush or besom to scatter the casts. Brushing in this way helps to reduce wear and tear on mower blades caused by the gritty nature of the casts and prevents them being smeared over the lawn by the mower, smothering the grass beneath and causing a patchy appearance.

moss control

If there is too much moss to control by raking, apply a mosskiller, such as lawn sand or a liquid formulation containing sulphate of iron. The moss will turn black, but wait until it then turns brown before raking out dead remains. Re-treat any patches where moss reappears about three weeks after the first application.

WEED AND FEED TIP To save time, use a combined weed and feed formulation, which will kill off the weeds with a selective chemical herbicide while it feeds the grass.

Early spring is the ideal time to aerate your lawn. This will help to get it back into condition and looking its best for the months of use ahead.

trimming a lawn edge

1 Use a half-moon edging tool to cut a clean edge to the lawn. On straight edges, stand on a plank and use it as a cutting line.

2 Neaten lawn edges, if necessary, using long-handled edging shears.

spring feeding

Start feeding lawns now, especially in milder areas where growth starts early. Use a spring or summer fertiliser which is high in nitrogen and phosphates to promote growth and root development of the grass. If you use a powdered or granular formulation, rather than liquid feed, wait for a day when the grass is dry and the soil is moist, so that the fertiliser settles on the soil. If there is no rain within 48 hours, water the lawn lightly to wash in the fertiliser.

trimming lawn edges

The edge of a lawn often sags and crumbles as a result of frost action on the bare soil. Remove the narrowest strip possible to reinstate a clean edge; collect the trimmings and add them to the compost heap.

dealing with bare patches

Bare patches may be due to weeds smothering the grass, or part of the lawn being covered with an object; whatever the cause, the grass will eventually die due to lack of light. Spills of concentrated fertiliser or other chemicals may 'burn' the grass and kill it off in patches. Fortunately, these areas can be re-seeded to restore the lawn to its original condition (see below).

mowing the lawn

Once the soil temperature rises above 5–7°C (40–45°F), the grass starts growing and you need to mow. The exact timing will vary from year to year, depending on the weather. Make the first cuts with the mower blades set high (see Winter). As the rate of growth increases, the lawn will need more frequent mowing, and the height of cut can gradually be lowered. Aim to reduce the grass by a third of its height at each cutting; do not cut it too short, as this weakens the grass and exposes bare soil where moss and weeds can easily establish.

looking ahead . . .
☑ LATE SPRING Sow grass seed or lay turf for a new lawn.

re-seeding bare patches

1 First go over the area with a spring-tined rake. Rake vigorously to drag out all the old dead grass, including pieces of dead root, and to score the soil surface. Use a garden fork to break up the surface and ease soil compaction. Jab the tines into the soil to a depth of 2–3cm (1in).

2 Rake the soil to a depth of 1–2cm (½–¾in) to level it and to create a fine seedbed.

3 Sow grass seed evenly over the area, at a rate of about 30g per m² (1oz per sq yd), and lightly rake it in.

4 Cover the area with sacking until the seeds germinate; water in dry weather.

fruit

This is the turn of the year in the fruit garden, when stored crops come to an end and blossom heralds the harvest to come. Check and feed all your fruit ready for the new season, and remember to protect early flowers on wall-trained fruit whenever frost is forecast.

now is the season to . . .

- **check fruits** in store frequently as the end of the keeping season approaches, and use up the good samples quickly.
- **inspect supports** for trained fruit, and replace or repair them if necessary. Check and loosen ties before new growth starts. Tie in new stems while they are flexible.
- **thin spurs on trained** apples and pears (see opposite); complete this and all winter pruning, except for stone fruits, as soon as possible (see Winter).
- **prune new bush** and cane fruit before growth starts (see opposite).
- **plant autumn-fruiting raspberries,** and cut old canes in existing rows down to the ground.
- **tie in new blackberry canes** if not done in autumn (see below).

- **plant perpetual strawberries** for fruit later this year. Remove the first flush of flower buds from summer-fruiting varieties planted in autumn and all buds from those put in now, to allow plants to build up strength.
- **divide alpine strawberries,** and sow new plants under glass (see page 57).
- **weed and lightly cultivate** round all fruits, before feeding and mulching (see below).
- **protect blossom from frost,** especially early flowering apricots and peaches (see opposite).
- **watch for signs of pests and disease,** including scale insects (see page 57).
- **start early vines** under glass into growth (see page 56).
- **pollinate early blossom** on greenhouse fruits (see page 56).
- **remove grease bands** from fruit trees in April.
- **water new fruits in a dry spell,** especially those near walls and fences where the soil is sheltered from rain.
- **pick forced rhubarb** under pots.

tying in blackberries and hybrid berries

In mild gardens, new stems are usually trained in autumn, after the old fruited canes are removed, but in colder gardens the young canes are loosely bundled along a wire for protection (see Autumn). You can untie these now and fan the canes out evenly on the wires, securing them with string or plastic twists. Very long canes can be cut off at the top wire, or you can tie them along the wire as a thick rope, or arch them above the supports, tying the tips to the top wire to form gentle loops.

feeding and mulching

All fruit plants, except very large trees, respond to feeding in March or early April. Apply a general-purpose fertiliser at the rate of 100–140g per m² (3–4oz per sq yd), using the higher rate on poor or light soils. After pruning and weeding, sprinkle the fertiliser evenly over a slightly larger area than is shaded by the branches, and lightly rake in. After two weeks, mulch with a 5–8cm (2–3in) layer of garden compost or well-rotted manure.

Forced rhubarb is one of very few crops to be harvested in the fruit garden in early spring, but there is much to do now to ensure good fruit crops later in the year.

pruning new bush and cane fruits

Most new cane and bush fruits need formative pruning so that they grow into the desired shape. You can do this straight after planting, or wait until early in their first spring.

- **raspberries, blackberries and hybrid berries** Cut each cane to a bud 15–23cm (6–9in) above ground.
- **blackcurrants** Cut all stems to about 5cm (2in) high. Retain the best four or five shoots that appear later; if these are less than 45–60cm (18–24in) long at the end of the season, cut growth back again next spring.
- **gooseberries, red currants and white currants** Cut back all shoots by half to an upward-pointing bud. Prune cordons and other trained forms by cutting back main branches by half, and all sideshoots to 2–3cm (1in). Remove all growth on the lower 10–15cm (4–6in) of the main stem to establish a clear 'leg'.

protecting blossom

Wall-trained fruits that flower early are more at risk from spring frosts than those in the open garden, because of the still conditions that prevail near boundaries and garden structures. Protect the blossom by draping plants with fleece or net curtaining at night.

Strawberries need similar protection, or you can cover plants with cloches. If the open flowers do get frosted, it is possible to wash off the frost early, before sunshine can damage the frozen blooms and turn the centres black. Fit a fine spray attachment to a hosepipe or hand sprayer and mist the flowers until all signs of frost have gone.

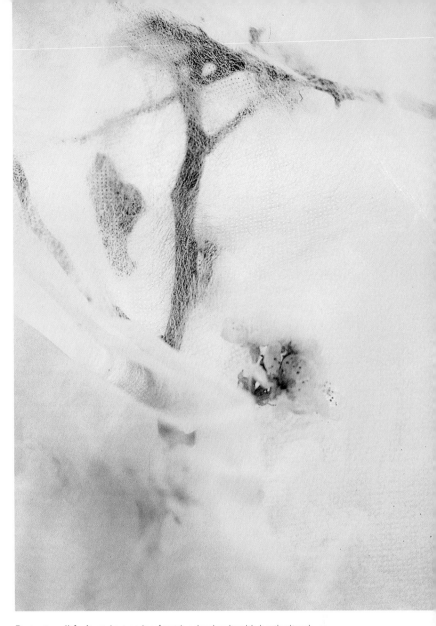

Protect wall fruit against spring frost by draping it with horticultural fleece at night. Remove it by day to allow access for pollinating bees.

thinning spurs on trained apples and pears

1 **Thin fruiting spurs** that have become crowded or cross each other by cutting some out at their base, or where they branch.

2 **Remove any young shoots and buds** that are going to become inaccessible, emerge close to main branches or point in the wrong direction.

3 **Aim to leave an open, balanced** arrangement of sideshoots to admit plenty of air and light; clear away all prunings when you have finished.

fruit/2

fruit under glass

Apricots, peaches and vines will be coming into flower in the greenhouse, while forced rhubarb and strawberries should be ready for picking. Discard rhubarb crowns after forcing, but plant strawberries in the garden after hardening off; they may crop again in late summer. Alpine strawberries make attractive plants, and sowing seeds under glass now is a good way to build up stocks of unusual varieties.

pollinating and thinning

Apricots, peaches and strawberries grown in the greenhouse often flower before many pollinating insects are about, especially if the weather is cold. On a warm day, open wide the ventilators and doors, but otherwise you will need to fertilise the open flowers yourself, around midday if possible. Early outdoor apricots and peaches on warm walls may also flower too early for insects, and they will benefit from hand pollination too.

In a mild season, the earliest varieties can set a heavy crop of fruitlets by the end of March, and these should be thinned as soon as possible to ensure good-sized fruits. Reduce clusters to leave one or, at the most, two fruitlets in each. Thin crowded stems to leave a fruitlet every 5–8cm (2–3in). If all these develop, you should thin them further in late spring.

greenhouse grapes

In unheated greenhouses, grape vines will be coming into leaf and flower, especially if the stems are sprayed every day or two with warm water to stimulate the buds to open. If you lowered the main stems in winter to encourage the buds to break evenly (see Winter), you can retie them on their wires when the majority of buds show early leaf. In heated greenhouses and conservatories, the vines will be flowering now, so tap the stems every day with a cane to fertilise the flowers.

thinning grapes

● **as trusses often set too many fruits,** thin a heavy set when grapes are the size of small peas, to prevent the developing fruits from crowding each other. You may need to do this in April in a warm greenhouse, but wait until early summer in an unheated one. Using a pair of pointed, long-bladed scissors, remove most of the grapes in the centre of the bunch, and the smallest grapes around the point of the bunch, but leave plenty in the widest part or 'shoulders'; aim to leave at least a pencil thickness between grapes.

● **pinch out the shoots** at the second leaf beyond a truss of setting fruit.

If insects have not done the job of pollination (above), use a soft, small paintbrush to stroke the centre of each bloom lightly (left) and transfer the pollen from one flower to another.

alpine strawberries

Many alpine strawberries do not make runners in the same way as large-fruited kinds, but instead grow into large clumps like a border perennial. Although these will fruit if left alone, yield and quality are greatly improved if you split large clumps into smaller segments every few years (see below).

raising from seed

Use a soil-based compost, and sow the seeds sparingly in trays or pots. Cover them thinly with compost and keep them in a propagator or greenhouse at about 18°C (64°F) until seedlings appear. Prick these out individually into small pots when they have two true leaves, and plant out in May or June.

dealing with scale insects

1 **Check plants** in early spring for the brownish scales, particularly on the woody stems of vines, apricots and peaches.

2 **Wipe them off** using a cotton bud or a soft cloth, dipped in alcohol.

dividing alpine strawberries

1 **Shear off the old foliage** during early March and dig up the clump with a fork.

2 **Either cut a plant** into several portions or simply tear it apart with your hands; discard the old woody centre.

3 **Replant the young outer portions** about 30cm (12in) apart in fresh ground that has been dug and manured. They make an attractive edging to a bed in the kitchen garden.

scale insects

These minute sap-feeding insects can attack fruit trees and vines, especially those growing under glass. They shelter under waxy oval scales on shoots and branches where they lay their eggs safe from most insecticides, so you will have to remove them by hand (see above). Spraying with insecticide is effective only against the migrating juveniles, which usually emerge in early summer outdoors, but much earlier under heated glass. Inspect stems closely in warm spells during spring and summer, and spray if the minute crawling insects are seen. Spray again a fortnight later to catch survivors and late hatchings, if possible before they can develop their protective scales.

there is still time to . . .

● **check blackcurrants for big bud mites**; infected buds are conspicuous and are easily removed for destruction (see Winter).

● **cover rhubarb** outdoors with forcing pots, boxes or buckets to produce early tender stalks.

● **cover strawberries** with cloches or polythene tunnels to advance their harvest by a few weeks.

● **protect peaches** and nectarines from peach leaf curl by covering the trees with screens, and by applying a copper-based fungicide spray.

looking ahead . . .

☑ LATE SPRING Prune stone fruits such as plums and cherries.
☑ Plant out alpine strawberries.
☑ SUMMER Thin grapes in unheated greenhouses.
☑ LATE SUMMER Summer-prune trained fruit.
☑ Cut down summer-fruiting raspberries.
☑ AUTUMN Cut down blackberries and hybrid berries after fruiting.

vegetables

Although there is no real end to the cropping year in a well-planned kitchen garden, early spring feels like the year's beginning as the weather improves.
This is the best time to sow seed under cover and plant out a wide range of hardy vegetables.

now is the season to . . .

■ **order seeds** and young vegetable plants for delivery later. Although young plants and seedlings are becoming available in garden centres, do not be tempted to buy these too early in cold areas unless you can provide them with the protection they may need.

■ **inspect stored vegetables** at regular intervals and remove any showing signs of mould or rot before they infect their neighbours. Use up quickly those that show signs of growth or withering. Stored crops could include beetroot, carrots, garlic, onions, potatoes, shallots, swedes and turnips.

■ **begin to harden off** and plant out hardy crops, such as peas, started off in pots under glass in winter.

■ **continue preparing seedbeds** (see Winter). Break the soil down to a roughly level surface, so that it can dry out during sunny or windy weather. This will help you to create a fine surface, or tilth, when the seedbed is raked level (see Late Spring).

■ **monitor the soil temperature** to see how quickly it is

To test the soil temperature, insert an outdoor thermometer into the upper 8–10cm (3–4in) layer of earth and leave it for about an hour.

warming up. Many seeds need temperatures of 5–7°C (40–45°F) in the upper layer of soil before they will germinate.

■ **warm the soil** before sowing or planting by covering areas with cloches, low polythene tunnels or black plastic sheeting. If the weather is dry and windy, remove the covers to allow the soil to dry before sowing (see Winter).

■ **make early sowings** of crops such as beetroot, broad beans, carrot, lettuce, peas, radish, spinach and turnips when soil conditions become suitable. Choose early varieties of these crops where possible.

■ **plant onions sets,** early potatoes, asparagus and globe artichokes (see page 63).

■ **prepare trenches** for planting runner beans, peas, marrows or pumpkins in late spring or early summer (see below).

■ **dig areas as they become clear** of crops and compost the plant waste. Dig in any overwintering green manures.

■ **if the soil is wet,** dig trenches 15–20cm (6–8in) deep and wide at 1.2m (4ft) intervals. This creates mini raised beds in between, with improved drainage.

Digging shallow trenches creates raised beds, allowing you to plant or sow even on heavy soil or a high water table.

■ **protect seedbeds and seedlings from birds** by covering them with fleece or netting, or using bird scarers. Brassicas are particularly vulnerable, and wood pigeons will feed on any cauliflowers they can reach.

■ **watch for slugs** and early signs of other pests (see opposite).

■ **during dry periods, take the opportunity** to hoe off weed seedlings, but remember that disturbing the soil encourages more weed seeds to germinate as the weather turns milder.

Cover the kitchen waste with soil dug from the next section.

trench composting

You can compost a small supply of waste in a trench as a source of nourishment and consistent moisture for tall peas, runner beans, marrows, squash and pumpkins. Mark out a trench 30cm (12in) wide where they are to grow. Dig out a short section at one end, the depth of a spade blade. Fill the trench to half its depth with kitchen and vegetable waste, and cover with soil.

Continue until the trench has been filled along its length; cover the last section with the soil from the first. Leave to settle for a month or two. For beans on 'wigwams', or pumpkins, dig a pit 1m (3ft) across for each plant and fill in the same way.

avoiding later pest problems

Pests and diseases become more prevalent as the weather turns milder. Slugs start to feed soon after hatching, but if this first generation can be controlled it will be months before the population builds up to epidemic proportions.

protecting seedlings **from slugs**

The juicy young leaves of seedlings will always attract slugs but there are various ways to deter them.

1 **Scatter grit** around young plants, using a pot as a guide

2 **Buy a proprietary slug pot** filled with a toxic mixture

3 **Cut a serrated collar** from a plastic bottle using pinking shears

4 **Place the base** of a clear plastic bottle filled with old beer near young plants, to act as a trap – or use upturned grapefruit skins

- **look out for aphids** by inspecting the outer leaves of cabbages, cauliflowers and other vegetables.
- **control blackfly** on broad beans by pinching out the growing tips when they begin to flower.
- **clear away all plant debris** to the compost heap rather than bury it, as it provides food for hatching slugs at this time.

You can buy lettuce and brassicas as young plants. If weather conditions or soil are unsuitable for immediate planting, transplant into pots or modular trays and grow on under glass or on a windowsill until you can plant out.

harvesting **now**

- asparagus • brussels sprouts
- calabrese • celeriac • jerusalem artichokes • kale • leeks • parsnips
- salad onions • spring greens
- sprouting broccoli • winter cabbage and cauliflower • winter lettuce
- winter radish • winter spinach

Sprouting broccoli

sowing and planting

Early spring is the time for putting into practice the plans you made during the winter months, and for sowing and planting the crops you enjoy eating. The weather and your garden conditions play a part in the precise timing of your sowing and planting, as do the varieties you choose.

varieties

If you look through seed catalogues or along a stand of seed packets, you will see that some crops, such as peas, carrots and potatoes, have early and maincrop varieties. Maincrops are sown later in the season than earlies, and usually take longer to mature. You can sow some early varieties of carrot in late summer, as they are quick to mature, but with lettuce it is vital to sow the right variety for the season.

'Purple Cape' is a winter cauliflower variety, with purple-red curds, harvested in March.

One way to mark a straight drill is to press the handle of a rake or hoe into the soil to make a groove.

Seed tape with pre-spaced seed saves thinning crops such as lettuce, radish and carrots, which are easily sown too thickly.

Vegetable seeds come in a wide and colourful array of shapes and sizes; the bigger they are, the easier to space correctly.

sowing into a coldframe

1 Using the corner of a hoe, make straight, shallow drills in a seedbed you have prepared and raked to a fine tilth.

2 If the soil is dry, trickle water into the drills before sowing the seeds.

3 Sow the seeds thinly and cover them lightly with soil. Water gently through a fine rose before closing the lid of the coldframe. The seeds should have germinated in 14–21 days.

Space young leeks or other crops closer than recommended if you wish to harvest and eat them as baby, or mini, vegetables.

spacing crops

Plants grow better without too much competition, which is why regular weeding and correct spacing are important. It is worth thinning seedlings in stages rather than all in one go, to avoid gaps, conserve moisture and suppress weeds. Later thinnings can often be used in salads, or as immature or baby vegetables, leaving the rest wider-spaced to mature fully. You may in any case prefer smaller roots and cabbages, in which case grow them closer together; the seed packet usually states whether a variety is suitable for growing this way.

extended harvesting

For the harvesting period to last as long as possible, make a number of small successional sowings every few weeks and include early, maincrop and seasonal varieties. Protecting early and late crops with cloches is another way to extend the harvest. With peas and beans, regular picking in itself prolongs the season.

The yield you can expect from a crop is greatly influenced by growing conditions. If your soil is well prepared, regularly enriched with organic matter and kept weed free, your yield will be much higher than where the soil is dry, weedy and exhausted. Other influencing factors are the weather and your choice of variety; some varieties simply yield more heavily than others.

Use cloches to protect early and late salad crops and extend the harvest.

timing

Many crops can be sown or planted over several months. Bear in mind that most seeds and young plants can only grow when the soil temperature reaches a minimum requirement; the danger of sowing too early is not frost, but that seeds will sit in cold, damp soil and rot before they germinate. Many of the earlier sowings will be more successful under glass – a greenhouse or coldframe – or with cloche protection than in open ground. Sowings made under glass in modular trays incur less root disturbance than those made in trays or pots and then pricked out. This is a useful way of getting a head start and avoiding the unpredictability of the weather at the start of the year. Using modular trays is also a way to minimise root disturbance when transplanting vegetables, as they are planted with an intact rootball, avoiding the risk of tearing young roots as you tease seedlings apart.

vegetables/3

sowing and planting by crop

Spring is the best sowing and planting time for many crops, including perennial asparagus and both globe and jerusalem artichokes.

peas and beans

- **sow early varieties of peas** in 8–10cm (3–4in) pots, two or three seeds per pot, then place in a cool greenhouse or coldframe, if not already done in late winter. The plants will be large enough for planting out by mid-spring, with those sown in a length of guttering (see Late Spring) a little later. Plant them 8–10cm (3–4in) apart, preferably in pre-warmed soil to avoid any check to growth.
- **as the weather warms, remove cloches** from autumn-sown peas, but harden them off first by removing alternate cloches during the day and ventilating them increasingly at night for a couple of weeks.
- **thin peas sown in autumn or late winter** by removing alternate plants.
- **sow early peas and broad beans outdoors** as a follow-on crop to those raised in pots, or sown outdoors under cloches or polythene tunnels.
- **harden off and plant out** broad beans sown in pots under cover in winter, 25–30cm (10–12in) apart.

Traditional forcing pots are used to cover kale plants, forcing a crop of tender young shoots.

cabbage family

- **finish harvesting last year's brussels sprouts** as the last 'buttons' swell; snap off the leafy tops and use as greens.
- **sow brussels sprouts, sprouting broccoli** and varieties of summer cabbage and cauliflower in pots or in a seedbed for transplanting in May or June.
- **harvest kale** by picking the young shoots, leaving the large outer leaves intact to fuel the plants' growth.
- **continue to harvest winter cabbages,** cutting the whole head, and start picking the secondary crop of leafy greens produced by the stumps of previously harvested cabbages (see Winter).
- **transplant autumn-sown** spring cabbages early, spacing plants about 30cm (12in) apart (see Autumn).
- **spring greens** planted in autumn will be ready for harvest. Pick some of the young leaves, as more will develop, or remove alternate plants so that those left will form a head.

onion family

- **finish planting shallots, and plant onion sets** early on a well-drained site. Check them regularly until they have started to root, as birds foraging for food often move them about. Replant them if necessary.
- **inspect stored onions and garlic;** dispose of any showing signs of rot or mould, and quickly use up any that are shooting.
- **lift mature leeks** as required. If you need the ground for planting other crops in April, lift any that remain and heel them in spare ground out of the sun.
- **continue to sow leeks and onions** in modular trays or pots in the greenhouse. Sow four or five seeds per pot to transplant in late spring.
- **sow salad onions** from late March in short rows.

Plant onion sets 1cm (½in) deep and 10–15cm (4–6in) apart in rows 25cm (10in) apart.

Where mice are a problem, start onion sets in pots to plant out once they are bigger.

root crops

● **make first sowings** of early varieties of beetroot, carrot and turnip unless the soil is cold and wet, in which case wait for it to warm up. For the earliest sowings, use cloches, or cover the soil for a week or two with plastic sheeting to provide warmer conditions and encourage rapid seed germination. SOWING CARROTS TIP Cover carrots with fleece tucked into the soil to give an earlier crop and to protect against carrot fly.

● **sow kohl rabi and parsnips** outdoors in late March or April. As parsnips are slow to germinate, sow radish or beetroot in between as markers; these fast-maturing crops will be ready for pulling before the parsnip roots start to develop.

● **sow celeriac** under cover in modular trays.

planting early potatoes

METHOD 1 **When each chitted potato** has formed four or five shoots 2–3cm (1in) long, dig a trench 10cm (4in) deep and place them in it, rose end up, and 25–30cm (10–12in) apart; fill in with soil.

METHOD 2 **Plant the chitted tubers** in individual holes, using a trowel, at the same depth and distance, in rows 40–50cm (15–20in) apart. Fill in each hole with soil.

potatoes

It is advisable to buy seed potatoes that are certified disease-free stock, rather than be tempted to plant tubers you have bought from the greengrocer or supermarket. The size of seed potatoes depends on the variety, but they should be about the size of a hen's egg. Before planting, you need to sprout, or chit, potatoes indoors (see Winter). Do this first with earlies, for planting out in March or early April, and two to three weeks later for maincrop varieties, planted in late spring. Soil temperature at the planting depth should be at least 6°C (43°F) for four or five days before planting, so that the shoots will grow unchecked.

salad crops

● **continue to protect early sowings** with cloches or low polythene tunnels, giving ventilation on sunny days. Thin when necessary; there may be pickings in a mild season.

● **make successional sowings of lettuce,** radish and spinach in the open ground, preferably warmed by plastic sheeting.

perennial crops

Globe artichokes and asparagus, in particular, need a lot of space and should be planted in a sheltered, sunny position. The soil should be well drained, deeply dug, enriched with plenty of rotted manure or garden compost and cleared of all traces of perennial weeds. These long-term crops need two years to establish before you can enjoy a harvest.

● **take globe artichoke offsets** or buy small plants. Cut offsets from the edge of an established plant and set them just deep enough to stand upright, about 5cm (2in); each plant will need about 1m² (10sq ft). Cover with fleece if frost threatens.

● **asparagus crowns** must not be allowed to dry out, so plant as soon as possible (see below). Young plants are also sold in pots ready for transplanting, or you can raise plants from seed sown in modular trays under glass. Start to harvest established plants when spears are 15cm (6in) tall.

● **jerusalem artichokes** will tolerate light shade. Plant tubers 30cm (12in) apart and 10cm (4in) deep in well-prepared soil. The plants grow tall, reaching 3m (10ft), and will crop this year.

planting asparagus crowns

2 Plant the crowns 10–15cm (4–6in) deep, spreading out the roots, crab-wise, either side of the ridge. Space them 30cm (12in) apart in rows 45cm (18in) apart. Earth over the trench and fork in more compost. On heavy soils, plant the crowns more shallowly, but earth up the stems as they grow.

1 Dig a trench 45cm (18in) deep and incorporate plenty of well-rotted organic matter. Make a shallow ridge down the centre.

herbs

With spring in the air there is a rapid revival of growth, so finish tidying up and dividing large clumps of perennial herbs, and start feeding the young plants. Begin sowing, at first under glass and later outdoors, and planting hardy herbs outside and in containers.

now is the season to . . .

■ **tidy herb beds and borders** before new growth gets under way. Clear the dead foliage of herbaceous herbs such as salad burnet and fennel, then weed and prick over the soil with a fork.

■ **feed perennial herbs** such as marjoram and tarragon with bone meal or a high-potash granular fertiliser.

■ **warm the ground** before sowing by covering prepared soil with cloches, plastic sheeting or a light coldframe to encourage rapid germination. Start sowing two to three weeks later.

■ **thin autumn-sown** seedlings.

■ **pot up rooted cuttings** under glass into 8cm (3in) pots of soil-based compost.

■ **check any layers of thyme**, rosemary, sage and other herbs started the previous year. Pot them up if they have rooted.

■ **propagate perennial herbs** by division (see opposite).

■ **finish laying out** new herb gardens (see Autumn).

■ **prune lavender, sage and rosemary** in a mild season; avoid cutting back into old wood, which may not regenerate.

and if you have time . . .

■ **plant out potted** hardy herbs used indoors over winter after feeding with general fertiliser and hardening them off for 10–14 days. Keep tender herbs frost free in a coldframe or greenhouse until late spring.

repotting tender herbs

French lavender (*Lavandula stoechas*), rosemaries such as *R. officinalis* 'Prostratus', and lemon verbena can be trimmed to shape now, before potting on or repotting. Cut out dead wood, shorten very long shoots and remove one or two older branches on lemon verbena; lightly clip evergreens to a balanced shape.

● **pot on young plants** into the next size pot, using a soil-based compost and putting plenty of drainage material in the bottom.

● **repot larger specimens** by carefully knocking them from their pots. Tease the outer 2–3cm (1in) of compost from the roots, shortening any that spiral all round the pot, and replace in the same container, working fresh soil-based compost between the roots with your fingers.

dividing basil

1 **First acclimatise** the plant by standing the pot in its plastic sleeve in a cool, well-lit place. Gradually turn down the sleeve a little more each day. Water gently if dry.

2 **When you can remove** the plastic sleeve without the plants drooping, gently tap out the contents of the pot.

3 **Slice the rootball** into several segments with a sharp knife. Pot up each piece in a 10cm (4in) pot of soil-based compost, water gently and stand in a lightly shaded place.

4 **Once the plants recover** and stand upright, you can grow and pot them on in the usual way.

dividing bought herbs

You can divide up pots of culinary herbs, such as parsley, coriander and basil, bought from a supermarket (see above).

herbs to sow now

IN A WARM GREENHOUSE IN LATE MARCH ● basil ● coriander ● dill ● marjoram ● parsley ● rue

IN A COOL GREENHOUSE OR COLDFRAME ● lemon balm ● lovage ● sage ● sorrel ● summer savory

OUTDOORS ● borage ● caraway ● chervil ● chives ● fennel

planting a herb tower

A terracotta 'tower' with several planting pockets around the sides is ideal for growing a basic selection of culinary herbs or a collection of the same herb, such as thymes or basils, in different varieties.

planting a thyme tower

1 Spread a layer of gravel, 5cm (2in) deep, in the base of the pot and in the centre of it stand a length of perforated watering pipe, or plastic drainpipe with holes drilled every 10cm (4in). Pour in a handful or two of gravel to keep the pipe in place, and fill around it with soil-based compost up to the level of the first planting pocket.

2 Set a thyme plant in position, then add compost up to the level of the next planting hole.

4 Use a watering can to fill the pipe with water, which will percolate through to all layers.

3 Continue adding compost and planting thymes in the pockets. Fill to just below the rim of the pot and finish by planting two or three thymes on top.

The finished tower (right) can become a focal point, especially when the thymes are in flower.

dividing perennial herbs

By dividing perennial herbs you can produce smaller and younger plants that will grow more vigorously.

● **early in the season** you can divide chives, lemon balm, marjoram, mint, sorrel and tarragon.

● **late in the season** you can divide any of the above, plus lovage, pennyroyal, rue, salad burnet, thyme, winter savory and any herbs growing in cold gardens.

● **dig up clumps**, split them with a spade or sharp knife, or tear them apart with your fingers, and replant the outer portions in fresh soil, discarding the woody centre.

there is still time to . . .

● **order annual herb seeds** before the main sowing season, or get ahead by buying seedlings or dividing pots of herbs sold for kitchen use (see opposite).

● **take root cuttings** of bergamot, chamomile, mint, hyssop, sweet cicely, sweet woodruff and tarragon (see Winter).

looking ahead . . .

☑ SUMMER Plant out tender herbs and those raised from seed, cuttings, layers and divisions.
☑ LATE SUMMER Pot up herbs for winter use.

the greenhouse

The greenhouse is at the centre of early spring activities. Its protected surroundings allow early sowings, but you do need to be organised, as seedlings of all kinds jostle for space with cuttings and overwintering plants. As the weather warms up, and on sunny days, ventilate and water more often.

now is the season to . . .

■ **gradually increase watering** as temperatures rise. Pots and trays can dry out rapidly on warm sunny days, so keep newspapers handy to shade seedlings in particularly bright weather.

■ **ventilate more freely,** especially on still sunny days, but remember to close the vents at night.

■ **harvest strawberries and rhubarb** forced in winter. Discard forced rhubarb crowns at the end of the season.

■ **check heaters** are working efficiently before seeds of all kinds start to germinate.

■ **keep insulation in place** for a few more weeks. If the season is very warm, remove fixed insulation cautiously, but keep newspapers and fleece handy for sudden cold spells.

■ **monitor pests** (see opposite) and guard against diseases such as damping-off (see page 72).

■ **sow your home-saved seeds** at the appropriate time, after checking that they are still in good condition (see page 73).

■ **sow greenhouse crops** such as tomatoes and cucumbers, and if outdoor conditions are unsuitable sow vegetables like peas, broad beans, lettuce and summer cabbages.

■ **continue sowing annual bedding** plants and hardy annuals (see page 28).

■ **prick out seedlings** as soon as they can be handled easily (see page 29).

■ **pot up rooted cuttings** that have overwintered under glass.

■ **pot on rootbound plants** when they show signs of new growth (see opposite).

■ **let bees fertilise indoor fruits** such as apricots, peaches and strawberries by opening vents wide on mild days, or pollinate the open flowers by hand (see page 56).

■ **tie up grape vines** as soon as their buds break and train new shoots (see page 56).

■ **revive tender perennials** (see opposite).

■ **take cuttings** from the new shoots of tender perennials.

The fluffy, scented flowers of mimosa (*Acacia dealbata*) are deliciously fragrant. In frost-prone areas this tender shrub must be grown in an unheated greenhouse.

■ **propagate tender succulents** (see page 69).

■ **take cuttings of begonias,** chrysanthemums, dahlias and gloxinias forced in winter, when their shoots are about 8cm (3in) long (see Winter).

■ **cut forced** *Anemone coronaria* for the house; continue to water and feed plants when flowering finishes.

■ **liquid-feed greenhouse pot plants** such as calceolarias and cinerarias as they come into flower.

■ **pot up lily bulbs** for early flowers. Plant out those that have flowered, after feeding and hardening off.

and if you have time . . .

■ **pot up lily-of-the-valley** for fragrant indoor blooms.

reviving tender perennials

1 Tidy the plant by cutting back leggy stems, which will promote healthy new growth.

2 Remove the plant from its pot and tease out the roots using a pencil or plant label.

3 Re-pot into a larger container and fill the space round the sides with new compost.

4 Pack the compost down firmly with a cane and water carefully.

awakening overwintered perennials

From early March you can revive tender perennials such as pelargoniums, fuchsias, marguerites (*Argyranthemum*), heliotrope and coleus that have been kept barely moist and dormant over winter. Move plants to a well-lit position. Prune hard by shortening thin stems and sideshoots to about 2–3cm (1in), and remove all dead material. Give a little water; if this runs straight through, stand pots in a tray of water for a while until the compost is uniformly moist. Once young shoots appear, increase watering, take soft-tip cuttings if required and repot or pot on into larger containers if you want to plant them out in late spring.

potting up lily-of-the-valley

It is not too late to dig up some roots of lily-of-the-valley to enjoy the heavily fragrant white bells indoors. Make sure the roots have plenty of pinkish white, pointed tips and plant several roots in a 10–13cm (4–5in) pot, with the tips just below the surface. Water and keep cool in a well-lit place.

potting on

As soon as roots poke through the bottom of a pot, start checking whether the plant needs a larger container by gently tapping it from the pot. If only a few roots are visible at the edges it is not ready, so slide the plant back in the pot and settle it by firmly knocking the base of the pot on the staging. The right moment for potting on is when there are plenty of roots round the sides, but before they encircle the rootball. Choose a pot 2–3cm (1in) larger for plants in pots up to 13cm (5in), or 5cm (2in) wider for those in larger pots (see right).

monitoring pests

Many pests can survive winter cosseted in the warmth of a greenhouse and start multiplying very early in the year. To check for their presence, hang sticky yellow traps just above plants and inspect regularly, brushing the plant leaves first to disturb any flying pests. Raise the traps as plants grow, and move them round the greenhouse every week or so.

potting on a tender shrub

1 Spread a drainage layer of gravel or crocks in the bottom of the new pot and cover with a little compost. Stand the potted plant in the centre, still in its pot, and add or remove compost until the rims are level. Twist the smaller pot to free it, then lift it out, leaving behind a neatly moulded hole.

2 Tap the plant from its pot, fit it in the hole and settle it in place by patting or knocking the pot on the staging. Water from above to consolidate the compost.

the greenhouse/2

propagation

This is the prime time for sowing seeds. The basic technique is the same for vegetables and flowers, although the amount of heat and light individual crops require may differ. For this reason, make a point of always reading the instructions on the seed packet before you start to sow. As new growth gets under way, it is also time to take cuttings of soft shoots and succulents. If you have a cool or unheated greenhouse, you can give seeds and cuttings the higher temperatures they require by using a heated propagator.

sowing techniques

You can sow seeds indoors in a variety of containers including trays, modular trays, pans or, if there are just a few of them, in small pots. The standard method is the same for all these containers (see right), but make sure they are scrupulously clean and use fresh seed compost to avoid possible problems. After sowing, place the container in a propagator or cover it with a sheet of glass to prevent the compost from drying out, but remove this as soon as germination takes place.

seeds large and small

Space large seeds, such as nasturtiums and sweet peas, individually at regular intervals in a tray, or sow two or three seeds in small pots and press them down into the compost.

Tiny seeds produced by plants such as petunias and begonias are difficult to sow. Mix them thoroughly with some dry silver sand and sprinkle this over the surface to distribute evenly.

Nasturtium (*Tropaeolum* 'Alaska')

sowing seeds

1 **Overfill the container** with moist seed compost and level off with a piece of board.

2 **Press lightly** with a tamping board to firm and level the surface of the compost.

3 Tip some of the seeds into one hand, and sprinkle a pinch at a time evenly and sparingly across the surface.

4 **For seeds** needing darkness, sieve a thin layer of compost over the surface. Mist with water or stand the tray in shallow water until the surface is moist.

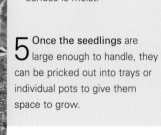

5 Once the seedlings are large enough to handle, they can be pricked out into trays or individual pots to give them space to grow.

taking aeonium cuttings

1 **Cut sideshoots** off at their base with a sharp knife or snap them off cleanly by hand.

2 **Pull off the lower leaves** and insert the bare stem upright in a small pot of sandy cuttings compost or a soil-based compost blended with extra grit.

A collection of succulents, including aloe and agave, sit on metal trays filled with gravel, which ensures the free drainage these plants need.

taking cuttings of succulents

Tender succulents such as aeoniums, echeverias and kalanchoes kept dry through winter can be watered now to plump up their leaves and start them growing. Branching kinds like *Aeonium arboreum* often produce sideshoots that root easily to make vigorous new plants (see above). Water and keep in a warm place out of full sun until rooted. If you want lots of plants, insert individual leaves (those you removed from the stems) in a tray of gritty compost and place in a propagator.

propagators

The easiest and best way to provide the right amount of warmth for germinating seeds or rooting cuttings – and to confine this heat to the plants that need it – is to use a covered propagator. Some models are shaped like small coldframes, or simply trays with clear lids, often fitted with ventilators but without additional heating. Other models are more sophisticated, with a thermostatically controlled heating element and perhaps a misting unit.

You can make your own propagator by constructing a box on the greenhouse staging,

The hinged lid of this home-made propagator is covered with clear plastic sheeting for insulation and to cut out bright light.

topped with a clear, hinged lid. For additional heat, buy a soil-heating cable of adequate wattage for the temperature range you require, and lay this in a bed of horticultural sand at the bottom of the case. Fit a thermostat, with the control box on the outside, together with a maximum-minimum thermometer to monitor temperatures. A simpler method is to buy a propagating tray with a self-contained heating element and capillary mat for watering. Stand containers of seeds or cuttings on the tray and cover them individually with plastic domes or all together with the clear top supplied. Narrow windowsill models are available for holding two to five seed trays, allowing you to raise seed indoors.

looking ahead . . .

☑ LATE SPRING Start hardening off young bedding and overwintering tender plants to acclimatise them to outside conditions.
☑ Continue to take soft-tip cuttings.
☑ SUMMER Move out summer bedding and tender plants for the patio.
☑ Introduce biological pest controls.

there is still time to . . .

● **sow varieties of** half-hardy bedding annuals that germinate and grow fast (see page 28).
● **buy plug plants** and seedlings of vegetables and annual flowers to pot up or prick out in a cool greenhouse.

the healthy garden

Propagating and caring for young plants are some of the top priorities as life returns to the garden.
Finish clearing winter debris and making structural repairs so that the garden is tidy and pleasant to sit in.

early spring checklist

Use this checklist to make sure you have not overlooked any important seasonal jobs.

- **tidy beds and borders,** clearing away plant debris and cutting dead stems back to ground level. Divide perennials and alpines if necessary.
- **check all supports and plant ties;** loosen any that are tight.
- **complete repairs to structures** such as fences and paths.
- **finish planting bare-rooted trees, shrubs and roses** as soon as possible. Container-grown shrubs and herbaceous perennials can be safely planted throughout spring. Check recent plantings and firm in any disturbed by wind and frost.
- **prune roses** and renovate overgrown hedges and shrubs.
- **dig in green manure,** sown in late summer last year, two or three weeks before the soil is required.
- **start digging light soils** and cultivate heavy soils left rough over winter, if the surface is dry and workable.
- **prepare seedbeds,** and cover them with cloches or plastic sheeting for a week or two, ready for early sowings.
- **continue to protect plants of borderline hardiness** in case of hard frost. Remove the covers in mild weather so that plants can harden off.
- **check stocks of compost,** pots, trays and other propagating materials, ready for the main sowing season.

- **press on with early sowing under glass,** prick out seedlings when large enough to handle, and keep a flow of young plants moving through the greenhouse to a coldframe.
- **sow and plant vegetables outside** when conditions are favourable (see pages 62–3).
- **revive overwintered tender plants,** and take cuttings from the young shoots.
- **watch for early signs of pests and diseases,** especially in heated greenhouses.
- **check that stored bulbs and tubers** are still in good condition, and start them into growth at the appropriate time.
- **repot or pot on houseplants,** and propagate them by cuttings or division.
- **divide outdoor perennials** in fine weather (see Late Spring).
- **complete repairs to damaged lawns** and start mowing as the grass begins to grow. If you want to make a new lawn from turf or seed, prepare the ground now.
- **clear new ground** and tackle perennial weeds as early as possible (see opposite).

Protect seedbeds and vulnerable seedlings from birds by laying netting over the soil.

positive health care

Early spring is an ideal time to check your plants over for ailments. Frost and wind damage should be obvious by winter's end, allowing you to do any essential remedial pruning, such as cutting out dead and diseased wood or disfigured evergreen foliage. The first signs of spring and summer disorders such as mildew or aphids may be evident now, especially in a dry or warm season.

Aphids cluster on fresh new shoots and buds; rub off by hand or spray with insecticide.

Green manure like this crop of phacelia and mustard should be dug into the soil a few weeks before planting to improve its condition and fertility.

Powdery mildew affects leaves (left) and stems (right) in a warm, dry spring following a mild winter that allowed dormant spores to survive. Cut out affected stems and spray with fungicide.

Watch out for weeds too, and control these while they are still small. Hoe round established plants on a warm, dry day to kill annual weed seedlings, and use a trowel or border spade to dig up invasive perennial weeds such as thistles, couch grass, horsetail and ground elder.

clearing weed-infested ground

Nettles, thistles, ground elder, couch grass and other perennial weeds are tenacious plants that can often revive from the smallest fragment of root, as well as from dormant seeds in the soil. Clearing perennial weeds is an essential preliminary task when making or reclaiming a garden.

clearing by hand

Although slow and labour-intensive, digging out weeds by hand is the most reliable method, provided you then hoe off or hand-pull surviving weeds as they appear. Divide the ground into manageable areas and deal with each separately. Dig the ground to split the matted roots into smaller groups, then carefully fork through the loosened soil, shaking the soil from each forkful and picking out the weeds. Pick all weed fragments from the surface. Work over the whole area in this way, then fork through lightly once more to expose missed roots. If possible, allow two to three weeks for surviving weeds to sprout and be removed before sowing or planting.

using weedkillers

A systemic weedkiller such as glyphosate kills all plant parts, including the roots. It works best on young vigorous growth, so do not apply during periods of drought or cold weather when plants are less active. Slash or mow down tall topgrowth and clear. When the new foliage is about 15cm (6in) high, apply a solution of weedkiller according to the manufacturer's instructions. Leave for at least seven days, and then dig in the remains of the growth. Allow time for surviving roots to start growing again, and spray once more; some persistent weeds, such as ground elder, may need two to three applications.

ROTAVATING TIP If you plan to clear the ground using a rotary cultivator, delay this until summer. The blades will chop up weed roots, leaving most on the surface where they dry quickly and can be raked off. Repeat every two weeks in hot weather and after two months the ground should be weed-free.

mulching

This method takes the longest time, but involves minimal effort and no chemicals. Mow the weeds as short as possible and then cover the ground with a light-excluding mulch.

● **old carpets are effective,** especially if laid on top of black plastic sheeting. Most weeds will have died after a year, but keep in place for two years to kill couch grass and ground elder. Thick black plastic sheeting tucked into the soil also works well.

● **thick cardboard** or complete newspapers can be laid over the weeds, preferably in autumn. Overlap them generously; cover with a 15cm (6in) layer of old manure, garden compost, leaf-mould or other organic material. Next spring, plant potatoes or brassicas into the mulch, and spread a straw layer between plants; this gives you a useful crop of vegetables while the mulch controls the weeds.

● **pull up any weed shoots** that break through, or spot-treat them with weedkiller.

clearing weeds

There are several ways of tackling perennial weed clearance, none of them instantly successful, but you will find that persistence generally pays off.

Use a long, slim trowel to dig out the long taproot of perennial weeds like dandelion.

Hoeing is the best way to tackle annual weeds, but take care round the stems of established plants.

You can paint the young leaves of perennials such as ground elder with a systemic weedkiller.

the healthy garden/2

avoiding propagation problems

Fluctuating temperatures mean that early spring is a fickle season under glass, and ventilation becomes increasingly important as plants start growing from seed or cuttings. The soft growth is very susceptible to pests and diseases, and you need to be sensitive to the needs of these young plants to avoid common problems.

damping-off disease

This very troublesome disease can result in the death of many kinds of seedlings, both indoors and out. It is caused by a range of virulent soil-borne fungi, which are particularly liable to affect fast-growing annual bedding flowers, and also some vegetables, while they are very young.

Seedlings develop dark leaves and then collapse in patches, their white stems becoming as thin as hairs, turning brown and shrivelling at soil level. The condition can quickly affect a whole tray or bed of seedlings. Treatment is difficult and control depends on precautionary good hygiene.

- **use fresh seed compost** (low in nutrients), and sterilise garden soil used for compost mixes (see right).
- **wash and disinfect old pots,** containers and seed labels.
- **mix extra horticultural sand into compost** to improve drainage for susceptible plants such as nemesia and antirrhinums, and cover seeds with a thin layer of sand.
- **sow sparsely,** and prick out or thin before the seedlings are overcrowded.
- **use modular trays,** sowing a few seeds in each cell, to confine infection, which spreads easily throughout ordinary seed trays.

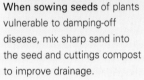
When sowing seeds of plants vulnerable to damping-off disease, mix sharp sand into the seed and cuttings compost to improve drainage.

Sowing seeds in individual disposable pots or modular trays will help to reduce the risk of disease spreading.

- **water containers from below** using mains water, as rainwater from butts is often a source of the fungi. Avoid overwatering.
- **water with a copper-based fungicide** after sowing and pricking out.
- **keep seedlings at the right temperature,** ideally in a heated propagator: cold draughts and cool, wet soils or composts are lethal.

sterilising soil for compost

If you make your own composts, it is important to sterilise garden soil before adding it to the mix in order to kill most of the disease pathogens and weed seeds. You can do this by using a chemical disinfectant, available for this purpose, or by pasteurising the soil in a conventional or microwave oven.

- **in a conventional oven** Spread moist soil 8–10cm (3–4in) deep in a tray, cover with kitchen foil and heat at 80°C (175°F) for 40 minutes. Uncover and leave to cool.
- **in a microwave oven** First sieve out the stones and organic material. Weigh 2kg (4lb 8oz) of soil into a bowl, cover and cook on maximum for five minutes. Spread on a tray to cool.
- **do not sterilise** garden compost or leaf-mould, as heat can reduce their food value.

Half-hardy annuals such as antirrhinums grown under glass are readily affected by damping-off disease, which can decimate sowings. Reduce the risk of infection by using clean equipment and fresh compost and watering with a copper-based fungicide.

testing old seed

1 Spread and moisten two or three thicknesses of absorbent paper in a saucer or shallow pan, and sprinkle a few seeds on the surface.

2 Cover with plastic film and keep in a warm place, in light or darkness according to the type of seed. Do not allow the paper to dry out.

3 Leave for up to three weeks and watch for signs of germination. If half or more start to grow, the seed will be worth sowing.

testing seeds

All seeds eventually lose their ability to germinate. If yours are more than two or three years old, or might have been exposed to damp or heat, test a sample before sowing to see how well they germinate (see left).

USING OLD SEED TIP Mix together all the old seed varieties that showed poor germination, and scatter them fairly thickly on a bare patch of soil. Before the plants flower, dig them in as green manure.

making liquid feed

You can make your own liquid fertiliser by growing comfrey or nettles and harvesting the plants, then soaking the leaves in a net in a bucket of water for about two weeks.

making liquid fertiliser

1 Shear off the fresh young growth of comfrey or nettles in spring, using a pair of garden shears.

2 Pack the leaves into a net bag and tie it at the top.

3 Suspend this in a tank or bucket of water for 10–14 days, occasionally squeezing the bag. Dilute the resulting liquor to look like weak tea before applying.

why seeds fail to germinate

There are many reasons why seeds fail to germinate. The most common causes are:

• **using old seed** that has lost its viability, or its ability to germinate

• **using stale compost** left over from a previous season, or a potting mixture rather than a special seed compost

• **using compost** that is too wet, or that has been allowed to dry out before seedlings emerge

• **surroundings** too cold or too hot

• **compost pressed too firmly** after sowing, or compacted by heavy watering from above

• **seeds covered with compost** when they need light, or buried too deeply

A well-planted garden in early spring is wreathed with blossom, studded with early bulbs and alight with flowering shrubs and clumps of narcissus and Lenten roses. Breathtaking carpets of bulbs will take the eye away from leafless branches and bare canopies. Most early spring bulbs naturalise and spread unaided, but if you note star performers which suit the garden now, you can lift and divide them later. Early flowering cherries, camellias and early rhododendrons will make fine specimen trees, while even the tiniest of gardens can enjoy great variety through alpines, many of which bloom in early spring.

plant selector

Helleborus hybridus 'Pluto'

perennials

Most non-woody durable plants are herbaceous (that is, they die down in winter), but some of the most important that flower in early spring are evergreen. Plant in the dormant season, preferably in autumn.

purple, blue and violet

1 Corydalis flexuosa

The long season of this compact perennial begins in early spring, when ferny leaves are topped by sprays of tubular flowers in various shades of blue. The foliage can be light green, blue-green or purplish green with red marks. In dry summers the leaves die down, but re-emerge in the autumn, sometimes with a scattering of flowers. Cultivars include the aptly named 'China Blue', 'Père David', with sky-blue flowers, and 'Purple Leaf', the most purplish in flower and leaf. Hardy.

Height: 30cm (12in) **Spread:** 25cm (10in)
Site: Partial shade. Humus-rich and moist but well-drained soil
Compost: Soil-based (John Innes No. 2)
Use: Container, shady border, underplanting for shrubs, woodland garden
Good companions: *Erythronium dens-canis*, *Galanthus* 'S. Arnott', *Tiarella wherryi*

2 Omphalodes verna
Blue-eyed mary, Creeping forget-me-not

Spreading mats of green tapered leaves provide good ground cover between shrubs. In spring sprays of small blue flowers with a white eye are a bonus. Hardy.

Height: 20cm (8in) **Spread:** 30cm (12in)
Site: Partial shade, shade. Humus-rich and moist but well-drained soil
Use: Ground cover, shady border, wild garden, woodland garden
Good companions: *Galanthus nivalis*, *Primula vulgaris*, *Pulmonaria angustifolia* 'Munstead Blue'

3 Primula auricula 'Blue Velvet'
Border auricula

The border auriculas are a group of evergreen primulas that thrive in the open garden. They have leathery, sometimes white-mealy leaves and produce erect stems that carry terminal clusters of usually fragrant, flat-faced flowers. 'Blue Velvet' has plush, rich blue-purple flowers with a white centre. Hardy.

Height: 15cm (6in) **Spread:** 20cm (8in)
Site: Sun, partial shade. Humus-rich and moist but well-drained soil
Use: Sunny or lightly shaded border

Good companions: *Narcissus* 'Cedric Morris', *Polygonatum* x *hybridum*, *Primula auricula* 'Old Yellow Dusty Miller'

4 Primula 'Miss Indigo'
Primrose

This primrose forms a characteristic rosette of bright green, deeply veined leaves. Nestling among these are rich purple, double flowers, the petals finely edged in creamy white. Hardy.
Height: 15cm (6in) **Spread:** 30cm (12in)
Site: Partial shade, sun. Humus-rich and moist but well-drained soil
Compost: Soil-based (John Innes No. 2) or soil-less
Use: Container, front of border, woodland garden
Good companions: *Galanthus elwesii*, *Primula vulgaris* 'Alba Plena', *Scilla siberica* 'Spring Beauty'

5 Pulmonaria saccharata 'Frühlingshimmel'
Jerusalem sage, Lungwort

Like many pulmonarias, this has grey-spotted leaves. From late winter to late spring it produces sprays of pale pink buds, red-brown at the base, that open to clear mauve-blue flowers. Hardy.
Height: 25cm (10in) **Spread:** 60cm (2ft)

Site: Partial shade. Humus-rich and moist but well-drained soil
Use: Ground cover, shady border, wild garden, woodland garden
Good companions: *Corydalis ochroleuca*, *Narcissus* 'February Gold', *Waldsteinia ternata*

6 Symphytum 'Hidcote Blue'
Comfrey

This leafy plant has green rough-textured foliage and makes a good filler between shrubs, but is potentially invasive. Red buds are gathered on a coiled stem and as this unrolls the tubular flowers change to blue and white. Hardy.
Height and spread: 45cm (18in)
Site: Partial shade, sun. Moist but well-drained soil
Use: Underplanting for shrubs, wild garden, woodland garden
Good companions: *Digitalis purpurea*, *Euphorbia amygdaloides* 'Purpurea', *Lunaria annua*

pink and mauve

7 Bergenia 'Schneekönigen'
Elephant's ears

Clump-forming perennial with large leaves partially curled at the edges. The large, very pale pink flowers are borne throughout spring. Hardy.
Height: 40cm (16in) **Spread:** 60cm (2ft)
Site: Sun, partial shade. Well-drained, preferably moist soil
Use: Front of border, gravel garden, ground cover
Good companions: *Allium hollandicum* 'Purple Sensation', *Deutzia* x *rosea*, *Stachys byzantina* 'Silver Carpet'

8 Bergenia stracheyi
Elephant's ears

One of the smallest of the bergenias, this forms a clump of upright oval leaves, which in early spring cradle short-stemmed sprays of fragrant pink flowers. The Alba Group is white flowered. Hardy.
Height: 20cm (8in) **Spread:** 25cm (10in)
Site: Sun, partial shade. Moist but well-drained soil
Use: Front of border, woodland garden
Good companions: *Epimedium* x *rubrum*, *Galanthus nivalis*, *Geranium sanguineum*

9 Bergenia 'Sunningdale'
Elephant's ears

Clump-forming evergreen with spoon-shaped red-backed leaves that develop rich bronze tints in autumn and winter. During spring bright red stems carry sprays of vivid purplish pink flowers. Hardy.
Height and spread: 40cm (16in)
Site: Sun, partial shade. Well-drained, moist soil
Use: Front of border, gravel garden, ground cover
Good companions: *Artemisia arborescens*, *Bergenia* 'Ballawley', *Cistus ladanifer*

10 Epimedium grandiflorum 'Rose Queen'
Barrenwort, Bishop's mitre

The deep pink flowers have white-tipped spurs and are held clear of the foliage, which is of great beauty. The young leaves emerge bronzed in spring and later turn green. Hardy.
Height: 25cm (10in) **Spread:** 30cm (12in)
Site: Partial shade. Moist but well-drained soil
Use: Ground cover, shady border, woodland garden
Good companions: *Geranium macrorrhizum* 'Ingwersen's Variety', *Tellima grandiflora* 'Purpurteppich', *Viburnum* x *bodnantense* 'Dawn'

11 Primula 'Guinevere'
Primula

Evergreen perennial with heavily corrugated bronze-purple leaves and erect stems that carry heads of yellow-centred, mauve-pink flowers. Hardy.
Height: 15cm (6in) **Spread:** 25cm (10in)
Site: Partial shade, sun. Humus-rich and moist but well-drained soil
Compost: Soil-based (John Innes No. 2) or soil-less
Use: Container, front of border, woodland garden
Good companions: *Galanthus* 'S. Arnott', *Narcissus* 'Dove Wings', *Polemonium* 'Lambrook Mauve'

red and russet

1 Pulmonaria rubra 'David Ward'
Lungwort

The coral red flowers are a vivid feature in spring, but at least of equal value is the evergreen foliage. The pale green leaves are edged with creamy white and form large rosettes. Hardy.

Height: 30cm (12in) **Spread:** 1m (3ft)

Site: Partial shade, shade. Humus-rich and moist but well-drained soil

Use: Ground cover, shady border, woodland garden

Good companions: *Brunnera macrophylla*, *Cornus controversa* 'Variegata', *Pulmonaria saccharata* 'Frühlingshimmel'

yellow

2 Epimedium perralderianum
Barrenwort, Bishop's mitre

Evergreen foliage plant with glossy, deep green toothed leaves, bronze-tinted when young. The bright yellow flowers have short spurs. Hardy.

Height: 30cm (12in) **Spread:** 60cm (2ft)

Site: Partial shade. Moist but well-drained soil

Use: Ground cover, shady border, woodland garden

Good companions: *Corydalis ochroleuca*, *Epimedium* x *warleyense* 'Orangekönigin', *Mahonia japonica*

3 Euphorbia amygdaloides var. robbiae
Mrs Robb's bonnet

Spreading evergreen with red-tinted upright stems densely set with dark green leaves that have reddish backs. Greenish yellow flowerheads are borne in spring and early summer. Potentially invasive, but useful in shade where soil is poor. Harmful if ingested and contact with the milky sap may cause skin reactions. Hardy.

General care: Cut flower stems to the base in summer when flowering is over.

Height and spread: 60cm (2ft)

Site: Partial shade. Well-drained, preferably moist soil

Use: Shady border, wild garden, woodland garden

Good companions: *Helleborus foetidus*, *Pachysandra terminalis*, *Vinca minor* 'La Grave'

4 Euphorbia characias subsp. wulfenii
Milkweed, Spurge

Evergreen shrubby perennial that makes a large clump of stiff stems crowded with blue-grey leaves. From early spring until early summer large yellow-green flowerheads top the clump. Harmful if ingested and contact with the milky sap may cause skin reactions. Hardy.

General care: Cut flower stems to the base in summer when flowering is over.

Height and spread: 1.2m (4ft)

Site: Sun. Well-drained soil

Use: Gravel garden, sunny border

Good companions: *Eryngium* x *tripartitum*, *Sedum* 'Herbstfreude', *Stipa gigantea*

5 Euphorbia rigida
Milkweed, Spurge

Evergreen with initially upright stems covered with blue-green narrow leaves. Plants tend to sprawl in spring when the stems produce heads of long-lasting yellow-green flowers. Harmful if ingested and contact with the milky sap may cause skin reactions. Hardy.

Height: 45cm (18in) **Spread:** 60cm (2ft)

Site: Sun. Well-drained soil

Use: Gravel garden, raised bed, rock garden, sunny border

Good companions: *Cytisus* x *praecox* 'Allgold', *Lavandula* x *intermedia* Dutch Group, *Ruta graveolens* 'Jackman's Blue'

6 Primula auricula 'Old Yellow Dusty Miller'
Border auricula

This evergreen primula (see 3, *Primula auricula* 'Blue Velvet', page 76) has spoon-shaped leaves dusted with white meal and rich yellow flowers with white-mealy eyes. Hardy.

Height: 15cm (6in) **Spread:** 25cm (10in)

Site: Sun or partial shade. Humus-rich and moist but well-drained soil

Use: Sunny or lightly shaded border

Good companions: *Myosotis sylvatica* 'Royal Blue', *Narcissus* 'Jack Snipe', *Tulipa* 'Orange Emperor'

7 Primula vulgaris
Primrose

The bright green, deeply veined leaves form a more or less evergreen clump. The odd flower may be found in late winter, but the main season is spring, when plants produce clusters of pale yellow, often fragrant flowers. Hardy.

Height: 20cm (8in) **Spread:** 35cm (14in)

Site: Partial shade. Moist but well-drained soil

Compost: Soil-based (John Innes No. 2) or soil-less

Use: Container, front of border, wild garden, woodland garden

Good companions: *Anemone blanda*, *Chionodoxa luciliae* Gigantea Group, *Muscari aucheri*

cream and white

8 Bergenia ciliata
Elephant's ears

Unlike the majority of bergenias, the large rounded leaves of this species are hairy, and it is only reliably evergreen in frost-free areas. The white flowers are carried in sprays on red-tinted stems. The petals emerge from brown-pink bases. Hardy.

Height: 30cm (12in) **Spread:** 45cm (18in)

Site: Sun. Well-drained, preferably moist soil

Use: Front of border, gravel garden

Good companions: *Eryngium alpinum*, *Osteospermum jucundum*, *Verbena bonariensis*

9 Pachyphragma macrophyllum

The smell of the small four-petalled flowers is rank, but the billowing mass creates snowy brightness under deciduous trees and shrubs. Mounds of overlapping rounded leaves make good cover throughout summer and persist until the new leaves emerge the following spring. Hardy.

Height: 30cm (12in) **Spread:** 75cm (2ft 6in)

Site: Partial shade. Moist but well-drained soil

Use: Ground cover, wild garden, woodland garden

Good companions: *Euphorbia amygdaloides* 'Purpurea', *Geranium phaeum* 'Album', *Helleborus foetidus* Wester Flisk Group

10 Primula vulgaris 'Alba Plena'
Primrose

White double forms of the primrose (see 7, above) have been cultivated for centuries. 'Alba Plena' often begins flowering in winter and picks up momentum in early spring. The flowers have several layers of pure white, deeply notched petals around a muddled centre. Hardy.

Height: 15cm (6in) **Spread:** 30cm (12in)

Site: Partial shade. Moist but well-drained soil

Compost: Soil-based (John Innes No. 2) or soil-less

Use: Container, front of border, wild garden, woodland garden

Good companions: *Aquilegia* 'Hensol Harebell', *Galanthus* 'Atkinsii', *Helleborus hybridus*

11 Pulmonaria 'Sissinghurst White'
Jerusalem cowslip, Lungwort, Spotted dog

The bristly evergreen foliage is covered with grey-white spots. In the shade that it prefers the white funnel-shaped flowers, which open from pale pink buds, strike a cool note. Hardy.

Height: 30cm (12in) **Spread:** 45cm (18in)

Site: Partial shade. Humus-rich and moist but well-drained soil

Use: Ground cover, shady border, wild garden, woodland garden

Good companions: *Anemone sylvestris*, *Magnolia denudata*, *Omphalodes cappadocica*

hellebores

The long-lasting muted magnificence of hellebores in flower often begins in late winter and their fingered, sometimes evergreen leaves are pleasing over many months. Most hellebores do well in a wide range of conditions, but are generally at their best in dappled shade under a canopy of deciduous trees or shrubs, in moist but well-drained soil that is preferably neutral to alkaline. All parts are harmful if eaten.

1 Helleborus torquatus Party Dress Group

Cultivars of *H. torquatus* are usually deciduous; the leaves are composed of numerous tapered leaflets and appear after flowers begin to open in late winter or early spring. The nodding or outward-facing double flowers of the Party Dress Group are greenish brown to pink and are borne profusely. Hardy.

Height and spread: 30cm (12in)

Good companions: *Asplenium scolopendrium, Cyclamen hederifolium, Lonicera* x *purpusii* 'Winter Beauty'

2 Helleborus orientalis subsp. guttatus

Lenten rose

The leathery fingered leaves overwinter, but are usually blemished and therefore best removed by the time the nodding or outward-facing single flowers open in late winter or early spring. These are creamy white, sometimes tinted pink, with green centres surrounded by red-purple speckling. Hardy.

Height and spread: 45cm (18in)

Good companions: *Eranthis hyemalis, Primula* 'Miss Indigo', *Primula vulgaris*

3 Helleborus x sternii 'Boughton Beauty'

This hybrid combines subtly coloured flowers with handsome, dark green, usually toothed foliage, over which plays a flicker of silver. The stems and veins of the three-lobed leaves are maroon or purplish pink and the single flowers, dark pink in bud opening to greenish pink, are filled with cream stamens. Not fully hardy.

Height and spread: 50cm (20in)

Good companions: *Erythronium dens-canis, Galanthus nivalis, Sarcococca hookeriana* var. *digyna*

4, 5, 6, 7, 8 Helleborus hybridus

Lenten rose

The dark green leaves of this clump-forming evergreen perennial have often become shabby by late winter, but the nodding saucer-shaped flowers are subtly tinted with intriguing deep shades. A vast number of un-named seedlings come in a wide colour range that extends from off-white and greenish cream or yellow through pink and red to dark plum. Buy Lenten roses when in flower to be sure of selecting colours you like. Many seedlings have single flowers (5, 7), but some are double or anemone-centred (8). The Ashwood Garden hybrids (4) offer a selection of good quality un-named plants. Named forms, such as 'Pluto' (6), tend to be expensive. Hardy.

Height and spread: 45cm (18in)

Good companions: *Galanthus elwesii, Lilium martagon* 'Album', *Philadelphus* 'Manteau d'Ermine'

annuals & biennials

At this time of year short-lived plants raised as biennials give good value over many weeks. Those that flower in early spring combine well with bulbs to add colour to formal beds and containers.

purple, blue and violet

1 Viola x wittrockiana Princess Series
Pansy

The pansies are short-lived evergreen perennials usually grown as annuals or biennials. The season of winter-flowering kinds extends into spring and even into early summer. In the small-flowered Princess Series the colour range includes white, cream, yellow, blue and purple. Hardy.

General care: Sow seed outdoors in summer for winter and early spring flowers or under glass in late winter for spring and summer flowers.

Height: 15cm (6in) **Spread:** 30cm (12in)

Site: Sun, partial shade. Moist but well-drained soil

Compost: Soil-based (John Innes No. 2) or soil-less

Use: Container, formal bedding, front of border

Good companions: *Hyacinthus orientalis* 'Carnegie', *Narcissus* 'Little Gem', *Scilla siberica*

red, russet and maroon

2 Bellis perennis 'Kito'
Double daisy

For lawn purists the common daisy is a tiresome perennial weed, but doubles have been cultivated, usually as biennials, since the sixteenth century. 'Kito' is readily raised from seed, and has very double red-pink flowerheads. The spoon-shaped leaves are bright green. Hardy.

General care: Sow seed outdoors in early summer and plant out in early autumn.

Height: 15cm (6in) **Spread:** 15cm (6in)

Site: Sun, partial shade. Moist but well-drained soil

Compost: Soil-based (John Innes No. 2) or soil-less

Use: Bedding, sunny or shady border, container, edging

Good companions: *Crocus vernus* 'Pickwick', *Iris* 'Natascha', *Tulipa* 'Heart's Delight'

3 Erysimum cheiri 'Blood Red'
Wallflower

The wallflower is a short-lived perennial and plants naturalised in old brickwork often survive for several years. As a garden plant it is almost invariably treated as a biennial and valued for its upright stems crowded with fragrant velvety flowers in spring. 'Blood Red' has relatively early scented flowers of an intense deep red. Hardy.

General care: Sow seed outdoors in late spring or early summer and plant out in mid-autumn.

Height: 45cm (18in) **Spread:** 30cm (12in)

Site: Sun. Well-drained soil, preferably limy

Compost: Soil-based (John Innes No. 2)

Use: Container, formal bedding, sunny border

Good companions: *Fritillaria imperialis*, *Tulipa* 'Estella Rijnveld', *Tulipa* 'Purissima'

4 Primula Prominent Series
Polyanthus

The polyanthus primulas are short-lived evergreen perennials usually grown as biennials. Sturdy stems carry a truss of scented flowers above a rosette of deeply veined leaves. In this dwarf selection the brightly coloured or white flowers, usually with a conspicuous yellow eye, appear in late winter or early spring. Hardy.

General care: Sow seed in summer and plant out in autumn.

Height and spread: 15–20cm (6–8in)

Site: Sun, partial shade. Moist but well-drained soil

Compost: Soil-based (John Innes No. 2) or soil-less

Use: Container, formal bedding, front of border

Good companions: *Bellis perennis* 'Kito', *Hyacinthus orientalis* 'Anna Marie', *Tulipa* 'Cape Cod'

5 Primula Silver-laced Group
Polyanthus

Like Gold-laced Group primulas (see Late Spring), these short-lived semi-evergreen perennials are often grown as biennials, but are less widely available. Upright stems carry four to eight flowers, which have a yellow eye and mahogany lobes outlined in white. Hardy.

General care: Sow seed outdoors in early summer and plant out in autumn. Divide plants after flowering or in autumn.

Height: 25cm (10in) **Spread:** 30cm (12in)

Site: Partial shade. Fertile and moist but well-drained soil

Compost: Soil-based (John Innes No. 2) or soil-less

Use: Container, formal bedding, greenhouse or conservatory, shady border

Good companions: *Fritillaria meleagris*, *Narcissus* 'Rip van Winkle', *Primula* Cowichan Garnet Group

bulbs

Much of the colour that brings the garden to life in early spring comes from bulbs. The term is used loosely to cover all those perennials that develop underground storage organs.

purple, blue and violet

1 Anemone coronaria Saint Bridgid Group
Windflower

The wild plant, a native of the Mediterranean with knobbly tubers and prettily divided leaves, bears single flowers that are white or various shades of blue and red. Saint Bridgid anemones have double or semi-double flowers in a richer colour range, much valued for cutting. Hardy.

General care: For flowers in late winter or early spring plant in early to mid-autumn with the top of the corm about 8cm (3in) deep. Plant in mid-spring for flowers in summer.

Height: 30cm (12in) **Spread:** 15cm (6in)

Site: Sun. Well-drained soil

Compost: Soil-based (John Innes No. 2) with added grit

Use: Container, sunny border, raised bed

Good companions: *Chaenomeles speciosa* 'Nivalis', *Paeonia lactiflora* 'Festiva Maxima', *Tulipa* 'Purissima'

2 Chionodoxa luciliae Gigantea Group
Glory of the snow

This fleshy bulb produces narrowly strap-shaped leaves and sprays of usually three mid-blue flowers with a white eye. Hardy.

General care: Plant in early to mid-autumn with the top of the bulb about 8cm (3in) deep.

Height: 20cm (8in) **Spread:** 5cm (2in)

Site: Sun. Well-drained soil

Compost: Soil-based (John Innes No. 2)

Use: Container, front of border, raised bed, rock garden

Good companions: *Crocus chrysanthus* 'Cream Beauty', *Iris* 'Joyce', *Tulipa* 'Heart's Delight'

3 Chionodoxa sardensis
Glory of the snow

Small slender bulb with sprays of up to 12 eye-catching starry flowers that are vivid blue with a very small white eye. Hardy.

General care: Plant in early to mid-autumn with the top of the bulb about 8cm (3in) deep.

Height: 15cm (6in) **Spread:** 5cm (2in)

Site: Sun. Well-drained soil

Compost: Soil-based (John Innes No. 2)

Use: Container, front of border, raised bed, rock garden

Good companions: *Bellis perennis*, *Galanthus* 'S. Arnott', *Primula* 'Guinevere'

4 Ipheion uniflorum

The bulb smells slightly of garlic, as do the linear pale green leaves if bruised. In early to mid-spring, each bulb produces pale to purplish blue, upward-facing starry flowers, the segments usually with a darker centre line. 'Wisley Blue' has violet-blue flowers. Leave bulbs undisturbed to develop into dense clumps. Not fully hardy.

General care: Plant in autumn or straight after flowering with the top of bulb 8cm (3in) deep.
Height: 15cm (6in) **Spread:** 5cm (2in)
Site: Sun. Moist but well-drained soil
Compost: Soil based (John Innes No. 2) with added leaf-mould and grit
Use: Front of border, rock garden
Good companions: *Campanula persicifolia*, *Lilium regale*, *Paeonia lactiflora* 'Karl Rosenfield'

5 Muscari aucheri
Grape hyacinth

In early to mid-spring this bulbous species produces rather narrow leaves and upright stems topped by a tight stack of small bell-shaped blue flowers that narrow at the mouth. Hardy.

General care: Plant in autumn with the top of the bulb about 10cm (4in) deep.
Height: 20cm (8in) **Spread:** 5cm (2in)
Site: Sun. Moist but well-drained soil
Compost: Soil-based (John Innes No. 2)
Use: Sunny border, raised bed, rock garden
Good companions: *Chionodoxa forbesii* 'Pink Giant', *Magnolia stellata*, *Tulipa clusiana*

6 Puschkinia scilloides

Starry flowers, about six to a loose spray, are pale blue with a darker centre line to each segment. Variety *libanotica* is usually all white. Hardy.

General care: Plant in early autumn with the top of the bulb about 8cm (3in) deep.
Height: 20cm (8in) **Spread:** 5cm (2in)
Site: Sun, partial shade. Well-drained soil
Compost: Soil-based (John Innes No. 2)
Use: Container, front of border, raised bed, rock garden, underplanting for perennials and shrubs
Good companions: *Muscari botryoides* 'Album', *Tulipa clusiana*, *Tulipa humilis* Violacea Group

7 Scilla bifolia
Squill

In late winter or early spring this small bulb produces a loose spray of about 10 starry flowers. Usually purplish to turquoise-blue, there are also white and pink-flowered forms. Hardy.

General care: Plant in late summer or early autumn with the top of the bulb about 8cm (3in) deep.

Height: 15cm (6in) **Spread:** 5cm (2in)
Site: Sun, partial shade. Humus-rich, well-drained soil
Compost: Soil-based (John Innes No. 2) with added leaf-mould and grit
Use: Container, front of border, raised bed, rock garden, underplanting for perennials and shrubs
Good companions: *Lonicera* 'Winter Beauty', *Narcissus* 'Jack Snipe', *Puschkinia scilloides* var. *libanotica*

8 Scilla mischtschenkoana
Squill

This dwarf bulb flowers in late winter or early spring, when leaves are still short. The flowers, usually four to a stem, are pale blue, darker on the backs of the segments and with a dark line down the centre of each. Hardy.

General care: Plant in late summer or early autumn with the top of the bulb 8cm (3in) deep.
Height: 10cm (4in) **Spread:** 5cm (2in)
Site: Sun, partial shade. Humus-rich, well-drained soil
Compost: Soil-based (John Innes No. 2) with added leaf-mould and grit
Use: Container, front of border, raised bed, rock garden, underplanting for perennials and shrubs
Good companions: *Chaenomeles* x *superba* 'Pink Lady', *Chionodoxa forbesii* 'Pink Giant', *Narcissus* 'Dove Wings'

9 Scilla siberica 'Spring Beauty'
Siberian squill

Brilliant blue flowers, usually several to a bulb, hang on loose stems over strap-like leaves. Hardy.
General care: Plant in early autumn with the top of the bulb about 8cm (3in) deep.

Height: 15cm (6in) **Spread:** 5cm (2in)
Site: Sun, partial shade. Humus-rich, well-drained soil
Compost: Soil-based (John Innes No. 2) with added leaf-mould and grit
Use: Container, front of border, raised bed, rock garden, underplanting for perennials and shrubs
Good companions: *Galanthus elwesii*, *Narcissus obvallaris*, *Primula vulgaris*

pink and mauve

10 Chionodoxa forbesii 'Pink Giant'
Glory of the snow

The delicate pink, white-centred stars of this vigorous bulb are useful for contrasting with the more usual blue flowers of the species. Hardy.

General care: Plant in early to mid-autumn with the top of the bulb about 8cm (3in) deep.
Height: 20cm (8in) **Spread:** 5cm (2in)
Site: Sun. Well-drained soil
Compost: Soil-based (John Innes No. 2)
Use: Container, front of border, raised bed, rock garden
Good companions: *Chionodoxa luciliae* Gigantea Group, *Scilla siberica* 'Spring Beauty', *Tulipa* 'Heart's Delight'

11 Corydalis solida 'George Baker'

Tuberous plant with ferny grey-green leaves, fleshy stems and small pink-red snapdragon-like flowers. Needs a sheltered position. Hardy.

General care: Plant in autumn with the top of the tuber about 10cm (4in) deep.
Height: 25cm (10in) **Spread:** 15cm (6in)
Site: Sun, partial shade. Sharply drained soil
Compost: Soil-based (John Innes No. 2) with added grit
Use: Container, raised bed, rock garden
Good companions: *Crocus angustifolius*, *Crocus minimus*, *Geranium cinereum* 'Ballerina'

pink and mauve (continued)

1 Hyacinthus orientalis 'Anna Marie'
Hyacinth

The powerfully scented spikes of the numerous hyacinth cultivars are densely set with waxy bell-shaped flowers. 'Anna Marie' is pale pink, but other colours are available. Prepared bulbs can be forced for winter flowering. Hardy.

General care: Plant in autumn with the top of the bulb about 10cm (4in) deep.

Height: 25cm (10in) **Spread:** 8cm (3in)

Site: Sun, partial shade. Well-drained soil

Compost: Soil-based (John Innes No. 2) or bulb fibre if planting in containers without drainage holes

Use: Container, formal bedding, front of border

Good companions: *Bellis perennis*, *Hyacinthus orientalis* 'Jan Bos', *Primula* 'Guinevere'

2 Tulipa 'Apricot Beauty'
Single early flowering tulip

The soft salmon-pink cups are edged with orange. Single Early Group tulips can be forced for winter flowering. Hardy.

General care: Plant in late autumn or early winter with the top of the bulb 10–15cm (4–6in) deep.

Height: 40cm (16in) **Spread:** 15cm (6in)

Site: Sun. Well-drained soil

Compost: Soil-based (John Innes No. 2)

Use: Border, container, formal bedding

Good companions: *Erysimum cheiri* 'Ivory White', *Primula* Gold-laced Group, *Viola* x *wittrockiana* Universal Series

3 Tulipa 'Couleur Cardinal'
Triumph Group tulip

Most Triumph tulips flower in mid-spring, so are useful for beds that need to be cleared early for summer bedding. 'Couleur Cardinal' is compact.

The single cups have plum outer petals, but are glowing crimson inside. Hardy.

General care: Plant in late autumn or early winter with the top of the bulb 10–15cm (4–6in) deep.

Height: 35cm (14in) **Spread:** 15cm (6in)

Site: Sun. Well-drained soil

Compost: Soil-based (John Innes No. 2)

Use: Border, container, formal bedding

Good companions: *Anemone coronaria* De Caen Group, *Muscari aucheri*, *Myosotis sylvatica* 'Royal Blue'

4 Tulipa 'Peach Blossom'
Double early flowering tulip

Peak flowering time for these tulips is mid-spring, but they can be forced for winter blooms. 'Peach Blossom' has deep pink flowers, the base often green-tinged cream. Hardy.

General care: Plant in late autumn or early winter with the top of the bulb 10–15cm (4–6in) deep.

Height: 30cm (12in) **Spread:** 15cm (6in)

Site: Sun. Well-drained soil

Compost: Soil-based (John Innes No. 2)

Use: Border, container, formal bedding

Good companions: *Bellis perennis*, *Hyacinthus orientalis* 'Ostara', *Tulipa* 'Heart's Delight'

red and russet

5 Anemone coronaria De Caen Group
Windflower

The single flowers of these vigorous anemones are in various shades of red, pink and white. Hardy.

General care: For flowers in late winter or early

spring, plant in early to mid-autumn with the top of the corm about 8cm (3in) deep. Plant in mid-spring for flowers in summer.

Height: 25cm (10in) **Spread:** 15cm (6in)

Site: Sun. Well-drained soil

Compost: Soil-based (John Innes No. 2) with added grit

Use: Container, sunny border, raised bed

Good companions: *Centaurea cyanus*, *Consolida ajacis* Giant Imperial Series, *Gladiolus* 'The Bride'

6 Hyacinthus orientalis 'Jan Bos'
Hyacinth

Although this early cultivar produces a slimmer spike than many hyacinths, the stem is still densely set with fragrant, bright crimson-red bells. Prepared bulbs are suitable for forcing. Hardy.

with the top of the bulb 10–15cm (4–6in) deep.
Height: 20cm (8in) **Spread:** 15cm (6in)
Site: Sun. Well-drained soil
Compost: Soil-based (John Innes No. 2)
Use: Border, container, formal bedding, raised
bed, rock garden
Good companions: *Iris* 'George', *Primula*
'Guinevere', *Tulipa humilis* Violacea
Group

10 **Tulipa 'Madame Lefeber'**
Fosteriana tulip

One parent of the Fosteriana Group of tulips is
red-flowered *T. fosteriana*, a species that
produces single bowl-shaped flowers in mid-
spring. The sheeny, searing red flowers of this
hybrid are borne slightly earlier. Hardy.
General care: Plant in late autumn or early winter
with the top of the bulb 10–15cm (4–6in) deep.
Height: 35cm (14in) **Spread:** 15cm (6in)
Site: Sun. Well-drained soil
Compost: Soil-based (John Innes No. 2)
Use: Border, container, formal bedding
Good companions: *Bellis perennis* 'Kito',
Erysimum cheiri 'Blood Red', *Hyacinthus orientalis*
'Jan Bos'

11 **Tulipa praestans 'Fusilier'**

The relatively small red flowers are carried in
bouquets of up to five per stem over slightly
downy grey-green leaves. Hardy.
General care: Plant in late autumn or early winter
with the top of the bulb 10–15cm (4–6in) deep.
Height: 30cm (12in) **Spread:** 15cm (6in)
Site: Sun. Well-drained soil
Compost: Soil-based (John Innes No. 2)
Use: Border, container, formal bedding, raised
bed, rock garden
Good companions: *Muscari aucheri*, *Myosotis
sylvatica* 'Royal Blue', *Primula* Prominent

12 **Tulipa 'Red Riding Hood'**
Greigii tulip

Greigii tulips have handsome leaves with dark
markings. This is one of the best, with bright
scarlet single flowers and attractively maroon-
mottled foliage. Hardy.
General care: Plant in late autumn or early winter
with the top of the bulb 10–15cm (4–6in) deep.
Height: 20cm (8in) **Spread:** 15cm (6in)
Site: Sun. Well-drained soil
Compost: Soil-based (John Innes No. 2)
Use: Border, container, formal bedding, raised
bed, rock garden
Good companions: *Armeria maritima*
'Düsseldorfer Stolz', *Festuca glauca* 'Seeigel',
Muscari botryoides 'Album'

General care: Plant in autumn with the top of the
bulb about 10cm (4in) deep.
Height: 25cm (10in) **Spread:** 8cm (3in)
Site: Sun, partial shade. Well-drained soil
Compost: Soil-based (John Innes No. 2) or bulb
fibre if planting in containers without drainage holes
Use: Container, formal bedding, front of border
Good companions: *Muscari aucheri*, *Primula*
Cowichan Garnet Group, *Viola* Sorbet Series

7 **Tulipa clusiana var. chrysantha**
Lady tulip

In early to mid-spring this graceful plant bears a
large yellow flower, stained red or brown-purple
on the outside. *T. clusiana* itself is white with
crimson-pink markings. Hardy.
General care: Plant in late autumn or early winter
with the top of the bulb about 10cm (4in) deep.
Height: 30cm (12in) **Spread:** 8cm (3in)
Site: Sun. Well-drained soil
Compost: Soil-based (John Innes No. 2)
Use: Border, container, formal bedding
Good companions: *Aubrieta* 'Greencourt Purple',
Campanula carpatica, *Daphne cneorum* 'Eximia'

8 **Tulipa hageri 'Splendens'**

In early to mid-spring this tulip bears up to four
large star-shaped flowers to a stem. Each one is
up to 9cm (3½in) across, crimson-scarlet, tinged
green on the outside with a black base and
brown-red inside. Hardy.
General care: Plant in late autumn or early winter
with the top of the bulb about 10cm (4in) deep.
Height: 30cm (12in) **Spread:** 15cm (6in)
Site: Sun. Well-drained soil
Compost: Soil-based (John Innes No. 2)
Use: Border, container, formal bedding, raised
bed, rock garden
Good companions: *Aurinia saxatilis* 'Citrina',
Tulipa orphanidea Whittallii Group, *Tulipa urumiensis*

9 **Tulipa 'Heart's Delight'**
Kaufmanniana tulip

The flowers of this low-growing mottle-leaved
tulip are carmine-red on the outside, paler at the
margins, and off-white inside, giving an overall
impression of pinkish red. The base is yellow with
red marks. Hardy.
General care: Plant in late autumn or early winter

red and russet (continued)

1 Tulipa 'Shakespeare'
Kaufmanniana tulip

The blooms of this sturdy tulip, which flowers in the first half of spring, are an unusual blend of salmon and scarlet with yellow at their base. Hardy.

General care: Plant in late autumn or early winter with the top of the bulb 10–15cm (4–6in) deep.

Height: 25cm (10in) **Spread:** 15cm (6in)

Site: Sun. Well-drained soil

Compost: Soil-based (John Innes No. 2)

Use: Border, container, formal bedding, raised bed, rock garden

Good companions: *Chionodoxa forbesii* 'Pink Giant', *Hyacinthus orientalis* 'Jan Bos', *Muscari aucheri*

yellow and orange

2 Fritillaria imperialis
Crown imperial

Sturdy stems carry tiers of glossy green leaves for up to two-thirds of their height and then are topped by more leaves, below which hangs a ring of bell-shaped flowers up to 5cm (2in) across. The most common colour is reddish orange, but there is considerable variation: 'Rubra' and 'Rubra Maxima' are deep orange-red; 'Lutea' and 'Lutea Maxima' are bright yellow. Hardy.

General care: Plant the large hollow-crowned bulb on its side on a bed of coarse sand about 20cm (8in) deep.

Height: 75cm (2ft 6in) **Spread:** 30cm (12in)

Site: Sun, partial shade. Well-drained soil. Good on lime

Use: Border

Good companions: *Muscari aucheri, Stipa gigantea, Tulipa orphanidea* Whittallii Group

3 Tulipa 'Cape Cod'
Greigii tulip

This hybrid has handsomely mottled foliage. The yellow flowers are shaded apricot on the outside and tinted bronze around the black base inside. The segments have a central red stripe. Hardy.

General care: Plant in late autumn or early winter with the top of the bulb 10–15cm (4–6in) deep.

Height: 20cm (8in) **Spread:** 15cm (6in)

Site: Sun. Well-drained soil

Compost: Soil-based (John Innes No. 2)

Use: Border, container, formal bedding, raised bed, rock garden

Good companions: *Achillea* x *lewisii* 'King Edward', *Haplopappus glutinosus, Helianthemum* 'Wisley Primrose'

4 Tulipa 'Orange Emperor'
Fosteriana tulip

The large flowers of this vigorous hybrid are usually borne in mid-spring over broad grey-green leaves. They are glowing orange, less intense inside, with a yellow base. Hardy.

General care: Plant in late autumn or early winter with the top of the bulb 10–15cm (4–6in) deep.

Height: 40cm (16in) **Spread:** 15cm (6in)

Site: Sun. Well-drained soil

Compost: Soil-based (John Innes No. 2)

Use: Border, container, formal bedding

Good companions: *Crocus vernus* 'Remembrance', *Erysimum cheiri* 'Orange Bedder', *Tulipa* 'Prinses Irene'

5 Tulipa orphanidea Whittallii Group

The impression of this subtly coloured tulip is of bronzed orange, but the outer segments are tinged green and the base inside is black. The almost spherical flowers open to a star. Hardy.

General care: Plant in late autumn or early winter with the top of the bulb about 10cm (4in) deep. Clumps are best left undisturbed.

Height: 35cm (14in) **Spread:** 10cm (4in)

Site: Sun. Well-drained soil

Compost: Soil-based (John Innes No. 2)

Use: Border, container, raised bed, rock garden

Good companions: *Crocus angustifolius, Crocus chrysanthus* 'Zwanenburg Bronze', *Iris danfordiae*

6 Tulipa 'Prinses Irene'
Triumph Group tulip

In mid-spring this hybrid bears cup-shaped orange flowers with a purple 'flame' on the outer segments. Hardy.

General care: Plant in late autumn or early winter with the top of the bulb 10–15cm (4–6in) deep.

Height: 35cm (14in) **Spread:** 15cm (6in)

Site: Sun. Well-drained soil
Compost: Soil-based (John Innes No. 2)
Use: Border, container, formal bedding
Good companions: *Primula* Gold-laced Group,
Tulipa 'Couleur Cardinal', *Viola* x *wittrockiana*
Ultima Series

7 Tulipa urumiensis

Linear, grey-green leaves form a flat rosette from
which rises a short stem carrying one or two
starry flowers. These are bright yellow inside and
bronze-yellow on the exterior. Hardy.
General care: Plant in late autumn or early winter
with the top of the bulb about 10cm (4in) deep.
Height: 35cm (14in) **Spread:** 10cm (4in)
Site: Sun. Well-drained soil
Compost: Soil-based (John Innes No. 2)
Use: Border, container, raised bed, rock garden
Good companions: *Rhodanthemum
hosmariense*, *Sedum* 'Bertram Anderson', *Tulipa
orphanidea* Whittallii Group

cream and white

8 Anemone nemorosa
Wood anemone

This creeping rhizomatous plant can spread
rampantly. The white nodding flowers are often
flushed pink or mauve; 'Allenii' is mauve-blue,
'Alba Plena' is white and double. Hardy.
General care: Best planted after flowering, while
plants are still in leaf. Alternatively, plant fresh
rhizomes horizontally about 5cm (2in) deep in
early autumn.
Height: 10cm (4in) **Spread:** 25cm (10in)
Site: Partial shade. Moist, humus-rich but well-
drained soil
Use: Underplanting for shrubs, woodland garden

Good companions: *Galanthus nivalis*, *Narcissus*
'Dove Wings', *Viola riviniana* Purpurea Group

9 Leucojum vernum
Spring snowflake

In late winter or early spring strap-shaped deep
green leaves emerge with a leafless stem that
carries one or two white drooping flowers. The
segments are tipped with green. Hardy.
General care: Plant in late summer or early autumn
with the top of the bulb about 10cm (4in) deep.
Height: 25cm (10in) **Spread:** 10cm (4in)
Site: Sun, partial shade. Moist, humus-rich soil
Use: Border, in grass, waterside
Good companions: *Astilbe* x *arendsii* 'Irrlicht',
Cornus alba 'Kesselringii', *Leucojum aestivum*
'Gravetye Giant'

10 Ornithogalum oligophyllum
Star-of-bethlehem

The bright green linear leaves lie almost flat with
above them a cluster of up to five unscented
flowers that are almost wholly green on the
outside and glistening white inside. Hardy.
General care: Plant in autumn with the top of the
bulb about 10cm (4in) deep.
Height: 10cm (4in) **Spread:** 15cm (6in)
Site: Sun. Well-drained soil
Use: Naturalised in short grass, raised bed, rock
garden

Good companions: *Aurinia saxatilis*
'Citrina', *Euphorbia myrsinites*,
Tulipa orphanidea Whittallii Group

11 Tulipa 'Purissima'
Fosteriana tulip

Stems rise from bright green leaves carrying
large, long-lasting flowers that open milky white
then turn pure white with a soft yellow centre.
Hardy.
General care: Plant in late autumn or early winter
with the top of the bulb 10–15cm (4–6in) deep.
Height: 35cm (14in) **Spread:** 12cm (5in)
Site: Sun. Well-drained soil
Compost: Soil-based (John Innes No. 2)
Use: Border, container, formal bedding
Good companions: *Buxus sempervirens*,
Hyacinthus orientalis 'Anna Marie', *Viola* x
wittrockiana Universal Series

12 Tulipa turkestanica

A few grey narrow leaves accompany up to
seven flowers on a slender stem. The star-like
flowers are ivory with a yellow centre. Hardy.
General care: Plant in late autumn or early winter
with the top of the bulb about 10cm (4in) deep.
Height: 30cm (12in) **Spread:** 8cm (3in)
Site: Sun. Well-drained soil
Compost: Soil-based (John Innes No. 2)
Use: Border, container, formal bedding, raised
bed, rock garden
Good companions: *Crocus chrysanthus* 'Cream
Beauty', *Euphorbia myrsinites*, *Tulipa urumiensis*

daffodils

In spring, yellow or white daffodils make an enormous impact in the garden – in borders or naturalised in grass – and as cut flowers. They vary in vigour, size, number of flowers and colour, but the structure of the flower is essentially always the same – six petals around a short cup or long trumpet – apart from double forms. Plant in late summer or early autumn in a well-drained sunny or partially shaded site, with the top of the bulb at a depth twice its height. In containers, use soil-based (John Innes No. 2) compost with added grit. Daffodils described here are hardy and can be forced for winter flowering.

1 Narcissus 'Dutch Master'
Trumpet daffodil

This all-yellow hybrid conforms to the classic daffodil pattern – a ring of six petals backing a trumpet at least as long as the petals.

Height: 40cm (16in)
Spread: 10cm (4in)
Good companions: *Forsythia giraldiana*, *Lonicera* x *purpusii* 'Winter Beauty', *Narcissus* 'Saint Keverne'

2 Narcissus 'Jack Snipe'
Cyclamineus daffodil

The flowers of this vigorous Cyclamineus daffodil (see 4) are long-lasting, from early to mid-spring. The white petals are swept back from a short lemon-yellow trumpet.
Height: 20cm (8in) **Spread:** 8cm (3in)
Good companions: *Primula vulgaris*, *Pulmonaria officinalis* 'Sissinghurst White', *Viburnum farreri*

3 Narcissus 'Tête-à-Tête'

This dwarf daffodil is very compact, early and bears one to three bright yellow flowers on each stem, the long cups slightly darker than the swept-back petals. It is excellent for growing in containers indoors or outside, alone or with other small bulbs or shrubby plants.
Height: 15cm (6in) **Spread:** 5cm (2in)
Good companions: *Narcissus* 'Little Gem', *Salix reticulata*, *Scilla siberica* 'Spring Beauty'

4 Narcissus 'February Gold'
Cyclamineus daffodil

Hybrids derived from the bright yellow *N. cyclamineus* are generally considerably larger than this dwarf moisture-loving daffodil, but share the sharply angled single flowers of their common parentage, with segments swept back from a relatively long trumpet. They flower in late winter and early spring. This vigorous hybrid has yellow petals and a long, slightly richer-coloured frilled trumpet.
Height: 30cm (12in) **Spread:** 8cm (3in)
Good companions: *Chimonanthus praecox*, *Chionodoxa luciliae* Gigantea Group, *Clematis macropetala* 'Maidwell Hall'

5 Narcissus 'Dove Wings'
Cyclamineus daffodil

One of the first Cyclamineus daffodils to flower (see 4, above). 'Dove Wings' has a pale yellow trumpet and white petals.
Height: 30cm (12in) **Spread:** 8cm (3in)
Good companions: *Anemone blanda*, *Narcissus* 'Jack Snipe', *Primula vulgaris* 'Alba Plena'

6 Narcissus 'Little Gem'
Dwarf trumpet daffodil

Several dwarf daffodils that flower in early spring make an attractive alternative to large

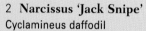

trumpet daffodils. 'Little Gem' is sturdy and compact with bright yellow petals and trumpet.

Height: 15cm (6in) **Spread:** 10cm (4in)

Good companions: *Crocus chrysanthus* 'Zwanenburg Bronze', *Iris histrioides* 'Major', *Veronica peduncularis* 'Georgia Blue'

7 Narcissus 'Barrett Browning'
Small-cupped daffodil

The small-cupped daffodils flower in early to mid-spring and produce a single bloom to a stem, with a cup up to a third the length of the flower segments. 'Barrett Browning' has a bright orange cup surrounded by white segments.

Height: 40cm (16in) **Spread:** 15cm (6in)

Good companions: *Myosotis sylvatica* 'Royal Blue', *Primula* Gold-laced Group, *Tulipa* 'Prinses Irene'

8 Narcissus obvallaris
Tenby daffodil

In early spring, stiff stems bear single flowers with petals pointing forward around a slightly frilled trumpet. Petals and trumpet are an almost uniform rich yellow. This sturdy daffodil is excellent for naturalising in the wild garden.

Height: 30cm (12in) **Spread:** 8cm (3in)

Good companions: *Crocus speciosus*, *Eranthis hyemalis, Galanthus nivalis*

9 Narcissus 'Rip van Winkle'
Double daffodil

Double daffodils tend to be knocked around by rough weather, but this dwarf is a good garden plant, each flower a bright yellow mophead of numerous pointed segments.

Height: 15cm (6in) **Spread:** 5cm (2in)

Good companions: *Hyacinthoides non-scripta, Narcissus obvallaris, Tulipa sprengeri*

10 Narcissus 'Sun Disc'
Jonquil

Most of the jonquils have very narrow leaves and round stems that bear two or three sweetly scented small-cupped flowers. 'Sun Disc' bears a single small rounded flower per stem. It is yellow at first but pales to cream.

Height: 20cm (8in) **Spread:** 5cm (2in)

Good companions: *Crocus chrysanthus* 'Cream Beauty', *Hypericum olympicum, Tulipa urumiensis*

11 Narcissus 'Liberty Bells'
Triandrus daffodil

Narcissus triandrus is a dainty species, having several small-cupped flowers to a stem. The charming hybrids that share these characteristics usually flower around the middle of spring. In mid-spring, 'Liberty Bells' bears two lemon-yellow flowers to a stem.

Height: 30cm (12in) **Spread:** 8cm (3in)

Good companions: *Hyacinthus orientalis* 'Ostara', *Tulipa* 'Couleur Cardinal', *Viola* Sorbet Series

12 Narcissus 'Saint Keverne'
Large-cupped daffodil

In general, large-cupped daffodils are a showy group with trumpets that are more than a third the length of the petals. 'Saint Keverne' is almost uniformly yellow, with broad petals. It is excellent for naturalising in grass or borders.

Height: 45cm (18in) **Spread:** 15cm (6in)

Good companions: *Berberis darwinii, Kerria japonica* 'Pleniflora', *Muscari armeniacum*

spring-flowering crocuses

The strong colours of crocuses make a considerable impact from winter to early spring, particularly when they are grown densely in containers or as large colonies in grass, where drifts of one colour are more effective than random mixtures. Many are also good for raised beds and rock gardens. Plant crocuses in autumn, the smaller species as early as possible, with the top of the corm 5–8cm (2–3in) deep in well-drained gritty soil, or in soil-based compost (John Innes No. 2) with added grit. All crocuses described here are hardy.

1 Crocus vernus 'Pickwick'
Dutch crocus

The large goblet-shaped flowers of the vigorous Dutch crocuses open out in sunshine to reveal bright orange stigmas. This cultivar is pale mauve striped purple and has a purple base.

Height: 12cm (5in) **Spread:** 5cm (2in)
Good companions: *Corylus avellana* 'Contorta', *Crocus x luteus* 'Golden Yellow', *Narcissus* 'Rijnveld's Early Sensation'

2 Crocus flavus

Scented bright yellow to orange flowers, up to four to a corm, are produced with the leaves.

Height: 8cm (3in) **Spread:** 5cm (2in)
Good companions: *Crocus chrysanthus* 'Ladykiller', *Scilla bifolia*, *Tulipa* 'Cape Cod'

3 Crocus angustifolius
Cloth of gold crocus

Small, intense orange-yellow flowers with mahogany-stained outer segments that recurve when fully open. Flowers are produced in late winter or early spring at the same time as leaves.

Height and spread: 5cm (2in)
Good companions: *Crocus minimus*, *Tulipa orphanidea* Whittallii Group, *Tulipa urumiensis*

4 Crocus x luteus 'Golden Yellow'
Dutch yellow crocus

Each corm produces up to five vivid orange-yellow flowers at the same time as the leaves, in late winter or early spring. This crocus does not set seed, but cormlets are produced freely so that colonies steadily expand.

Height: 10cm (4in) **Spread:** 5cm (2in)
Good companions: *Colchicum speciosum* 'Album', *Crocus speciosus*, *Crocus vernus* 'Purpureus Grandiflorus'

5 Crocus minimus

In early to mid-spring each corm produces one or two flowers with the leaves. The outer segments are buff with deep purple markings, the inner segments mauve-purple around the orange-yellow stigmas.

Height: 8cm (3in) **Spread:** 5cm (2in)
Good companions: *Crocus korokolwii*, *Pulsatilla vulgaris*, *Tulipa hageri* 'Splendens'

6 Crocus vernus 'Jeanne d'Arc'
Dutch crocus

This Dutch crocus (see 1, above) is pure white with a hint of violet at the base.

Height: 12cm (5in) **Spread:** 5cm (2in)
Good companions: *Betula utilis* var. *jacquemontii* 'Silver Shadow', *Crocus vernus* 'Remembrance', *Narcissus* 'Dove Wings'

7 Crocus vernus 'Remembrance'
Dutch crocus

One of the first of the Dutch crocuses (see 1, above) to flower, this cultivar bears violet-purple goblets with a bright green sheen over leaves with a white midrib.

Height: 12cm (5in) **Spread:** 5cm (2in)
Good companions: *Anemone blanda*, *Eranthis hyemalis*, *Narcissus* 'February Gold'

8 Crocus vernus 'Purpureus Grandiflorus'
Dutch crocus

The fine satin sheen of this Dutch crocus (see 1, above) shows off its rich purple colouring.

Height: 12cm (5in) **Spread:** 5cm (2in)
Good companions: *Colchicum* 'Rosy Dawn', *Crocus vernus* 'Jeanne d'Arc', *Crocus vernus* 'Pickwick'

climbers

Climbers twine, cling with small stem roots or clasp with tendrils. Those that flower in early spring bring welcome colour to walls, fences and architectural supports. Plant in the dormant season.

purple, blue and violet

1 Akebia quinata
Chocolate vine

The brown-purple flowers of this semi-evergreen climber are somewhat hidden in spring by the five-lobed leaves, but their pervasive spicy scent betrays their presence. After a hot summer purple, sausage-shaped fruits may follow and are produced most freely if two plants are grown close together. Hardy.

General care: Prune lightly immediately after flowering.

Height: 8m (25ft) **Spread:** 4m (12ft)

Site: Sun, partial shade. Moist but well-drained soil

Use: Pergola, tree climber, wall

Good companions: *Clematis montana* var. *rubens* 'Elizabeth', *Rosa* 'Aimée Vibert', *Wisteria sinensis*

pink and mauve

2 Clematis alpina 'Ruby'

The colour range of the alpine clematis, all spring-flowering, slender deciduous climbers, is centred on blue and white. Most are in flower by mid-spring, but 'Ruby' often produces occasional blooms in summer. It is a useful alternative in red-pink with greenish white petal-like stamens. Hardy.

General care: Plant with the base in shade. Prune lightly immediately after flowering.

Height: 3m (10ft) **Spread:** 1.5m (5ft)

Site: Sun, partial shade. Fertile, humus-rich and well-drained soil. Good on lime

Compost: Soil-based (John Innes No. 3)

Use: Container, shrub climber, training on tripod, wall

Good companions: *Clematis macropetala*, *Tulipa* 'Couleur Cardinal', *Tulipa* 'Purissima'

3 Clematis macropetala 'Maidwell Hall'

This slender deciduous clematis is usually in bloom by mid-spring and often continues into early summer. The freely produced deep mauve flowers appear double because petal-like stamens fill the centre. Fluffy seed heads follow. Hardy.

General care: Plant with the base in shade. Prune lightly immediately after flowering.

Height: 3m (10ft) **Spread:** 1.5m (5ft)

Site: Sun, partial shade. Fertile, humus-rich and well-drained soil. Good on lime

Compost: Soil-based (John Innes No. 3)

Use: Container, shrub climber, training on tripod, wall

Good companions: *Clematis* 'Abundance', *Rosa* 'Parade', *Solanum laxum* 'Album'

cream and white

4 Clematis armandii

This vigorous evergreen species is a very fine plant, with glossy dark green leaves and in early spring numerous clusters of scented white flowers. Hardy.

General care: Plant with the base in shade. Prune lightly immediately after flowering.

Height: 5m (15ft) **Spread:** 4m (12ft)

Site: Sun, partial shade. Fertile, humus-rich and well-drained soil. Does well on lime

Use: Arch, pergola, wall

Good companions: *Lonicera periclymenum* 'Serotina', *Rosa* 'Madame Alfred Carrière', *Rosa* 'Veilchenblau'

5 Hedera colchica 'Dentata Variegata'
Bullock's heart ivy, Persian ivy

Evergreen self-clinging plant that is equally at home on a large wall or making effective ground cover. The large unlobed leaves have curled-under edges and are grey-shaded bright green with irregular creamy yellow margins that become milky white as the leaves mature. Hardy.

General care: Prune at any time to restrict growth.

Height: 5m (15ft) **Spread:** 4m (12ft)

Site: Sun, partial shade. Well-drained soil

Use: Ground cover, wall

Good companions: *Buxus sempervirens*, *Hedera colchica* 'Dentata', *Prunus laurocerasus*

green

6 Holboellia coriacea

Fragrant evergreen twining climber with clusters of purplish male blooms carried at stem ends, greenish female ones lower down. Inedible purple fruits appear after a hot summer. Not fully hardy.

General care: Prune lightly after flowering.

Height: 6m (20ft) **Spread:** 2.5m (8ft)

Site: Sun, partial shade. Humus-rich and well-drained soil

Use: Arch, pergola, tree climber, wall

Good companions: *Buddleja crispa*, *Solanum crispum* 'Glasnevin', *Trachelospermum jasminoides*

shrubs & trees

Massed blossom often precedes or eclipses the beautiful foliage tints of
early spring when deciduous trees and shrubs start to break into leaf.
Plant in the dormant season, preferably in autumn or early spring.

purple, blue and violet

1 Erica x darleyensis 'Kramer's Rote'
Darley dale heath

Like other darley dale heaths, this bushy
evergreen is lime-tolerant and flowers over a long
season in winter and spring. The foliage is bronze
tinted and the flowers are magenta. Hardy.

General care: Trim plants in spring, after flowering.

Height: 30cm (12in) **Spread:** 60cm (2ft)

Site: Sun. Well-drained soil

Compost: Soil-based, preferably lime-free
(ericaceous)

Use: Container, ground cover, heather garden,
raised bed, rock garden

Good companions: *Erica carnea* 'King George',
Erica x *darleyensis* 'Furzey', *Juniperus* x *pfitzeriana*
'Wilhelm Pfitzer'

2 Rhododendron Blue Tit Group

This dense evergreen dwarf bush has foliage that
is yellow-green when young, but later turns mid-
green. The small funnel-shaped flowers are borne
in clusters of two or three at the tips of the
stems and are soft mauve-blue. Excellent for a
sunny rock or heather garden. Hardy.

Height and spread: 1m (3ft)

Site: Partial shade. Lime-free, humus-rich but
well-drained soil

Compost: Soil-based (ericaceous)

Use: Container, heather garden, rock garden

Good companions: *Disanthus cercidifolius*,
Gaultheria mucronata 'Bell's Seedling', *Ledum
groenlandicum*

3 Rhododendron 'Penheale Blue'

Free-flowering, compact evergreen shrub with
small glossy leaves, this can be grown in full sun.
In early and mid-spring it bears dense clusters of
funnel-shaped flowers that are violet-blue with
red undertones. Hardy.

Height and spread: 1.2m (4ft)

Site: Partial shade, sun. Lime-free, humus-rich
but well-drained soil.

Compost: Soil-based (ericaceous)

Use: Container, heather garden bed, rock garden

Good companions: *Acer japonicum* 'Vitifolium',

Hamamelis x *intermedia* 'Pallida', *Rhododendron*
'Golden Torch'

4 Salix gracilistyla 'Melanostachys'

This deciduous shrub is startling in spring before
the leaves develop. The blackish catkins have
brick-red anthers, the combination creating a
purplish effect on the naked branches. The leaves
are silky grey before they turn glossy green and
are retained well into autumn. Hardy.

Height: 3m (10ft) **Spread:** 4m (12ft)

Site: Sun. Moist but well-drained soil

Use: Border, waterside

Good companions: *Cornus alba* 'Kesselringii',
Miscanthus sinensis 'Silberfeder', *Salix irrorata*

5 Vinca minor 'La Grave'
Lesser periwinkle

Vinca minor itself is a low evergreen shrub with
trailing branches and glossy pointed leaves. It is a
vigorous coloniser and stems root readily. This
large-flowered selection bears purplish blue
flowers in spring and early summer. Of similar
vigour, f. *alba* is a white-flowered form, but
variegated forms, such as blue-flowered
'Argenteo-Variegata' with creamy leaf margins,
spread less aggressively. All forms flower best if
grown in full sun. Hardy.

Height: 15cm (6in) **Spread:** Indefinite

Site: Sun, partial shade. Well-drained soil

Use: Ground cover

Good companions: *Euphorbia amygdaloides*
'Purpurea', *Hedera helix* 'Ivalace', *Iris foetidissima*

pink and mauve

6 Chaenomeles x superba 'Pink Lady'
Flowering quince, Japanese quince

This deciduous shrub is one of several hybrids
that make spiny spreading bushes. It often starts
flowering on bare stems in winter and continues
into late spring. Bright pink cup-shaped flowers
open from strongly coloured buds. Hardy.

General care: Prune immediately after flowering,
on wall-trained specimens cutting back flowered
shoots to within three or four buds of a
permanent framework of branches.

Height: 1.5m (5ft) **Spread:** 2m (6ft)

Site: Sun, partial shade. Well-drained soil

Use: Border, wall

Good companions: *Chionodoxa forbesii* 'Pink
Giant', *Galanthus elwesii*, *Muscari armeniacum*

7 Daphne bholua var. glacialis 'Gurkha'

Rather upright deciduous shrub that begins
flowering in winter and extends into early spring.
The purplish pink flowers are borne in clusters on
stem tips and have a strong sweet scent. Hardy.

Height: 2.5m (8ft) **Spread:** 1.5m (5ft)

Site: Sun, partial shade. Humus-rich and moist
but well-drained soil

Use: Border, woodland garden

Good companions: *Geranium phaeum*, *Magnolia*
x *loebneri* 'Leonard Messel', *Omphalodes
cappodocica*

8 Erica erigena 'Irish Dusk'
Irish heath, Mediterranean heath

This compact dark-leaved form of a low-growing
lime-tolerant species often starts to flower in
winter and bears spikes of honey-scented pink
flowers throughout spring. Hardy.

General care: Trim plants in late spring or early
summer, after flowering.

Height: 60cm (2ft) **Spread:** 45cm (18in)

Site: Sun. Moist but well-drained soil
Use: Ground cover, heather garden,
hedge
Good companions: *Erica carnea*
'Springwood White', *Erica erigena*
'Brightness', *Picea abies* 'Little Gem'

9 Magnolia campbellii subsp. mollicomata

Once it is mature, after 10 years, this deciduous
tree is magnificent in spring when it bears large,
upright pink or purplish pink blooms. Hardy.
Height: 15m (50ft) **Spread:** 10m (33ft)
Site: Sun. Moist but well-drained soil, preferably
lime-free
Use: Canopy in border, woodland garden
Good companions: *Davidia involucrata, Disanthus
cercidifolius, Viburnum plicatum* 'Mariesii'

10 Magnolia x loebneri 'Leonard Messel'

This densely branched, deciduous tall shrub or
small tree flowers before the foliage develops.
Purplish pink globular buds open to form a paler
star of 10–12 narrow, somewhat limp petals. Hardy.
Height: 8m (25ft) **Spread:** 6m (20ft)
Site: Sun. Moist but well-drained soil
Use: Canopy in border, specimen shrub,
woodland garden
Good companions: *Epimedium* x *youngianum*
'Niveum', *Omphalodes verna, Tiarella wherryi*

11 Pieris japonica 'Blush'

The glossy leaves of this evergreen compact
shrub are coppery when young. In late winter and
early spring it is covered with drooping sprays of
deep pink buds. These open to pale pink waxy
flowers that age to white. Hardy.

Height: 4m (12ft) **Spread:** 3m (10ft)
Site: Sun, partial shade. Lime-free, moist but
well-drained soil
Use: Border, woodland garden
Good companions: *Gaultheria mucronata*
'Wintertime', *Kalmia latifolia* 'Ostbo Red',
Rhododendron Temple Belle Group

12 Prunus x blireana
Ornamental plum

Slightly fragrant, pink semi-double flowers cover
the branches of this deciduous shrub or small
tree in early and mid-spring. Copper-purple leaves
begin to open before flowering finishes. Hardy.
Height and spread: 4m (12ft)
Site: Sun. Moist but well-drained soil
Use: Canopy in border, specimen shrub or tree
Good companions: *Brunnera macrophylla, Tiarella
cordifolia, Vinca minor* 'La Grave'

pink and mauve (continued)

1 Prunus cerasifera 'Pissardii'
Cherry plum, Myrobalan, Purple-leaved plum

In early and mid-spring the twiggy stems of this bushy deciduous tree are crowded with pink buds that open to almost white single flowers. The rich red young foliage turns purplish in summer. Edible purple fruits are only rarely produced. Hardy.

Height and spread: 8m (25ft)

Site: Sun. Moist but well-drained soil

Use: Canopy in border, hedge, specimen tree

Good companions: *Anemone* x *hybrida* 'Honorine Jobert', *Fuchsia magellanica* 'Versicolor', *Geranium clarkei* x *collinum* 'Kashmir White'

2 Prunus dulcis
Common almond

This deciduous tree has finely tapered toothed leaves and spreads as it matures. In early spring the naked branches are covered with pink flowers. Velvety green fruits, which contain an edible nut, are freely produced in a warm climate only. Hardy.

Height and spread: 8m (25ft)

Site: Sun. Moist but well-drained soil

Use: Canopy in border, specimen tree

Good companions: *Anemone blanda, Colchicum* 'Rosy Dawn', *Colchicum speciosum* 'Album'

3 Prunus mume 'Beni-chidori'
Japanese apricot

Deciduous tree or shrub suitable for training against a wall, preferably warm and sheltered. In late winter and early spring the bare branches carry numerous crimson-pink, sweetly scented, single flowers. Edible fruits are only rarely produced in a cool temperate climate. Hardy.

General care: Delay pruning of wall-trained specimens until midsummer.

Height and spread: 8m (25ft)

Site: Sun. Moist but well-drained soil

Use: Canopy in border, specimen tree or shrub, wall

Good companions: *Abeliophyllum distichum, Nerine bowdenii, Primula auricula* 'Blue Velvet'

4 Prunus 'Pandora'
Ornamental cherry

This deciduous tree has ascending branches when young, but later becomes more spreading in growth. Specimens are covered with pale pink blossom in early spring, before the leaves appear. The foliage is bronze at first then green, and usually colours bright orange and red in autumn. Hardy.

Height: 9m (30ft) **Spread:** 8m (25ft)

Site: Sun. Moist but well-drained soil

Use: Canopy in border, specimen tree

Good companions: *Anemone blanda, Crocus vernus* 'Jeanne d'Arc', *Crocus vernus* 'Purpureus Grandiflorus'

5 Prunus triloba 'Multiplex'
Flowering almond

Deciduous shrub suitable for training against a wall, preferably warm and sheltered. Well-pruned plants will produce masses of clear pink double flowers in early to mid-spring. Hardy.

General care: As soon as flowering is over, cut all flowered shoots hard back.

Height and spread: 3m (10ft)

Site: Sun. Moist but well-drained soil

Use: Border, wall

Good companions: *Anemone coronaria* De Caen Group, *Hyacinthus orientalis* 'Carnegie', *Tulipa* 'Estella Rijnveld'

6 Rhododendron 'Anna Baldsiefen'

The foliage of this small evergreen shrub is light green in summer and bronze-red in winter. The vivid pink funnel-shaped flowers have wavy margins and are densely clustered. Hardy.

Height and spread: 1m (3ft)

Site: Partial shade. Lime-free, humus-rich and moist but well-drained soil

Compost: Soil-based (ericaceous)

Use: Border, container, woodland garden

Good companions: *Acer grosseri* var. *hersii, Magnolia* x *loebneri* 'Leonard Messel', *Rhododendron williamsianum*

7 Rhododendron ciliatum

This compact, domed evergreen shrub produces clusters of two to four nodding bell-shaped flowers that are scented and light pink. The dark green leaves are lighter underneath and have hairy margins. Hardy.

Height and spread: 2m (6ft)
Site: Partial shade. Lime-free, humus-rich and moist but well-drained soil
Use: Border, woodland garden
Good companions: *Fothergilla major* Monticola Group, *Halesia carolina*, *Rhododendron* 'Loder's White'

8 Rhododendron 'Cilpinense'

This evergreen hybrid makes a rounded bush of small dark green leaves with bristly margins. The many trusses of dark pink buds open to paler funnel-shaped flowers. Hardy.

General care: To protect flowers from frost damage, plant where there is overhead cover.
Height and spread: 1.2m (4ft)
Site: Partial shade. Lime-free, humus-rich and moist but well-drained soil
Compost: Soil-based (ericaceous)
Use: Border, container, woodland garden
Good companions: *Cornus kousa* var. *chinensis* 'Satomi', *Davidia involucrata*, *Magnolia campbellii* subsp. *mollicomata*,

9 Rhododendron 'Razorbill'

The deep pink, upward-facing tubular flowers of this compact evergreen shrub are borne in dense clusters. The small crinkled leaves are dark green. Hardy.

Height and spread: 1.2m (4ft)
Site: Partial shade. Lime-free, humus-rich and moist but well-drained soil
Compost: Soil-based (ericaceous)
Use: Border, container, woodland garden
Good companions: *Acer japonicum* 'Vitifolium', *Kalmia latifolia* 'Ostbo Red', *Rhododendron* 'Vanessa Pastel'

10 Rhododendron Temple Belle Group

Evergreen shrub with rounded pale green leaves that are attractive all year round. The nodding bell-shaped flowers, which are carried profusely in loose clusters, are a soft uniform mid-pink. Hardy.

Height and spread: 2m (6ft)
Site: Partial shade. Lime-free, humus-rich and moist but well-drained soil
Use: Border, woodland garden
Good companions: *Camellia* 'Cornish Snow', *Eucryphia* x *nymansensis* 'Nymansay', *Styrax japonicus*

11 Rhododendron williamsianum

The small heart or kidney-shaped leaves of this evergreen shrub are bright green with a blue-grey underside when mature, but bronze on opening. Red buds, borne singly or in small clusters, open to wide bells that age to pale pink. Hardy.

General care: To protect flowers from frost damage, plant where there is overhead cover.
Height: 1.5m (5ft) **Spread:** 1.2m (4ft)
Site: Sun, partial shade.
Use: Border, woodland garden
Good companions: *Magnolia denudata*, *Rhododendron* 'Palestrina', *Rhododendron* 'Penheale Blue'

12 Viburnum tinus 'Eve Price'
Laurustinus

Winter and spring-flowering evergreen shrub of dense growth. Ornamental heads of brown-pink buds open to pink-tinged white flowers. This form has relatively small leaves, 8cm (3in) long. Hardy.

General care: Trim or hard prune in spring only if required.
Height and spread: 2.5m (8ft)
Site: Sun, partial shade. Moist but well-drained soil
Compost: Soil-based (John Innes No. 3)
Use: Container, border, informal hedge, topiary
Good companions: *Helleborus argutifolius*, *Lonicera* x *purpusii* 'Winter Beauty', *Prunus lusitanica*

red and russet

1 Aucuba japonica 'Rozannie'
Spotted laurel

This is a plain-leaved cultivar of an evergreen shrub best known for its variegated forms. Small green flowers in early to mid-spring usually go unnoticed, but this self-pollinating cultivar produces a good crop of red berries in autumn that often persist until the following spring. All parts inedible. Hardy.

Height: 1.2m (4ft) **Spread:** 1m (3ft)

Site: Partial shade, sun, shade.

Compost: Soil-based (John Innes No. 3)

Use: Border, container, underplanting for trees

Good companions: *Geranium macrorrhizum* 'Ingwersen's Variety', *Geranium phaeum*, *Helleborus foetidus*

2 Chaenomeles x superba 'Nicoline'
Flowering quince, Japanese quince, Japonica

Spiny deciduous shrub that makes a somewhat tangled spreading bush, but flowers over a long period. The first of the semi-double scarlet cups open in clusters on bare stems. Hardy.

General care: Prune immediately after flowering, on wall-trained specimens cutting back flowered shoots to within three or four buds of a permanent framework of branches.

Height: 1.5m (5ft) **Spread:** 2m (6ft)

Site: Sun, partial shade

Use: Sunny or lightly shaded border, wall

Good companions: *Polemonium* 'Lambrook Mauve', *Tulipa* 'Peach Blossom', *Tulipa* 'Purissima'

3 Corylus maxima 'Purpurea'
Filbert

In late winter or early spring the naked branches of this deciduous large shrub are adorned with dangling purplish catkins that are tinged with pale yellow. From spring to autumn the very rich purple, heart-shaped leaves make a strong impact. The husks surrounding the edible nuts, which ripen in autumn, are also purplish. Hardy.

General care: To produce large leaves, cut stems back to near ground level in early spring and feed and mulch generously.

Height: 6m (20ft) **Spread:** 5m (15ft)

Site: Sun, partial shade. Well-drained soil. Good on chalk

Use: Canopy in border, specimen shrub

Good companions: *Euonymus alatus* 'Compactus', *Narcissus* 'Jack Snipe', *Sorbus sargentiana*

4 Pieris formosa var. forestii 'Wakehurst'

Evergreen shrub with eye-catching young growths that are brilliant scarlet then change to pink and cream before turning green. Although the buds are formed in the preceding autumn, the white flowers, which hang in sprays, do not open until the second half of spring. Not fully hardy.

Height: 4m (12ft) **Spread:** 5m (15ft)

Site: Sun, partial shade. Lime-free, humus-rich and moist but well-drained soil

Use: Border, heather garden, woodland garden

Good companions: *Hamamelis* x *intermedia* 'Diane', *Pieris japonica* 'Blush', *Rhododendron macabeanum*

5 Rhododendron Humming Bird Group

Compact, domed evergreen shrub with glossy round leaves. The nodding bell-shaped flowers have a waxy texture and are bright red with a scarlet glow inside. Hardy.

Height and spread: 1.5m (5ft)

Site: Partial shade. Lime-free, humus-rich and moist but well-drained soil

Compost: Soil-based (ericaceous)

Use: Border, container, woodland garden

Good companions: *Camellia* x *williamsii* 'Francis Hanger', *Rhododendron* 'Bow Bells', *Rhododendron williamsianum*

6 Ribes sanguineum 'Pulborough Scarlet'
Flowering currant

By mid-spring this upright deciduous shrub is usually well covered with numerous drooping sprays of small red flowers. Later the flower sprays are more upright. Despite the somewhat pungent smell, this is a vigorous and easy shrub of great value. Inedible dark berries are occasionally produced. Hardy.

General care: In late spring trim hedges. On free-standing specimens cut back flowered shoots and remove about a quarter of old stems.

Height: 2.5m (8ft) **Spread:** 2m (6ft)

Site: Sun. Well-drained soil

Use: Border, informal hedge

Good companions: *Cercis siliquastrum*, *Osmanthus* x *burkwoodii*, *Syringa vulgaris* 'Madame Lemoine'

7 Ribes speciosum
Fuchsia-flowered currant

The stems of this upright deciduous shrub are covered with red bristles. The rich red flowers, which dangle in little clusters, are usually open before mid-spring. Not fully hardy.

General care: In cold areas, worth training against a warm wall. In late spring cut back flowered shoots to within three or four buds of a permanent framework.

Height and spread: 2m (6ft)

Site: Sun. Well-drained soil

Use: Border, wall

Good companions: *Garrya elliptica* 'James Roof', *Iris unguicularis*, *Nerine bowdenii*

yellow and orange

8 Aucuba japonica 'Variegata'
Spotted laurel

Rounded evergreen shrub with glossy yellow-speckled leaves that are sparsely toothed. The colour is best in full sun. If there is a male plant nearby, this female cultivar bears good crops of berries that ripen red in autumn and usually last until the following spring. All parts are likely to cause a stomach upset if ingested. Hardy.

Height and spread: 3m (10ft)

Site: Partial shade, sun, shade.

Compost: Soil-based (John Innes No. 3)

Use: Border, container, underplanting for trees

Good companions: *Aucuba japonica* 'Rozannie', *Forsythia* x *intermedia* 'Lynwood', *Syringa vulgaris* 'Katherine Havemeyer'

9 Azara microphylla

Sprays of small dark green leaves make this evergreen small tree or large shrub a good foliage plant. In late winter and early spring fragrant, tiny, yellow petal-less flowers are clustered on the underside of shoots. Hardy.

General care: In late spring cut back flowered shoots of wall-trained specimens to within three or four buds of a permanent framework of branches.

Height: 8m (25ft) **Spread:** 4m (12ft)

Site: Sun, partial shade. Humus-rich and moist but well-drained soil

Use: Border, wall, woodland garden

Good companions: *Cornus alba* 'Elegantissima', *Cornus mas*, *Fuchsia magellanica* 'Riccartonii'

10 Berberis buxifolia

Evergreen or semi-evergreen shrub with dark green spine-tipped leaves that are grey on the underside. By mid-spring the arching stems carry numerous orange-yellow flowers, which hang singly or in pairs on long stems and are followed by inedible dark purple fruits. The more compact 'Pygmaea' grows to about 1m (3ft). Hardy.

General care: If required, trim after flowering.

Height: 2.5m (8ft) **Spread:** 3m (10ft)

Site: Sun, partial shade. Well-drained soil

Use: Border, informal hedge

Good companions: *Buddleja* 'Lochinch', *Caryopteris* x *clandonensis* 'Heavenly Blue', *Cotoneaster salicifolius* 'Rothschildianus'

11 Corylopsis pauciflora

Before coming into leaf this twiggy deciduous shrub bears short tassels of slightly fragrant pale yellow flowers that hang stiffly from the stems. The leaves open bronze-pink then turn bright green. Hardy.

Height: 1.5m (5ft) **Spread:** 2.5m (8ft)

Site: Partial shade. Lime-free, humus-rich and moist but well-drained soil

Use: Border, woodland garden

Good companions: *Hamamelis* x *intermedia* 'Arnold Promise', *Kirengeshoma palmata*, *Magnolia* 'Elizabeth'

yellow and orange (continued)

1 Corylopsis sinensis 'Spring Purple'

The sweetly scented, soft yellow flower tassels of this deciduous shrub are up to 10cm (4in) long. The young foliage is deep purple. Hardy.
Height: 3m (10ft) **Spread:** 2.5m (8ft)
Site: Partial shade. Humus-rich and moist but well-drained soil, preferably lime-free
Use: Border, woodland garden
Good companions: *Acer griseum*, *Cercidiphyllum japonicum*, *Leucothoe* Scarletta

2 Corylus avellana 'Aurea'
Hazel

This deciduous shrub is an ornamental rather than a nut-bearing form of the hazel. The drooping male catkins in late winter and early spring are pale yellow; the soft yellow leaves that follow create a more lasting effect. Hardy.

General care: For large leaves cut stems back annually to near base and feed generously.
Height and spread: 4m (12ft)
Site: Sun, partial shade. Well-drained soil. Good on chalk
Use: Border
Good companions: *Corylus maxima* 'Purpurea', *Euonymus alatus* 'Compactus', *Euonymus europaeus* 'Red Cascade'

3 Forsythia 'Beatrix Farrand'

Dense deciduous shrub with upright then arching stems that are covered in spring by numerous bright yellow nodding flowers. These are unusually large for a forsythia. Hardy.
General care: In late spring trim hedges. On free-standing shrubs cut back flowered shoots and cut to the base about a quarter of old stems.
Height and spread: 2m (6ft)
Site: Sun, partial shade. Moist but well-drained soil
Use: Border, hedge
Good companions: *Ceratostigma willmottianum*, *Fuchsia magellanica* 'Riccartonii', *Viburnum opulus* 'Compactum'

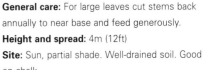

4 Forsythia × intermedia 'Lynwood'

This easy and reliable deciduous shrub is a tangle of branches that carry masses of deep yellow flowers before the leaves appear. Excellent for cutting as flowers will open indoors if stems are gathered while in bud. Hardy.

General care: In late spring trim hedges. On free-standing shrubs cut back flowered shoots and cut to the base about a quarter of old stems.

Height and spread: 3m (10ft)

Site: Sun, partial shade. Moist but well-drained soil

Use: Border, hedge

Good companions: *Hibiscus syriacus* 'Woodbridge', *Rosa* 'Geranium', *Rosa glauca*

5 Forsythia suspensa
Golden bell

Slender-stemmed deciduous shrub that is suitable for training against a wall. Small clusters of yellow starry flowers open on leafless stems in early to mid-spring.

General care: In late spring cut back flowered shoots and cut to the base about a quarter of old stems.

Height and spread: 3m (10ft)

Site: Sun, partial shade. Moist but well-drained soil

Use: Border, wall

Good companions: *Clematis* 'Bill MacKenzie', *Clematis* 'Gipsy Queen', *Rosa* 'Veilchenblau'

6 Hamamelis vernalis 'Sandra'
Ozark witch hazel

In late winter or early spring the bare stems of this deciduous shrub are set with many small, scented, clear yellow flowers. The young leaves that follow open purple then turn green, but retain a purplish colour on the underside. The foliage is brilliantly coloured in autumn. Hardy.

Height: 5m (15ft) **Spread:** 4m (12ft)

Site: Moist but well-drained soil

Use: Canopy in border, woodland garden

Good companions: *Corylopsis pauciflora*, *Rhododendron luteum*, *Rhododendron macabeanum*

7 Mahonia aquifolium 'Apollo'
Oregon grape

Compact form of a suckering evergreen shrub with leaves that open copper-tan then turn green and in winter are bronze-purple. Small yellow flowers are borne in dense clusters at the ends of stems in early spring and are followed by blue-black grape-like berries that can be used to make preserves. Hardy.

Height: 60cm (2ft) **Spread:** 1m (3ft)

Site: Partial shade, shade. Humus-rich and moist but well-drained soil

Use: Border, ground cover, woodland garden

Good companions: *Prunus laurocerasus* 'Otto Luyken', *Prunus lusitanica*, *Viburnum tinus* 'Gwenllian'

8 Ostrya carpinifolia
Hop hornbeam

By mid-spring this round-headed deciduous tree is decorated with dangling yellow male catkins. The fruit clusters that follow are hop-like and white. The toothed leaves are glossy dark green in summer, but turn yellow in autumn. Hardy.

Height and spread: 20m (65ft)

Site: Sun, partial shade. Well-drained soil

Use: Specimen tree, woodland garden

Good companions: *Cyclamen hederifolium*, *Helleborus hybridus*, *Polygonatum × hybridum*

9 Rhododendron 'Patty Bee'

Compact, rounded evergreen shrub with dark green leaves that become bronzed in winter. Pale yellow funnel-shaped flowers are borne very freely in the first half of spring. Hardy.

Height and spread: 75cm (2ft 6in)

Site: Sun, partial shade.

Compost: Soil-based (ericaceous)

Use: Border, container

Good companions: *Enkianthus campanulatus*, *Rhododendron* Blue Tit Group, *Rhododendron luteum*

10 Ribes odoratum
Buffalo currant

The yellow flowers of this deciduous shrub are produced in small, slightly drooping sprays. Usually open by mid-spring, they have a delicious and spicy scent. The bright green lobed leaves colour richly in autumn. Hardy.

General care: In late spring cut back flowered shoots and remove about a quarter of old stems.

Height and spread: 2m (6ft)

Site: Sun. Well-drained soil

Use: Border

Good companions: *Geranium* 'Johnson's Blue', *Geranium wallichianum* 'Buxton's Blue', *Rosa xanthina* 'Canary Bird'

11 Salix caprea 'Kilmarnock'
Kilmarnock willow

The branches of this small male tree hang down stiffly like the spokes of an umbrella. In late winter or early spring, silver catkins, yellowed by developing anthers, appear before the leaves open. Plants are grafted, so height varies. Hardy.

Height and spread: 2m (6ft)

Site: Sun. Moist but well-drained soil

Compost: Soil-based (John Innes No. 3)

Use: Border, container, specimen tree

Good companions: *Euphorbia polychroma*, *Geum rivale* 'Leonard's Variety', *Iris sibirica* 'Ego'

cream and white

12 Chaenomeles speciosa 'Nivalis'
Flowering quince, Japanese quince

The tangled branches of this spiny deciduous shrub are spangled with pure white cupped flowers over a long season, from late winter until late spring. Aromatic yellow-green fruits, often used in preserves, may follow. Hardy.

General care: Prune immediately after flowering, on wall-trained specimens cutting back flowered shoots to within three or four buds of a permanent framework of branches.

Height: 2.5m (8ft) **Spread:** 4m (12ft)

Site: Sun, partial shade. Well-drained soil

Compost: Sunny or lightly shaded border, wall

Use: Border, wall

Good companions: *Paeonia lactiflora* 'White Wings', *Tulipa clusiana*, *Tulipa* 'Spring Green'

Height: 40cm (16in) **Spread:** 75cm (2ft 6in)
Site: Sun. Well-drained soil
Compost: Soil-based, preferably lime-free
(ericaceous)
Use: Container, ground cover, heather garden,
raised bed, rock garden
Good companions: *Erica* x *darleyensis* 'Kramer's
Rote', *Erica vagans* 'Mrs D.F. Maxwell', *Juniperus
virginiana* 'Grey Owl'

cream and white (continued)

1 Daphne blagayana

Low evergreen or semi-green shrub with trailing
stems and leathery oval leaves. The strongly
scented milk-white flowers are gathered in
clusters of up to 30 at the end of stems.
Hardy.
Height: 40cm (16in) **Spread:** 1m (3ft)
Site: Partial shade. Humus-rich and moist but
well-drained soil
Use: Border, underplanting for shrubs and trees
Good companions: *Aquilegia vulgaris* 'Nivea',
Erythronium dens-canis, Helleborus niger

2 Erica x darleyensis 'Silberschmelze'
Darley dale heath

Like other darley dale heaths, this bushy
evergreen tolerates lime and flowers over a long
season. The scented white flowers are borne
from winter and through spring. The foliage is
deep green in summer but tinged red in winter,
and in spring there is a hint of cream at the tips.
Hardy.

3 Griselinia littoralis 'Variegata'
Broadleaf

This evergreen large shrub makes an attractive
windbreak or foliage plant in seaside gardens.
It has glossy leathery leaves that are bright green
streaked with grey-green and have creamy white
margins. Not fully hardy.
General care: If necessary, trim lightly in late
spring.
Height: 3m (10ft) **Spread:** 2m (6ft)
Site: Sun. Well-drained soil
Use: Border, informal hedge
Good companions: *Buddleja davidii* 'Black
Knight', *Escallonia* 'Apple Blossom', *Rosa*
'Blanche Double de Coubert'

4 Lonicera fragrantissima
Honeysuckle

Partially evergreen shrub that makes a spreading
red-stemmed bush, with dark green leaves that
are blue-green underneath. In late winter and
early spring, creamy white tubular flowers make
little impact visually, but their scent is delicious.
Dull red berries follow. Hardy.

General care: Immediately after flowering cut out
up to a quarter of old stems and cut back
remaining stems that have flowered to a strong
bud.
Height: 2m (6ft) **Spread:** 3m (10ft)
Site: Sun, partial shade. Well-drained soil
Use: Border
Good companions: *Buddleja alternifolia,
Ceanothus* x *delileanus* 'Topaze', *Perovskia* 'Blue
Spire'

5 Magnolia salicifolia
Willow-leaved magnolia

The fragrant, pure white starry flowers of this
deciduous tree are up to 10cm (4in) across and
open by mid-spring, before the foliage breaks.
The lance-shaped leaves are dull green with a
grey underside and are lemon scented when
bruised. Usually starts flowering when young.
Hardy.
Height: 9m (30ft) **Spread:** 6m (20ft)
Site: Sun, partial shade. Moist but well-drained
soil, preferably lime-free
Use: Canopy in border, specimen tree, woodland
garden
Good companions: *Clerodendrum trichotomum
var. fargesii, Hydrangea aspera* Villosa Group,
Hydrangea macrophylla 'Madame Emile Mouillère'

6 Magnolia stellata
Star magnolia

Slow-growing, compact deciduous shrub that spreads with age. Beautiful grey-green buds open to starry white flowers with up to 15 petals. Many cultivars with blush or pink flowers. Hardy.

Height: 3m (10ft) **Spread:** 4m (12ft)

Site: Sun, partial shade. Moist but well-drained soil

Use: Border, specimen shrub

Good companions: *Narcissus* 'Jack Snipe', *Scilla siberica* 'Spring Beauty', *Tulipa* 'Purissima'

7 Osmanthus x burkwoodii

Rounded, slow-growing evergreen shrub with glossy toothed leaves. By mid-spring there are small sprays of sweetly scented, white tubular flowers. Hardy.

General care: Trim hedges in late spring.

Height and spread: 3m (10ft)

Site: Sun, partial shade. Well-drained soil, preferably moist

Use: Border, hedge, topiary

Good companions: *Cornus alternifolia* 'Argentea', *Sarcococca hookeriana* var. *digyna*, *Viburnum tinus* 'Gwenllian'

8 Pieris floribunda
Fetter bush

In winter upright sprays of greenish white buds, borne at the tips of shoots, stand out against the dark green foliage of this rounded evergreen shrub. They open to small, white urn-shaped flowers. Hardy.

Height: 2m (6ft) **Spread:** 3m (10ft)

Site: Sun, partial shade. Lime-free, humus-rich and moist but well-drained soil

Use: Border, heather garden, woodland garden

Good companions: *Cornus controversa* 'Variegata', *Magnolia stellata*, *Rhododendron* 'Loder's White'

9 Pieris japonica 'Debutante'

Compact low-growing cultivar of a popular evergreen shrub for acid soils. The flower sprays are upright, but the individual white urn-shaped flowers dangle. Hardy.

Height and spread: 1m (3ft)

Site: Sun, partial shade. Lime-free, humus-rich and moist but well-drained soil

Use: Border, heather garden, woodland garden

Good companions: *Gaultheria mucronata* 'Wintertime', *Kalmia latifolia* 'Ostbo Red', *Pieris floribunda*

10 Prunus 'Taihaku'
Great white cherry

Vigorous deciduous tree that is dazzling in mid-spring when it is massed with large white single flowers. The leaves are copper-red when they unfurl, but become dark green as they age. Hardy.

Height: 8m (25ft) **Spread:** 9m (30ft)

Site: Sun, partial shade. Moist but well-drained soil

Use: Canopy in border, specimen tree

Good companions: *Crocus vernus* 'Jeanne d'Arc', *Crocus vernus* 'Pickwick', *Crocus vernus* 'Remembrance'

11 Prunus x yedoensis
Yoshino cherry

The arching branches of this deciduous tree carry masses of pale pink blossom before the leaves appear. The scented single flowers are carried in clusters of five or six. They remain pink in the centre, but age to near white. The foliage in summer is dark green. Hardy.

Height: 12m (40ft) **Spread:** 9m (30ft)

Site: Sun. Moist but well-drained soil

Use: Canopy in border, specimen tree

Good companions: *Colchicum* 'The Giant', *Crocus speciosus*, *Narcissus* 'Dove Wings'

12 Pyrus calleryana 'Chanticleer'

Narrowly upright deciduous tree with thorny branches and glossy leaves that turn red in late autumn. The single white flowers are borne in profusion and usually coincide with the development of the young leaves. They are followed by inedible small brown fruits. Hardy.

Height: 6m (20ft) **Spread:** 5m (15ft)

Site: Sun. Well-drained soil

Use: Avenue, border, specimen tree

Good companions: *Buddleja alternifolia*, *Crataegus persimilis* 'Prunifolia', *Malus* 'John Downie'

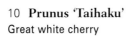

cream and white (continued)

1 Rhododendron 'Snow Lady'

Mound-shaped evergreen shrub with somewhat bristly leaves. Scented, pure white funnel-shaped flowers are borne in somewhat loose clusters of two to five. Hardy.

Height and spread: 1m (3ft)

Site: Sun. Lime-free, humus-rich and moist but well-drained soil

Compost: Soil-based (ericaceous)

Use: Border, container, rock garden

Good companions: *Gaultheria mucronata* 'Wintertime', *Rhododendron moupinense*, *Rhododendron* 'Penheale Blue'

2 Skimmia × confusa 'Kew Green'

Compact evergreen shrub that forms a dome of dark green glossy leaves. It is a male form and bears dense heads of scented, creamy white flowers. Old plants may exceed the dimensions given. Hardy.

Height: 2m (6ft) **Spread:** 1.5m (5ft)

Site: Partial shade, sun. Humus-rich, moist but well-drained soil

Use: Shady border, woodland garden

Good companions: *Aucuba japonica* 'Rozannie', *Lonicera* × *purpusii* 'Winter Beauty', *Prunus* 'Taihaku'

3 Spiraea thunbergii

The wiry stems and twigs of this spreading, usually deciduous shrub are covered with a 'snow' of small flowers in early to mid-spring, sometimes with an earlier flurry. The small, bright green narrow leaves turn orange-brown in autumn. Hardy.

General care: In late spring trim hedges. On free-standing specimens cut back flowered shoots and cut to the base up to a quarter of old stems.

Height: 1.5m (5ft) **Spread:** 2m (6ft)

Site: Sun. Moist but well-drained soil

Use: Border, informal hedge

Good companions: *Anemone hupehensis* 'Hadspen Abundance', *Tradescantia* Andersoniana Group 'Osprey', *Viburnum farreri*

4 Viburnum × burkwoodii 'Anne Russell'

Compact semi-evergreen shrub with heads of sweetly scented, waxy tubular flowers that are pink in bud but open white. The blooms last well on the plant, but not when cut. Hardy.

Height: 2m (6ft) **Spread:** 1.5m (5ft)

Site: Sun, partial shade. Moist but well-drained soil

Use: Border

Good companions:
Daphne bholua 'Jacqueline Postill', *Ilex crenata* 'Convexa', *Prunus* 'Pandora'

5 Viburnum farreri

Deciduous shrub initially of upright growth, but upper parts of mature stems arch out. It is winter flowering, but usually starts in late autumn and continues into early spring. The small, strongly scented tubular flowers are white, sometimes tinged pink, and carried in clusters. Hardy.

Height: 3m (10ft)

Spread: 2.5m (8ft)

Site: Sun, partial shade. Moist but well-drained soil

Use: Border, woodland garden

Good companions: *Aconitum* 'Ivorine', *Cornus kousa* var. *chinensis* 'Satomi', *Fuchsia magellanica* 'Versicolor'

6 Viburnum × juddii

Bushy deciduous shrub that bears sprays of sweetly scented, white tubular flowers that open from pink buds. Usually in flower by mid-spring and may continue into early summer. Hardy.

Height: 1.2m (4ft) **Spread:** 1.5m (5ft)

Site: Sun, partial shade. Moist but well-drained soil

Use: Border

Good companions: *Geranium* × *magnificum*, *Kolkwitzia amabilis* 'Pink Cloud', *Rosa* Mary Rose

silver and grey

7 Juniperus virginiana 'Grey Owl'

Evergreen conifer with almost horizontal branches that spread to make a wide shrub. The foliage is soft grey-green. Hardy.

Height: 2.5m (8ft) **Spread:** 4m (12ft)

Site: Sun. Well-drained soil

Use: Border, heather garden, sunny bank

Good companions: *Artemisia arborescens*, *Buddleja* 'Lochinch', *Cistus ladanifer*

8 Salix hastata 'Wehrhahnii'

Slow-growing deciduous shrub with dark purplish stems thickly set with silver-grey male catkins that turn yellow well before the bright green leaves develop. Hardy.

Height and spread: 1m (3ft)

Site: Sun. Moist but well-drained soil

Use: Border, waterside

Good companions: *Cornus alba* 'Kesselringii', *Salix gracilistyla* 'Melanostachys', *Salix irrorata*

9 Salix helvetica
Swiss willow

Bushy deciduous shrub with rounded silver-grey catkins that open from gold-brown buds at the same time as the leaves emerge. It is a good foliage plant, with grey-green leaves that are white on the underside.

Height: 60cm (2ft) **Spread:** 45cm (18in)

Site: Sun. Moist but well-drained soil

Use: Border, rock garden, waterside

Good companions: *Daphne cneorum* 'Eximia', *Hebe cupressoides*, *Saxifraga* 'Peter Pan'

10 Chamaecyparis lawsoniana 'Green Hedger'
Lawson cypress

The lawson cypress, a vigorous evergreen conifer that bears small cones, has numerous cultivars, including large trees and dwarf shrubs. 'Green Hedger' makes a dense conical tree and has bright green foliage. Hardy.

General care: Trim hedges between late spring and early autumn.

Height: 18m (60ft) **Spread:** 5m (15ft)

Site: Sun. Well-drained soil, preferably moist and lime-free

Use: Hedge, specimen tree, windbreak

Good companions: *Acer cappadocicum* 'Aureum', *Nyssa sylvatica*, *Quercus coccinea* 'Splendens'

11 Taxus baccata
Yew

Evergreen slow-growing conifer that makes a large shrub or broad tree. The spreading branches are covered with scaly red-brown bark and the short linear leaves are very dark green, yellow-green on the underside. In autumn female plants carry seeds with a bright red fleshy covering (aril), the only part of the plant that is not poisonous. Yew is an outstanding hedging plant and suitable for large-scale topiary. Do not use as a hedge next to grazing land. Mature free-growing specimens may exceed the dimensions given. Hardy.

General care: Trim hedges and topiary specimens in summer or early autumn.

Height: 9m (30ft) **Spread:** 8m (25ft)

Site: Sun, shade. Fertile well-drained soil

Use: Hedge, specimen shrub or tree, topiary

Good companions: *Anemone* x *hybrida* 'Honorine Jobert', *Aster pringlei* 'Monte Cassino', *Rosa* 'Nevada'

12 Taxus x media 'Hicksii'

Evergreen conifer of which one parent is the common yew (see 11, above). This clone makes a large dark shrub of somewhat open conical shape. Hardy.

General care: Trim hedges in summer and early autumn.

Height: 6m (20ft) **Spread:** 2.5m (8ft)

Site: Sun, partial shade. Fertile, well-drained soil

Use: Hedge, specimen shrub

Good companions: *Crataegus persimilis* 'Prunifolia', *Ginkgo biloba*, *Prunus* x *subhirtella* 'Autumnalis'

camellias

Plant these free-flowering evergreen shrubs in shady borders and woodland gardens in humus-rich and moist but well-drained soil, or in containers filled with soil-based (ericaceous) compost. Although all these are hardy, it is wise to position them under a canopy of trees or against a wall to avoid exposure to early morning sun, as rapid thawing of frost may spoil the delicate blooms.

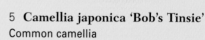

1 Camellia japonica 'Lavinia Maggi'
Spreading dark-foliaged shrub. Double white flowers with random pink and red splashes and no visible stamens.
Height and spread: 5m (15ft)
Good companions: *Acer griseum, Rhododendron moupinense, Rhododendron mucronulatum*

2 Camellia 'Leonard Messel'
Hybrid with dark green matt leaves and sumptuous, clear pink semi-double flowers.
Height: 4m (12ft) **Spread:** 3m (10ft)
Good companions: *Camellia x williamsii 'Saint Ewe', Cercidiphyllum japonicum, Magnolia denudata*

3 Camellia x williamsii 'Francis Hanger'
Free-flowering hybrid with wavy leaves and pure white single flowers with golden stamens. Drops its spent blooms.
Height: 5m (15ft) **Spread:** 3m (10ft)
Good companions: *Halesia carolina, Kalmia latifolia 'Ostbo Red', Smilacina racemosa*

4 Camellia japonica 'Jupiter'
Common camellia
Dark-foliaged upright shrub that bears numerous bright scarlet, single to semi-double flowers filled with a conspicuous bunch of golden stamens.
Height: 5m (15ft) **Spread:** 3m (10ft)
Good companions: *Gaultheria mucronata 'Bell's Seedling', Pieris floribunda, Rhododendron 'Penheale Blue'*

5 Camellia japonica 'Bob's Tinsie'
Common camellia
Dark-foliaged shrub. Small, red anemone-form flowers with conspicuous pink centre.
Height: 2m (6ft) **Spread:** 1m (3ft)
Good companions: *Camellia 'Cornish Snow', Gaultheria mucronata 'Wintertime', Leucothoe Scarletta*

6 Camellia x williamsii 'Donation'
Outstanding, very free-flowering upright hybrid. Large, bright pink semi-double flowers with darker veining. Drops its spent blooms.
Height: 5m (15ft) **Spread:** 3m (10ft)
Good companions: *Acer japonicum 'Vitifolium', Disanthus cercidifolius, Rhododendron 'Loder's White'*

7 Camellia 'Freedom Bell'
Compact dense shrub with toothed oval leaves that finish in a neat taper. Red semi-double flowers in late winter and early spring.
Height: 2.5m (8ft) **Spread:** 2m (6ft)
Good companions: *Camellia x williamsii 'Saint Ewe', Fothergilla major Monticola Group, Rhododendron 'Cilpinense'*

8 Camellia x williamsii 'Saint Ewe'
Free-flowering hybrid that makes a rounded shrub. Bright pink, cup-shaped single flowers.
Height: 4m (12ft) **Spread:** 3m (10ft)
Good companions: *Erythronium dens-canis, Primula 'Guinevere', Styrax japonicus*

alpines

Most small perennials and shrubs that thrive in well-drained conditions do not need a rock garden. They look good in a raised bed and many are suitable for containers or planted among paving. Plant in mild weather, between autumn and early spring.

purple, blue and violet

1 Aubrieta 'Doctor Mules'

Aubrietas produce evergreen mats of small greyish leaves. From early to late spring or even into early summer these are covered with four-petalled flowers in shades of pink, red or purple. 'Doctor Mules' is violet-purple. All are attractive trailing from retaining walls or the ledges of rock gardens. Hardy.

General care: To keep plants compact, trim after flowering in early summer.

Height: 5cm (2in) **Spread:** 60–75cm (2–2ft 6in)

Site: Sun. Well-drained soil. Good on lime

Use: Front of border, ground cover, paving, raised bed, rock garden, sunny bank

Good companions: *Aethionema* 'Warley Rose', *Arabis procurrens* 'Variegata', *Phlox subulata* 'McDaniel's Cushion'

2 Hepatica nobilis

Between late winter and mid-spring this slow-growing semi-evergreen perennial bears numerous upward or outward-facing flowers above a tuft of three-lobed leaves that are often mottled purple. The bowl-shaped flowers are usually purplish blue but can be pink, blue or white. Hardy.

Height: 10cm (4in) **Spread:** 15cm (6in)

Site: Partial shade, sun. Humus-rich and moist but well-drained soil. Good on lime

Use: Rock garden, woodland garden

Good companions: *Cyclamen coum*, *Galanthus* 'S. Arnott', *Saxifraga* 'Peter Pan'

3 Hepatica transsilvanica

The prettily scalloped three-lobed leaves of this semi-evergreen perennial are silvered by a fine down. Mauve-blue flowers are borne between late winter and late spring. Hardy.

Height: 15cm (6in) **Spread:** 20cm (8in)

Site: Partial shade, sun. Humus-rich and moist but well-drained soil. Good on lime

Use: Rock garden, woodland garden

Good companions: *Cyclamen hederifolium*, *Galanthus elwesii*, *Hepatica nobilis*

4 Primula × pubescens 'Mrs J.H. Wilson'

Crosses between *Primula auricula* and *P. hirsuta* produce rosettes of mealy grey-green leaves, above which stems bear several flowers in spring. The colour range extends from white and yellow to pink and purple, but the scented flowers of 'Mrs J.H. Wilson' are purple with a white eye. Hardy.

Height: 10cm (4in) **Spread:** 15cm (6in)

Site: Sun, partial shade. Humus-rich and moist but well-drained soil

Compost: Soil-based (John Innes No. 2) with added leaf-mould and grit

Use: Container, raised bed, rock garden

Good companions: *Adonis vernalis*, *Hepatica transsilvanica*, *Ramonda myconi*

5 Ramonda myconi

Evergreen perennial with dark green, corrugated hairy leaves. From mid to late spring it produces sprays of mauve-purple or violet flowers. Hardy.

General care: Best grown in a vertical crevice.

Height: 10cm (4in) **Spread:** 20cm (8in)

Site: Partial shade. Humus-rich and moist but well-drained soil. Good on lime

Compost: Soil-based (John Innes No. 2) with added leaf-mould and grit

Use: Container, dry wall, rock garden

Good companions: *Hepatica nobilis*, *Polygala chamaebuxus*, *Viola biflora*

6 Soldanella alpina
Alpine snowbell

Evergreen perennial with leathery leaves and mauve-purple bell-shaped flowers. Hardy.

General care: Surround the neck of the plant with a layer of grit and protect from wet in winter.

Height: 10cm (4in) **Spread:** 15–20cm (6–8in)

Site: Sun, partial shade. Humus-rich and moist but sharply drained soil

Compost: Soil-based (ericaceous) with added leaf-mould and grit

Use: Container, raised bed, rock garden

Good companions: *Crocus chrysanthus* 'Ladykiller', *Iris* 'Katharine Hodgkin', *Scilla mischtschenkoana*

purple, blue and violet
(continued)

1 Veronica peduncularis 'Georgia Blue'

Mat-forming evergreen perennial that often flowers through spring into summer. Short spikes of white-eyed blue flowers rise above creeping stems. Hardy.

Height: 10cm (4in) **Spread:** 60cm (2ft)
Site: Sun. Well-drained soil
Compost: Soil-based (John Innes No. 2) with added leaf-mould and grit
Use: Container, front of border, paving, raised bed, rock garden
Good companions: *Hebe cupressoides* 'Boughton Dome', *Leucojum vernum*, *Picea glauca* var. *albertiana* 'Conica'

pink and mauve

2 Primula clarkei

This miniature deciduous perennial flowers as the pale green, toothed leaves unfold. The flowers have deeply notched pink petals, but are pale yellow at the centre. Hardy.

Height: 5cm (2in) **Spread:** 15cm (6in)
Site: Partial shade. Moist but gritty well-drained soil
Compost: Soil-based (John Innes No. 2) with added leaf-mould and grit
Use: Container, raised bed, rock garden
Good companions: *Campanula carpatica*, *Polygola chamaebuxus*, *Primula nana*

3 Primula rosea

Deciduous perennial that flowers before the spoon-shaped toothed or scalloped leaves have fully developed. Up to 12 deep pink flowers with a yellow eye form a cluster at the top of each stem. Hardy.

Height: 15cm (6in) **Spread:** 20cm (8in)
Site: Partial shade. Lime-free, moist soil
Use: Bog garden, rock garden, waterside
Good companions: *Astilbe chinensis* var. *pumila*, *Hosta lancifolia*, *Leucojum vernum*

4 Saxifraga 'Cranbourne'
Kabschia saxifrage

The densely packed foliage of many Kabschia saxifrages is heavily encrusted with lime. The tight rosettes of this reliable hybrid are dark green and form a flat mat, over which are scattered almost stemless pink flowers. Hardy.

Height: 2–3cm (1in) **Spread:** 20cm (8in)
Site: Partial shade, sun. Alkaline and moist but gritty, sharply drained soil
Compost: Soil-based (John Innes No. 1) with added limestone chippings
Use: Container, raised bed, rock garden, trough
Good companions: *Saxifraga* 'Gloria', *Saxifraga* 'Gregor Mendel', *Saxifraga* 'Jenkinsiae'

5 Saxifraga 'Jenkinsiae'
Kabschia saxifrage

This fast-growing hybrid is one of the most reliable Kabschia saxifrages for outdoor rock gardens and raised beds. The pale pink flowers have a deep pink centre and are carried on stems above a mound of lime-encrusted rosettes. Hardy.

Height: 8cm (3in) **Spread:** 20cm (8in)
Site: Partial shade, sun. Alkaline and moist but gritty, sharply drained soil
Compost: Soil-based (John Innes No. 1) with added limestone chippings
Use: Container, raised bed, rock garden, trough
Good companions: *Crocus laevigata* 'Fontenayi', *Iris reticulata*, *Saxifraga* 'Gloria'

6 Saxifraga oppositifolia
Purple saxifrage

In the wild this evergreen perennial is found over an immense area and not surprisingly is variable. Plants in cultivation typically form creeping mats of dark green leaves that in spring are densely covered with stemless purple or pink flowers.

Height: 2–3cm (1in) **Spread:** 20–30cm (8–12in)
Site: Sun, partial shade. Moist but sharply drained soil
Compost: Soil-based (John Innes No. 1) with added leaf-mould and grit
Use: Container, raised bed, rock garden
Good companions: *Crocus laevigatus* 'Fontenayi', *Iris* 'J.S. Dijt', *Tulipa humilis* Violacea Group

red and russet

7 Polygala chamaebuxus var. grandiflora
Ground box

This low evergreen shrub flowers in mid-spring. The cream-and-yellow pea flowers of the species have a keel that ages to purple, but those of *P. chamaebuxus* var. *grandiflora* are more showy, with yellow-lipped purple to brown-crimson flowers. Hardy.

Height: 15cm (6in) **Spread:** 30cm (12in)

10 **Draba rigida var. bryoides**
Whitlow grass

The large genus *Draba* includes a number of small cushion or mat-forming species that are equipped to survive mountainous and arctic conditions. The 'cushion' of this example is composed of tiny rigid leaves. In mid-spring short stems carry several small, bright yellow cross-shaped flowers. Hardy.

General care: Surround the neck with a layer of grit and in winter protect outdoor plants from excess moisture with a raised pane of glass.

Height: 5cm (2in) **Spread:** 8cm (3in)
Site: Sun. Sharply drained gritty soil
Compost: Soil-based (John Innes No. 1) with added grit
Use: Container, raised bed, rock garden, trough
Good companions: *Crocus minimus, Iris reticulata, Saxifraga* 'Gregor Mendel'

11 **Saxifraga 'Gregor Mendel'**
Kabschia saxifrage

Rosettes of pale green leaves make a neat cushion above which short stems carry sprays of light yellow flowers. Good alpine houseplant. Hardy.

Height: 10cm (4in) **Spread:** 30cm (12in)
Site: Partial shade, sun. Moist but gritty, sharply drained, alkaline soil
Compost: Soil-based (John Innes No. 1) with added limestone chippings
Use: Container, raised bed, rock garden, trough
Good companions: *Primula marginata, Saxifraga* 'Gloria', *Saxifraga* 'Johann Kellerer'

cream and white

12 **Arabis alpina subsp. caucasica 'Variegata'**
Rock cress

This green and creamy yellow-variegated plant is less rampant than its plain-leaved counterpart, but is best used on large rock gardens or sunny banks where it will not overwhelm miniature neighbours. Short-stemmed sprays of fragrant white flowers are borne during spring and into summer. Hardy.

General care: Trim in summer after flowering to keep compact.

Height: 15cm (6in) **Spread:** 45cm (18in)
Site: Sun. Well-drained soil
Use: Front of border, sunny bank, raised bed, rock garden
Good companions: *Aethionema* 'Warley Rose', *Aubrieta* 'Doctor Mules', *Pinus mugo* 'Mops'

Site: Partial shade, sun. Humus-rich and moist but sharply drained soil
Compost: Soil-based (John Innes No. 2) with added leaf-mould or soil-less
Use: Container, rock garden
Good companions: *Adonis vernalis, Salix reticulata, Veronica peduncularis* 'Georgia Blue'

8 **Rhodohypoxis hybrids**

Rhodohypoxis baurii, the most commonly grown species of the genus, and numerous hybrids are tiny deciduous perennials with thickened corm-like rootstocks. Starry flowers are produced freely above narrow hairy leaves in spring and summer. They appear to have no centre because of the way the overlapping segments are arranged. Colours include shades of red, red-purple, pink and white. Not fully hardy.

General care: In winter protect plants outdoors from excessive wet with raised panes of glass.

Height and spread: 10cm (4in)
Site: Sun. Lime-free, moist but well-drained soil
Compost: Lime-free, soil-based (ericaceous) with added leaf-mould and sharp sand
Use: Container, raised bed, rock garden, trough
Good companions: *Lithodora diffusa* 'Heavenly Blue', *Picea mariana* 'Nana', *Salix reticulata*

yellow

9 **Adonis vernalis**

The very finely cut leaves of this perennial make a bright green tuft topped in early to mid-spring by golden-yellow cup-shaped flowers. Hardy.

Height: 30cm (12in) **Spread:** 40cm (16in)
Site: Partial shade. Humus-rich and moist but well-drained soil
Use: Lightly shaded border, rock garden
Good companions: *Campanula carpatica, Muscari aucheri, Scilla bifolia*

cream and white (continued)

1 Arabis procurrens 'Variegata'
Rock cress

Evergreen or semi-evergreen perennial that produces a mat of creamy white-edged green leaves and bears loose sprays of white flowers in spring. Hardy.

General care: Trim in summer after flowering to keep compact.

Height: 8cm (3in) **Spread:** 35cm (14in)

Site: Sun. Well-drained soil

Use: Front of border, sunny bank, raised bed, rock garden

Good companions: *Armeria maritima* 'Düsseldorfer Stolz', *Aubrieta* 'Greencourt Purple', *Phlox douglasii* 'Boothman's Variety'

2 Arenaria balearica
Corsican sandwort

Tiny bright green leaves make a dense mat that closely hugs moist surfaces. In spring and summer white starry flowers spangle this cover. Hardy.

Height: 2–3cm (1in) **Spread:** 45cm (18in)

Site: Partial shade. Moist but well-drained soil

Use: Paving, raised bed, rock garden

Good companions: *Campanula carpatica*, *Gentiana septemfida*, *Hebe cupressoides* 'Boughton Dome'

3 Persicaria tenuicaulis

Unlike some of its relatives, this deciduous or semi-evergreen species is slow to spread. It has small leaves and bears short spikes of scented white flowers in spring. Hardy.

Height: 10cm (4in) **Spread:** 30cm (12in)

Site: Sun, partial shade. Moist but well-drained soil

Use: Front of border, raised bed, rock garden

Good companions: *Campanula garganica*, *Diascia* 'Salmon Supreme', *Gentiana septemfida*

silver and grey

4 Picea pungens 'Montgomery'
Colorado spruce

Several dwarf cultivars of the Colorado spruce, an evergreen conifer from the Rocky Mountains, have blue-tinted foliage. 'Montgomery' slowly forms a broad cone that is dense with pointed grey-blue leaves. Hardy.

Height: 1.5m (5ft) **Spread:** 1.2m (4ft)

Site: Sun. Moist but well-drained soil, preferably lime-free

Use: Border, heather garden, raised bed, rock garden

Good companions: *Campanula cochleariifolia*, *Diascia barberae* 'Ruby Field', *Picea abies* 'Little Gem'

green

5 Salix reticulata
Willow

The ground-hugging stems of this deciduous dwarf willow are densely covered with dark green leaves that are conspicuously veined on the upper surface and grey with hairs on the underside. The spring catkins are yellow with pink tips and stand erect. Hardy.

Height: 10cm (4in) **Spread:** 30cm (12in)

Site: Sun. Moist but well-drained gritty soil

Use: Front of border, raised bed, rock garden

Good companions: *Astilbe chinensis* var. *pumila*, *Daphne blagayana*, *Persicaria tenuicaulis*

6 Thuja occidentalis 'Hetz Midget'
White cedar

There are numerous dwarf cultivars of the white cedar, an evergreen conifer grown for its timber. 'Hetz Midget' develops slowly into an almost spherical bush composed of dense sprays of green foliage. Hardy.

Height and spread: 75cm (2ft 6in)

Site: Sun. Moist but well-drained soil

Use: Border, heather garden, raised bed, rock garden

Good companions: *Campanula poscharskyana* 'Stella', *Thuja occidentalis* 'Rheingold', *Viola biflora*

Many of the vigorous waterside plants that require reliably moist soil throughout the year are slow to make growth in early spring, but a few are spectacularly conspicuous because of their flowers. Plant in the dormant season.

purple, blue and violet

1 **Primula denticulata**
Drumstick primula

Freely self-seeding perennial that produces rounded heads of tightly packed flowers in white as well as in shades of blue, purple, pink and red. The 'globe' appears first at ground level among the developing leaves before being pushed upwards on the stout 'stick'.

General care: Eliminate ruthlessly self-sown plants of poor colour.

Height: 30cm (12in) **Spread:** 25cm (10in)

Site: Partial shade, sun. Humus-rich and moist, even boggy soil

Use: Moist border, waterside

Good companions: *Iris sibirica* 'Ego', *Lobelia* 'Queen Victoria', *Primula pulverulenta* Bartley hybrids

pink and mauve

2 **Petasites fragrans**
Winter heliotrope

A ground-cover perennial with kidney-shaped leaves and heads of strongly fragrant, pale mauve to purple flowers that emerge with the foliage in late winter and early spring. Although useful for broad landscaping, even doing well on heavy clay, the fleshy roots are too invasive for small or medium-sized gardens. Not fully hardy.

Height: 30cm (12in) **Spread:** Indefinite

Site: Partial shade, shade. Moist soil

Use: Ground cover, waterside

Good companions: *Gunnera manicata*, *Metasequoia glytostroboides*, *Salix alba* subsp. *vitellina* 'Britzensis'

yellow and orange

3 **Caltha palustris var. palustris 'Plena'**
Giant marsh marigold

The stems of this vigorous perennial spread out widely, even extending over water, and root when they touch moist ground. The heart-shaped leaves are glossy green and the double 'button' flowers are rich yellow. Hardy.

General care: Grows in water up to 15cm (6in) deep.

Height: 60cm (2ft) **Spread:** 1m (3ft)

Site: Sun. Permanently moist soil

Use: Waterside

Good companions: *Euphorbia palustris*, *Iris pseudacorus* 'Variegata', *Myosotis scorpioides* 'Mermaid'

4 **Lysichiton americanus**
Yellow skunk cabbage

Long-lived perennial with short, thick rhizomes. Green-tinged yellow flowers emerge in early spring, when the waterside is almost bare. The true flowers are tiny and packed on a thick spike, the spadix, which is surrounded by a large bract, or spathe. Glossy 1m (3ft) leaves emerge as the flowers mature and clumps remain impressive throughout summer. Hardy.

Height: 1m (3ft) **Spread:** 1.2m (4ft)

Site: Sun, partial shade. Humus-rich, permanently moist soil

Use: Waterside

Good companions: *Gunnera manicata*, *Lysichiton camtschatcensis*, *Rheum palmatum* 'Atrosanguineum'

cream and white

5 **Lysichiton camtschatcensis**
Skunk cabbage

Long-lived perennial growing from thick short rhizomes. The flowers, which develop before the leaves are mature, consist of tiny, green true flowers packed on a thick spike, the spadix, surrounded by the swirl of a creamy white bract, or spathe. The large dark green leaves form a handsome clump. Hardy.

Height and spread: 75cm (2ft 6in)

Site: Sun, partial shade. Humus-rich, moist soil

Use: Waterside

Good companions: *Ligularia* 'The Rocket', *Lysichiton americanus*, *Zantedeschia aethiopica* 'Crowborough'

herbs & vegetables

Early spring is a busy time in the kitchen garden, for sowing and planting, but there are useful crops to harvest too, including overwintered vegetables such as leeks and sprouting broccoli and fast-growing salad vegetables.

herbs

1 Alexanders, Black lovage
Smyrnium olusatrum

Almost every part of this biennial or short-lived perennial can be used in salads, soups and stews for its strong angelica-and-celery flavour. Harvest leaves and shoots any time to use fresh, or just before flowering for drying. Hardy.

General care: Sow *in situ* in autumn or early spring, and thin seedlings to groups 45cm (18in) apart. To blanch young shoots for cooking and remove bitterness cover them with soil in March.

Height: 60cm–1.5m (2–5ft) **Spread:** 60cm (2ft)

Site: Sun or light shade. Moist but well-drained soil

Compost: Soil-based (John Innes No. 3)

Use: Border, container, herb garden

2 Anise hyssop
Agastache foeniculum

The fresh aniseed-flavoured leaves of this short-lived perennial can be used in teas, cold drinks, savoury rice and meat dishes. Mauve summer flowers attract bees and butterflies. Pick leaves and flowers for drying just as buds open. Hardy.

General care: Replenish stock by taking soft or semi-ripe cuttings in August or divide in spring.

Height: 1m (3ft) **Spread:** 60cm (2ft)

Site: Sun. Rich moist soil

Compost: Soil-based (John Innes No. 3)

Use: Border, container, herb garden

3 Chinese basil, Japanese shiso, Perilla
Perilla frutescens

The ruffled red or green leaves of this annual have a warm curry-like flavour. It is an essential ingredient of sushi, but young leaves and flower stalks can also be used raw in salads or cooked in soups and pickles. Tender.

General care: Sow under glass in spring, and plant out 30cm (12in) apart after the last frosts. Pick growing tips regularly to encourage bushy growth.

Height: 60cm (2ft) **Spread:** 38cm (15in)

Site: Sun or light shade. Well-drained soil

Compost: Soil-based (John Innes No. 3)

Use: Container, front of border, herb border

4 Lemon verbena
Aloysia triphylla (syn. Lippia citriodora)

The penetratingly fragrant pale green leaves of this deciduous shrub are used fresh for flavouring desserts, cakes, summer drinks and tisanes. Pale lilac flowers in summer. Best treated as a pot or summer bedding plant. Tender.

General care: Prune in spring and after flowering for bushy growth. Mulch plants in winter or bring indoors; check indoor plants for whitefly and red spider mites.

Height: 3m (10ft) **Spread:** 2m (6ft)

Site: Sun, sheltered. Light, well-drained soil

Compost: Soil-based (John Innes No. 3)

Use: Conservatory or greenhouse, container, herb border

5 Myrtle
Myrtus communis

Aromatic evergreen shrub or small tree. The spicy leaves complement rich meat dishes and the creamy white-and-gold flowers can be dried for potpourri. Harvest fresh leaves any time, leaves and flowers for drying when blooms are fully open. Can be clipped for topiary. Not fully hardy.

General care: Best grown in a container, especially while young. Overwinter under cover. Lightly trim to shape in spring and summer.

Height: 3m (10ft) **Spread:** 2.5m (8ft)

Site: Sun, sheltered. Fertile, well-drained soil

Compost: Soil-based (John Innes No. 3)

Use: Conservatory or greenhouse, container, herb garden, patio

6 Pennyroyal
Mentha pulegium

A compact, prostrate semi-evergreen perennial with tiny pungent leaves and purple flowers in summer. Used sparingly as a substitute for peppermint. Hardy.

General care: Water freely in summer. Plants may die in wet soils below -8°C (18°F), so overwinter some roots under cover.

Height: 15cm (6in) **Spread:** Indefinite

Site: Sun, light shade. Moist but very well drained soil

Compost: Soil-based (John Innes No. 3) with added grit

Use: Container, front of border, paving

Compost: Soil-based (John Innes No. 3)

Use: Border, container, herb garden

8 Sweet cicely
Myrrhis odorata

Sweet aniseed-flavoured perennial that makes a mound of delicate foliage. Leaves, roots and seeds are all useful for flavouring salads, dressings, ice cream and fruit. Gather seeds for drying in late summer; alternatively, cut down after flowering for more young foliage. Hardy.

General care: Plant 60cm (2ft) apart.

Height: 1m (3ft) **Spread:** 60cm (2ft)

Site: Light shade. Rich, well-drained soil

Compost: Soil-based (John Innes No. 3)

Use: Container, herb garden, wild garden

9 Sweet woodruff
Galium odoratum

Attractive ground-covering perennial with the scent of new-mown hay, used for flavouring cold drinks, tisanes and fruit cups. Harvest the foliage as it appears, and flowers and stalks in early summer; dry to heighten their flavour. Hardy.

General care: Plant 15–23cm (6–9in) apart.

Height: 15cm (6in) **Spread:** 30cm (12in)

Site: Light or semi-shade. Rich soil

Compost: Soil-based (John Innes No. 3)

Use: Container, ground cover, underplanting for shrubs

10 Thyme
Thymus species and cultivars

There are many upright or creeping evergreen thymes, some variegated, with pink, purple or white summer flowers. All are ornamental aromatic plants, but grey-green garden thyme (*T. vulgaris*) is the most useful for the kitchen. Use fresh at any time for stuffings and bouquet garni. For drying, gather just before flowering. Hardy.

General care: Plant 23cm (9in) apart. Trim after flowering. In very cold areas pot up and overwinter under cover.

Height: 30cm (12in) **Spread:** 30cm (12in)

Site: Sun. Poor, well-drained soil

Compost: Soil-based (John Innes No. 3)

Use: Container, edging, herb garden

7 Rosemary
Rosmarinus officinalis

Aromatic evergreen shrub with deep green, needle-like leathery leaves used for flavouring bread, meat, rice and egg dishes. The soft blue flowers are attractive to bees from mid-spring to early summer. There are many forms, including prostrate and variegated kinds. Leaves may be scorched after a cold winter. Plants usually recover if pruned back to healthy wood. Hardy.

General care: Plant 60cm–1m (2–3ft) apart. Trim after flowering and in early spring.

Height and spread: 1.5m (5ft)

Site: Sun, sheltered. Well-drained soil

vegetables

1 Broccoli, early sprouting
Brassica oleracea Italica Group

The immature flowering shoots of white or purple sprouting broccoli, available from January to the end of spring, are eaten lightly cooked. For continuity grow early and late varieties (see Late Spring), or sow a prepared mixture. Hardy.

Site: Sun, warm sheltered. Well-drained, non-acid soil

How to grow: Sow in April, thinly in rows in a nursery bed. Thin seedlings to 8cm (3in) apart, and in midsummer transplant 60cm (2ft) apart. Water well in dry weather. Cut shoots when 8–10cm (3–4in) long with sprigs of young foliage. Harvest frequently to encourage new shoots.

2 Cabbage, spring
Brassica oleracea Capitata Group

Varieties such as 'Pixie' and 'Duncan' make small juicy cabbages, while 'Vanguard' and 'Wintergreen' are leafy non-hearting 'greens'. To maximise yields, harvest alternate plants while small, leaving others to grow and heart up. Hardy.

Site: Sun, sheltered. Rich firm soil, with added lime if acid

How to grow: Sow two to three batches from early July to early August, thinly in rows in a nursery bed. Thin to 8cm (3in) apart, and transplant when seedlings are six weeks old, spacing hearted kinds 30cm (12in) apart each way, greens 25cm (10in) apart. Water well in dry weather and net against birds. In late winter feed with high-nitrogen fertiliser. Harvest as soon as large enough, leaving 5cm (2in) stumps to resprout.

3 Cauliflower, winter
Brassica oleracea Botrytis Group

Winter cauliflowers such as 'Armado April', 'Markanta' and richly coloured 'Purple Cape' are hardy varieties for mild areas.

Site: Sun, sheltered. Firm, neutral to alkaline soil

How to grow: Sow in May, in rows in a nursery bed, and thin to 8cm (3in) apart. Transplant when seedlings have four to six true leaves, 75cm (2ft 6in) apart each way. Water in well and keep moist in dry weather. Protect forming heads by breaking some of the outer leaves to lie across the curds. Start cutting heads while still small, as whole batches tend to mature together.

4 Corn salad, Lamb's lettuce, Mâche
Valerianella locusta

This mild salad annual has refreshing, slightly bitter leaves. It can be sown in spring for summer use, but is most valuable as a winter and early spring leaf crop. Hardy.

Site: Sun or light shade. Most soils

How to grow: Sow outdoors in July and August, thinly in broad rows 15cm (6in) wide. Thin seedlings to 10cm (4in) apart, transplanting some thinnings to a coldframe or greenhouse; select only the strongest seedlings. Keep moist at all times. Gather leaves or whole plants as required, first blanching plants under pots for one to two weeks if the flavour is too bitter. Sowings may be left unthinned for harvesting as cut-and-come-again crops – snip strips to 2–3cm (1in) high.

5 Endive
Cichorium endivia

This annual or biennial crop is similar to loose-leaved lettuce, but has a sharper flavour, which is less pronounced if plants are blanched. Curly-leaved varieties are sown in spring for summer use, but hardy varieties, such as 'Golda', can be harvested in winter and early spring, especially if protected to maintain quality.

Site: Sun, warm sheltered. Well-drained soil

How to grow: Sow in August and September, outdoors in a nursery bed or in modules under glass. Thin or transplant to 30cm (12in) apart each way. Water in dry weather. Blanch by covering with an upturned flowerpot or large plate 10–14 days before cutting. In exposed gardens cloche crops or transplant seedlings to a coldframe.

6 Good king henry, Mercury, Poor man's asparagus
Chenopodium bonus-henricus

The early shoots of this undemanding perennial are blanched for cutting in early spring; later the green arrow-shaped leaves can be picked and used like spinach. Self-seeds freely, so deadhead to keep under control. Hardy.

Site: Sun or light shade, sheltered. Well-drained soil

How to grow: Sow in spring in a nursery bed, thin to 10cm (4in) apart, then transplant in autumn

45cm (18in) apart each way. Heap soil 15cm (6in) high over mature plants in autumn and cut shoots in spring as they emerge. Stop cutting and remove soil mound in June, then mulch with compost. Divide plants every three to four years.

7 Leaf beet
Beta vulgaris Cicla Group
There are two main kinds of leaf beet: chard or seakale beet has thick stems and sculpted leaves, while perpetual spinach or spinach beet has large plain leaves that make a long-lasting weather-proof substitute for ordinary spinach, especially on drier soils. Hardy.
Site: Sun or light shade. Fertile, well-drained soil
How to grow: Sow *in situ*, two to three seeds per station 30cm (12in) apart each way, in March or April; sow again in August for transplanting to a coldframe for winter use. Water in dry weather and mulch well. Pick leaves as required or cut whole plants down to 2–3cm (1in). Water and feed with general fertiliser after a heavy picking.

8 Mustard and cress
Sinapsis alba and Lepidium sativum
These cut-and-come-again crops can be sown outdoors as edging or a catch crop between other vegetables. There are various kinds of cress, including Greek and finely cut-leaved varieties. All are sown two to three days before the mustard to ensure seedlings are ready together. Hardy.
Site: Light shade. Moist soils
How to grow: Sow *in situ* every two to three weeks between March and October (November in a greenhouse border). Broadcast the cress seeds in drills 15–30cm (6–12in) wide or in

patches and lightly rake in; oversow with mustard seeds two to three days later. Keep moist at all times. Cut with scissors when 5cm (2in) high, leaving short stumps to resprout.

9 Seakale
Crambe maritima
This perennial, which grows wild by the sea, is blanched under pots for cutting in early spring. It may be grown from seed or from root cuttings known as 'thongs'. Produces handsome flower and seed heads up to 60cm (2ft) across, which are popular with flower arrangers. Hardy.
Site: Sun or light shade, sheltered. Light well-drained soil
How to grow: Sow in a nursery bed in spring, and thin seedlings to 15cm (6in) apart. Transplant seedlings or plant thongs 45cm (18in) apart the following spring. Water in dry weather and mulch. Force two-year-old plants in January, covering them with an upturned bucket or forcing pot – the tender, white 15–20cm (6–8in) shoots will be ready for harvest two months later. Feed with general fertiliser after forcing, and replace after five to six years with root cuttings.

10 Shallot
Allium cepa Aggregatum Group
These multiplier onions – each bulb splits to produce a cluster of four to ten new ones – have a distinctive, almost perfumed flavour. Traditional varieties were planted in autumn, but modern kinds bolt if started too early. Not fully hardy.
Site: Sun. Rich, well-drained soil
How to grow: Plant virus-free bulbs 20cm (8in) apart each way in February or March, with their tips just showing. Water in dry weather and keep free of weeds. Gently lift clumps with a fork when leaves die down in midsummer, and leave to dry on the soil's surface. When the skins are papery and dry, separate bulbs and store them in nets or boxes in a cool, airy place for winter and spring use. Save smaller healthy bulbs to replant.

11 Spinach, summer
Spinacea oleracea
The flavour of well-grown spinach amply rewards the extra watering and mulching required. Start sowing this annual early in spring; on hot dry soils grow a bolt-resistant variety. Modern varieties crop all year with winter protection. Hardy.
Site: Sun, but lightly shaded in midsummer. Mulch soil with plenty of added organic matter
How to grow: Sow *in situ* every four to five weeks from April to July, and thin seedlings to 15cm (6in) apart. Water regularly in dry weather and mulch with compost. Harvest when plants have five to six true leaves; cut whole plants to leave stumps for resprouting, or pick some larger leaves. Clear and freeze crops that start to bolt.

12 Turnip
Brassica rapa
For summer use this mild crop is sown from spring onwards and harvested while the round or flat roots are still small and juicy. A winter-hardy variety, such as 'Manchester Market', can be sown late, and forced and blanched for an early spring crop of 'turnip tops'. Add lime to acid soil.
Site: Sun, but lightly shaded in midsummer. Mulch soil with plenty of added organic matter
How to grow: Sow summer crops outdoors every three to four weeks from March to July, thinning seedlings to 10cm (4in) apart in rows 20cm (8in) apart. Water little and often, and mulch when plants are larger. Harvest roots when 5cm (2in) across. For 'tops', sow in September and leave unthinned; give a general feed in February and let tops grow in the open, or feed in January and cover with a ridge of soil 15cm (6in) high to force and blanch the young shoots.

the greenhouse

Among the wide range of tender plants that flourish in a protected environment, including greenhouses and conservatories that are not heated, are many that bloom in the early days of spring.

purple, blue and violet

1 Hardenbergia violacea
Purple coral pea

Slender evergreen climber with wiry twining stems and leathery leaves, each composed of a single lance-shaped leaflet. In late winter and spring there are sprays of purplish blue pea flowers. There are several white and pink-flowered cultivars. Half hardy.

General care: Water sparingly in winter. Prune lightly immediately after flowering.

Height: 2m (6ft) **Spread:** 60cm (2ft)

Under glass: Full light. Soil-based compost (John Innes No. 2) with added leaf-mould and sharp sand

Use: Conservatory or greenhouse minimum 2°C (36°F)

2 Pericallis x hybrida Royalty Mix
Florists' cineraria

These short-lived dome-shaped perennials are usually grown as biennials for their long-lasting winter and early spring displays in shades of purple, blue, pink and red. Flowers are usually white-eyed and sometimes bicoloured. Tender.

General care: Discard plants when flowering is over.

Height and spread: 50cm (20in)

Under glass: Full light. Soil-based compost (John Innes No. 2)

Outdoor site: Sun. Well-drained soil

Use: Conservatory or greenhouse minimum 5°C (41°F), container, houseplant

3 Petrea volubilis
Purple wreath, Queen's wreath

A rapid and vigorous grower, outdoors in a favourable climate this twining evergreen climber may grow 12m (40ft). It has woody stems and rough leaves up to 20cm (8in) long. From late winter to summer arching sprays of violet-blue starry flowers make a showy display. Tender.

General care: Prune lightly immediately after flowering.

Height: 6m (20ft) **Spread:** 2.5m (8ft)

Under glass: Full light. Soil-based compost (John Innes No. 3)

Use: Conservatory or greenhouse minimum 10°C (50°F)

pink and mauve

4 Begonia manicata
Leopard begonia

Rhizomatous evergreen species with large, glossy somewhat fleshy leaves with a ring of red hairs just below each blade. In late winter and early spring airy sprays of small pink flowers are borne well above the foliage. Tender.

General care: Shade from hot sun.

Height and spread: 45cm (18in)

Under glass: Full light. Soil-based compost (John Innes No. 2) or soil-less

Use: Greenhouse or conservatory minimum 10°C (50°F), houseplant

5 Cattleya skinneri

Evergreen epiphytic orchid with erect cylindrical pseudobulbs, each producing two leathery oblong leaves. Showy purplish pink flowers with a partially white or cream lip are borne between late winter and early summer. Tender.

General care: Best grown in special orchid pots or baskets. Shade from hot sun.

Height and spread: 30cm (12in)

Under glass: Full light. Soil-less compost (epiphytic orchid mixture)

Use: Conservatory or greenhouse minimum 5°C (41°F)

6 Chamelaucium uncinatum
Geraldton wax

Wiry evergreen shrub with curious linear leaves that are triangular in cross-section and have a hooked tip. In spring and summer it bears clusters of small flowers, which have a cup-shaped centre surrounded by five petals, in pink, purple, red or white. In the open plants may grow to 4m (12ft) high. Half hardy.

General care: Water sparingly in autumn and winter. Prune lightly immediately after flowering.

Height: 2m (6ft) **Spread:** 60cm (2ft)

Under glass: Full light. Soil-based, lime-free (ericaceous) compost

Outdoor site: Sun. Lime-free, well-drained soil

Use: Conservatory or greenhouse minimum 7°C (45°F), sunny border

7 Dendrobium nobile

Semi-deciduous epiphytic orchid with stem-like pseudobulbs and narrow leaves that are notched at the tip. The fragrant flowers, usually borne in pairs, are white with pink or mauve tints and a maroon-blotched pale yellow lip. Tender.

General care: Grow on bark or in a slatted basket.

Height: 45cm (18in) **Spread:** 15cm (8in)

Under glass: Partial shade in late spring and summer, otherwise full light. Soil-less compost (epiphytic orchid mixture)

Use: Conservatory or greenhouse minimum 10°C (50°F)

8 Pleione formosana

Terrestrial or rock-perching orchid with a rounded pseudobulb. It produces a large flower, sometimes a pair, close to the ground. The white fringed lip at the centre of the pink segments is usually marked with red, purple or yellow. Half hardy.

General care: Plant in late spring with two-thirds of the pseudobulb exposed.

Height: 15cm (6in) **Spread:** 30cm (12in)

Under glass: Indirect light. Soil-based (John Innes No. 1) with added leaf-mould, or soil-less compost (epiphytic orchid mixture)

Outdoor site: Partial shade. Well-drained soil with added leaf-mould

Use: Conservatory or greenhouse minimum 2°C (36°F), sheltered rock garden

red and russet

9 Agapetes serpens

Evergreen shrub with lax stems closely set with small glossy leaves. In late winter or early spring the stems often carry numerous dangling urn-shaped flowers that are bright red with darker markings. Best trained as a climber. Half hardy.

General care: Shade from hot sun. Prune lightly immediately after flowering.

Height: 2.5m (8ft) **Spread:** 75cm (2ft 6in)

Under glass: Full light. Soil-based and lime-free (ericaceous) compost

Outdoor site: Partial shade. Lime-free and moist but well-drained soil

Use: Conservatory or greenhouse minimum 2°C (36°F), sheltered border, wall

yellow and orange

10 Acacia baileyana
Cootamundra wattle

The ornamental, grey-green ferny foliage of this evergreen small tree or large shrub is eclipsed in

late winter and spring by sprays of soft yellow pompons, in reality clusters of tiny flowers. In a garden plants may achieve twice the dimensions given for specimens in containers. Not fully hardy.

General care: Prune lightly after flowering.

Height: 4m (12ft) **Spread:** 2.5m (8ft)

Under glass: Full light. Soil-based compost (John Innes No. 2)

Outdoor site: Sun. Well-drained soil

Use: Conservatory or greenhouse minimum 4°C (39°F), wall

11 Ada aurantiaca

Evergreen epiphytic orchid that forms a clump of pseudobulbs, each of which produces a pair of narrow strap-shaped leaves. In late winter and spring arching stems carry up to 12 orange bell-shaped flowers with tapered segments. Tender.

General care: Grow on bark or in a small container. Shade from hot sun.

Height: 25cm (10in)

Spread: 20cm (8in)

Under glass: Full light. Soil-less compost (epiphytic orchid mixture)

Use: Conservatory or greenhouse minimum 10°C (50°F)

1 Clivia miniata

Evergreen perennial with a bulb-like base and rich green strap-shaped leaves. Stout stems carry heads of up to 20 orange-red funnel-shaped flowers in spring and summer. Tender.

General care: Shade from hot sun.

Height: 45cm (18in) **Spread:** 30cm (12in)

Under glass: Full light. Soil-based compost (John Innes No. 2)

Use: Conservatory or greenhouse minimum 10°C (50°F), houseplant

2 Kalanchoe blossfeldiana hybrids

These evergreen succulent perennials flower freely in late winter and spring, and will do so most of the year if exposed to light for less than 12 hours a day. Dense clusters of small yellow, orange, red, pink or white tubular flowers are carried above glossy toothed leaves. Tender.

General care: Shade from hot sun.

Height and spread: 30cm (12in)

Under glass: Full light. Soil-based compost (John Innes No. 2) with added grit

Use: Conservatory or greenhouse minimum 12°C (54°F), houseplant

3 Lachenalia aloides var. quadricolor
Cape cowslip

This South African bulb flowers in winter or early spring, when clusters of tubular bells dangle from a mottled erect stem. The buds are orange-red and the yellow open flowers are edged yellow-green on the outside with the inner segments tipped dark red. Half hardy.

General care: Plant in late summer or early autumn with the top of the bulb 2–3cm (1in) deep. Keep dry after the leaves have died down.

Height: 25cm (10in) **Spread:** 8cm (3in)

Under glass: Full light. Soil-based compost (John Innes No. 2)

Use: Conservatory or greenhouse minimum 2°C (36°F), houseplant

4 Lycaste cruenta

Epiphytic orchid with conical pseudobulbs, from the top and bottom of which grow lance-shaped leaves. Fragrant waxy flowers, with greenish yellow triangular outer segments and small yellow inner segments, are borne over a long season, but peak in early to mid-spring. Tender.

General care: Grow perched on bark or in a container.

Height and spread: 30cm (12in)

Under glass: Partial shade in late spring and summer, at other times full light. Soil-less compost (epiphytic orchid mixture)

Use: Conservatory or greenhouse minimum 12°C (54°F), houseplant

5 Primula kewensis

This evergreen perennial forms a rosette of light green, almost spoon-shaped leaves that are lightly dusted with white meal. Upright stems carry tiers of fragrant yellow flowers. Half hardy.

General care: Shade from hot sun and keep compost moist. The minimum temperature given below is needed for spring flowers.

Height: 45cm (18in) **Spread:** 20cm (8in)

Under glass: Full light. Soil-based compost (John Innes No. 2) with added leaf-mould and grit

Use: Conservatory or greenhouse minimum 10°C (50°F)

silver and grey

6 Begonia 'Silver Cloud'

Like many other *Begonia rex* hybrids, evergreen perennials grown for their highly ornamental foliage, this has a metallic finish. The large lobed leaves are spotted with silver between the veins. Tender.

General care: In winter water sparingly. Plants grown in containers can be moved outdoors in summer.

Height: 30cm (12in) **Spread:** 45cm (18in)

Under glass: Full light, partial shade. Soil-based compost (John Innes No. 2)

Use: Conservatory or greenhouse minimum 10°C (50°F), houseplant, patio

green

7 Adiantum raddianum 'Fritz Lüthi'
Delta maidenhair fern

Several forms of this variable evergreen fern are valued as indoor display plants for their elegantly arching, finely dissected triangular fronds. The long narrow fronds of 'Fritz Lüthi' are divided into many segments set at various angles, which gives an attractive effect of ruffled green lace. Tender.

General care: Maintain a humid atmosphere with good ventilation.

Height: 60cm (2ft) **Spread:** 75cm (2ft 6in)

Under glass: Indirect light. Soil-based compost (1 part John Innes No. 2, 1 part coarse sand, 3 parts peat or peat substitute) with a sprinkling of lime chippings

Use: Conservatory or greenhouse minimum 7°C (45°F), houseplant

8 Chamaedorea elegans
Parlour palm

The arching leaves of this slender evergreen foliage plant are composed of numerous blade-like leaflets, each about 30cm (12in) long. May produce inconspicuous yellow flowers and black fruits. Not fully hardy.

General care: Shade from hot sun.

Height and spread: 1.5m (5ft)

Under glass: Full or indirect light. Soil-based and lime-free (ericaceous) or soil-less compost

Use: Conservatory or greenhouse minimum 16°C (61°F), houseplant

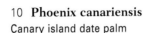

9 Cissus antarctica
Kangaroo vine

Vigorous evergreen climber capable of growing 6m (20ft) high in the wild. Each notched glossy leaf is matched by a forked tendril. Its main value is as a foliage plant, but small greenish summer flowers are followed by unpalatable black berries. Not fully hardy.

General care: Shade from hot sun.
Height: 3m (10ft) **Spread:** 1.2m (4ft)
Under glass: Full light. Soil-based compost (John Innes No. 2)
Use: Conservatory or greenhouse minimum 5°C (41°F), houseplant

10 Phoenix canariensis
Canary island date palm

Evergreen palm with a stout, very rough trunk that is scarred where old leaves have broken away. The large dark green leaves, which splay out from the top of the trunk, are composed of two rows of paired leaflets. In a hot climate cream or yellow flowers are followed by orange fruits, which although edible are not highly valued. Plants grown outdoors in a favourable climate may reach a height of 15m (50ft). Not fully hardy.

General care: Shade from hot sun. Plants grown in containers can be moved outdoors in summer.
Height: 5m (15ft) **Spread:** 3m (10ft)
Under glass: Full light. Soil-based compost (John Innes No. 2)
Use: Conservatory or greenhouse minimum 10°C (50°F), patio

11 Platycerium bifurcatum
Common staghorn fern

Epiphytic evergreen fern with two distinct types of fronds – sterile, wavy-edged round to heart-shaped ones that lie almost flat against their support, and fertile forked ones that may be erect, arching or pendent. Tender.

General care: Grow wired to bark or slabs of tree fern stem or in hanging baskets.
Height and spread: 1m (3ft)
Under glass: Bright but indirect light. Soil-based compost (John Innes No. 2) with equal parts leaf-mould or peat substitute, roughly chopped sphagnum moss and charcoal
Use: Conservatory or greenhouse minimum 5°C (41°F)

choosing the best plants

The following plant lists draw on all the plants described in the preceding pages of the Plant Selector, but they are grouped together here to help you choose plants for particular conditions, situations and uses.

plants for dry chalky soil

A large number of plants are automatically excluded from this list because they will not tolerate alkaline (limy) soil or they require moist conditions throughout the year. The improvement of shallow chalky soil by the addition of moisture-retaining organic matter allows lime-tolerant but moisture-loving plants, including clematis, hellebores and hepaticas, to be grown successfully. Some lime-loving plants, including many saxifrages, require plentiful moisture as well as gritty free-draining conditions.

- Arabis alpina subsp. caucasica 'Variegata'
- Arabis procurrens 'Variegata'
- Aubrieta 'Doctor Mules'
- Aucuba japonica (all)
- Bergenia (most)
- Chionodoxa (all)
- Corylus avellana 'Aurea'
- Corylus maxima 'Purpurea'
- Crocus (all)
- Erysimum cheiri 'Blood Red'
- Euphorbia characias subsp. wulfenii
- Euphorbia rigida
- Hedera colchica 'Dentata Variegata'
- Lonicera fragrantissima
- Taxus baccata
- Taxus × meadia 'Hicksii'
- Tulipa (all)

Tulipa turkestanica

plants for clay soil

Although the following plants generally succeed on close-textured clay soils, they do better when the ground has been improved by the addition of grit and organic matter such as well-rotted garden compost.

- Anemone nemorosa
- Aucuba japonica (all)
- Berberis buxifolia
- Bergenia (all)
- Caltha palustris var. palustris
- Chaenomeles (all)
- Corylus (all)
- Epimedium (all)
- Euphorbia amygdaloides var. robbiae
- Forsythia (all)
- Hamamelis vernalis 'Sandra'
- Hedera (all)
- Helleborus (all)
- Leucojum vernum
- Lonicera fragrantissima
- Lysichiton (all)
- Mahonia aquifolium 'Apollo'
- Narcissus (most)
- Petasites fragrans
- Primula rosea
- Prunus (all)
- Pulmonaria (all)
- Ribes sanguineum 'Pulborough Scarlet'
- Salix (most)
- Skimmia × confusa 'Kew Green'
- Symphytum 'Hidcote Blue'
- Taxus (all)
- Viburnum tinus 'Eve Price'

Narcissus 'Tête à Tête'

plants for moist shade

The following plants thrive in moist soils and tolerate partial shade and, in a few cases, full shade. Many will also grow in full sun provided the soil is reliably moist.

- Adonis vernalis
- Anemone nemorosa
- Arenaria balearica
- Aucuba japonica
- Camellia (all)
- Corydalis flexuosa
- Corylopsis pauciflora
- Corylopsis sinensis var. sinensis 'Spring Purple'
- Daphne blagayana
- Epimedium (all)
- Euphorbia amygdaloides var. robbiae
- Hamamelis vernalis 'Sandra'
- Helleborus (all)
- Hepatica (all)
- Leucojum vernum
- Mahonia aquifolium 'Apollo'
- Omphalodes verna
- Pachyphragma macrophyllum
- Primula (most)
- Pulmonaria (all)
- Ramonda myconi
- Rhododendron (all)
- Skimmia × confusa 'Kew Green'
- Symphytum 'Hidcote Blue'
- Viburnum tinus 'Eve Price'
- Viola (all)

Ramonda myconi

plants for acid soil

Plants marked with an asterisk* will only grow satisfactorily on soils that are free of lime. Other plants in the list thrive on acid soils, but may also grow on neutral or slightly alkaline soils.

- *Camellia* (all)*
- *Chamaecyparis lawsoniana* 'Green Hedger'
- *Corydalis flexuosa*
- *Corylopsis pauciflora* *
- *Corylopsis sinensis* var. *sinensis* 'Spring Purple'*
- *Erica* (all)
- *Hamamelis vernalis* 'Sandra'
- *Magnolia* (all)
- *Picea pungens* 'Montgomery'
- *Pieris* (all)*
- *Primula rosea* *
- *Rhododendron* (all)*
- *Rhodohypoxis* hybrids*

plants for coastal sites

Where windbreaks and hedges give protection from salt-laden winds, a wide range of plants can be grown in coastal gardens. Many benefit from the sea's moderating influence on temperatures.

- *Anemone coronaria*
- *Aubrieta* 'Doctor Mules'
- *Chaenomeles* (all)
- *Chamaecyparis lawsoniana* 'Green Hedger'
- *Chionodoxa* (all)
- *Crocus* (most)
- *Erica* (all)
- *Euphorbia* (all)
- *Forsythia* (all)
- *Griselinia littoralis* 'Variegata'
- *Juniperus virginiana* 'Grey Owl'
- *Narcissus* (most)
- *Osmanthus* x *burkwoodii*
- *Persicaria tenuicaulis*
- *Scilla* (all)
- *Spiraea thunbergii*
- *Veronica peduncularis* 'Georgia Blue'

flowers for cutting

The following list includes several spring-flowering shrubs and trees that if cut judiciously provide excellent material for arrangements. In addition to the following, many other plants, including winter-flowering pansies and early flowering bulbs, provide material for small, sometimes short-lived displays.

- *Anemone coronaria*
- *Camellia* (all)
- *Chaenomeles* (all)
- *Chamelaucium uncinatum*
- *Erysimum cheiri* 'Blood Red'
- *Forsythia* (all)
- *Hyacinthus orientalis* (all)
- *Narcissus* (all)
- *Primula auricula* (all)
- *Primula* Prominent Series
- *Primula* Silver-laced Group
- *Prunus* (most)
- *Salix* (most)
- *Tulipa* (all)
- *Viburnum farreri*

Salix hastata 'Wehrhahnii'

plants for dry shade

The following plants grow most vigorously where there is a regular supply of water, but generally succeed in such difficult conditions as the shady base of walls or where roots of overhead trees and shrubs are near the surface.

- *Aucuba japonica* cultivars
- *Bergenia* (most)
- *Epimedium grandiflorum* 'Rose Queen'
- *Epimedium perralderianum*
- *Euphorbia amygdaloides* var. *robbiae*
- *Hedera colchica* 'Dentata Variegata'
- *Pulmonaria* (all)
- *Symphytum* 'Hidcote Blue'

plants for sandy or gravelly soil

The following plants require free drainage and are mostly drought tolerant, although bulbs generally require a good supply of moisture in the growing season. The range of plants that can be grown in dry sunny gardens will be enlarged if the soil is improved by the addition of well-rotted organic matter.

- *Arabis alpina* subsp. *caucasica* 'Variegata'
- *Arabis procurrens* 'Variegata'
- *Aubrieta* 'Doctor Mules'
- *Berberis buxifolia*
- *Chionodoxa* (all)
- *Crocus* (all)
- *Erysimum cheiri* 'Blood Red'
- *Euphorbia characias* subsp. *wulfenii*
- *Euphorbia rigida*
- *Fritillaria imperialis*
- *Griselinia littoralis* 'Variegata'
- *Juniperus virginiana* 'Grey Owl'
- *Ornithogalum oligophyllum*
- *Puschkinia scilloides* var. *libanotica*
- *Tulipa* (all)

Crocus angustifolius

choosing the best plants/2

plants with variegated foliage

The leaves of the following plants are edged, spotted or otherwise marked with white, cream, yellow or grey.

- *Arabis alpina* subsp. *caucasica* 'Variegata'
- *Arabis procurrens* 'Variegata'
- *Aucuba japonica* 'Variegata'
- *Griselinia littoralis* 'Variegata'
- *Pulmonaria officinalis* 'Sissinghurst White'
- *Pulmonaria saccharata* 'Frühlingshimmel'

plants with colourful foliage

The colour of leaves often changes significantly from one season to the next. Some of the plants listed below are notable for the colour of their new leaves or for the bronze tints of the foliage in winter. For other colourful foliage see Shrubs, Trees and Climbers for Autumn Colour and Plants with Variegated Foliage.

- *Begonia* 'Silver Cloud'
- *Bergenia* 'Sunningdale'
- *Corylopsis sinensis* var. *sinensis* 'Spring Purple'
- *Corylus avellana* 'Aurea'
- *Corylus maxima* 'Purpurea'
- *Epimedium grandiflorum* 'Rose Queen'
- *Epimedium perralderianum*
- *Erica* x *darleyensis* 'Kramer's Rote'
- *Helleborus* x *sternii* 'Boughton Beauty'
- *Mahonia aquifolium* 'Apollo'
- *Picea pungens* 'Montgomery'
- *Pieris formosa* var. *forestii* 'Wakehurst'
- *Pieris japonica* 'Blush'
- *Prunus* x *blireana*
- *Prunus cerasifera* 'Pissardii'
- *Rhododendron* 'Anna Baldsiefen'
- *Tulipa* 'Cape Cod'
- *Tulipa* 'Heart's Delight'
- *Tulipa* 'Red Riding Hood'

spring-flowering plants for containers

As well as the plants listed here as suitable for general container gardening, a number of rock garden, or alpine, plants are suitable for troughs and all the greenhouse plants described on pages 114–117 can be grown in containers.

- *Anemone coronaria* (all)
- *Aucuba japonica* (all)
- *Bellis perennis* 'Kito'
- *Camellia* (all)
- *Chionodoxa* (all)
- *Clematis alpina* 'Ruby'
- *Clematis macropetala* 'Maidwell Hall'
- *Crocus* (all)
- *Erica* x *darleyensis* (all)
- *Erysimum cheiri* 'Blood Red'
- *Hedera canariensis* 'Gloire de Marengo'
- *Hyacinthus orientalis* (all)
- *Narcissus* (all)
- *Primula* 'Guinevere'
- *Primula* 'Miss Indigo'
- *Primula vulgaris* (all)
- *Puschkinia scilloides* var. *libanotica*
- *Rhododendron* (most)
- *Salix caprea* 'Kilmarnock'
- *Scilla* (all)
- *Tulipa* (all)
- *Viburnum tinus* 'Eve Price'
- *Viola* (all)

Tulipa 'Shakespeare'

Tulipa 'Orange Emperor'

shrubs, trees and climbers for autumn colour

In addition to their early spring flowers, in most years the foliage of the following plants colours well in autumn. The autumn display tends to be more reliable in a frost-free climate.

- *Hamamelis vernalis* 'Sandra'
- *Ostrya carpinifolia*
- *Prunus* 'Pandora'
- *Pyrus calleryana* 'Chanticleer'

plants with large or boldly shaped leaves

The leaves of the following plants are of architectural value in the garden.

- *Adiantum raddianum* 'Fritz Lüthi'
- *Akebia quinata*
- *Bergenia* 'Schneekönigen'
- *Bergenia stracheyi*
- *Bergenia* 'Sunningdale'
- *Clematis armandii*
- *Hedera canariensis* 'Gloire de Marengo'
- *Hedera colchica* 'Dentata Variegata'
- *Holboellia coriacea*
- *Lysichiton americanus*
- *Lysichiton camtschatcensis*
- *Pachyphragma macrophyllum*
- *Phoenix canariensis*

Bergenia stracheyi

plants with ornamental fruit, berries or seed heads

The plants in the following list are worthwhile because they have more than one feature of ornamental value.

- *Akebia quinata*
- *Aucuba japonica* 'Rozannie'
- *Aucuba japonica* 'Variegata'
- *Berberis buxifolia*
- *Clematis macropetala* 'Maidwell Hall'
- *Holboellia coriacea*
- *Mahonia aquifolium* 'Apollo'
- *Ostrya carpinifolia*
- *Pyrus calleryana* 'Chanticleer'

evergreen shrubs and trees

The following are useful for creating a year-round structure for the garden. Plants marked with an asterisk* are dwarf evergreen conifers.

- *Aucuba* (all)
- *Azara microphylla*
- *Berberis buxifolia*
- *Camellia* (all)
- *Chamaecyparis lawsoniana* 'Green Hedger'
- *Erica* (all)
- *Griselinia littoralis* 'Variegata'
- *Juniperus virginiana* 'Grey Owl'
- *Mahonia aquifolium* 'Apollo'
- *Osmanthus burkwoodii*
- *Picea pungens* 'Montgomery'*
- *Pieris* (all)
- *Polygala chamaebuxus*
- *Rhododendron* (all)
- *Skimmia* x *confusa* 'Kew Green'
- *Thuja occidentalis* 'Hetz Midget'*
- *Viburnum tinus* 'Eve Price'

Rhododendron Temple Belle Group

plants with fragrant flowers

The age of a flower, time of day and temperature all affect the strength of floral scents and their appreciation is highly personal. These plants are worth siting carefully so that their perfumes can be enjoyed.

- *Akebia quinata*
- *Arabis alpina* subsp. *caucasica* 'Variegata'
- *Azara microphylla*
- *Clematis armandii*
- *Corylopsis sinensis* var. *sinensis* 'Spring Purple'
- *Crocus flavus* subsp. *flavus*
- *Daphne bholua* var. *glacialis* 'Gurkha'
- *Daphne blagayana*
- *Dendrobium nobile*
- *Erica* x *darleyensis* 'Silberschmelze'
- *Erica erigena* 'Irish Dusk'
- *Erysimum cheiri* 'Blood Red'
- *Hamamelis vernalis* 'Sandra'
- *Hyacinthus orientalis* (all)
- *Lonicera fragrantissima*
- *Lycaste cruenta*
- *Magnolia salicifolia*
- *Narcissus* (all)
- *Osmanthus burkwoodii*
- *Persicaria tenuicaulis*
- *Petasites fragrans*
- *Primula auricula* (most)
- *Primula kewensis*
- *Primula* Prominent Series
- *Primula* x *pubescens* 'Mrs J.H. Wilson'
- *Primula vulgaris*
- *Prunus mume* 'Beni-chidori'
- *Prunus* x *yedoensis*
- *Rhododendron ciliatum*
- *Ribes odoratum*
- *Skimmia* x *confusa* 'Kew Green'
- *Viburnum* x *burkwoodii* 'Anne Russell'
- *Viburnum farreri*
- *Viburnum* x *juddii*

plants for ground cover

Close planting of shrubs and perennials will help to create an attractive weed-excluding cover. However, effective cover can only be achieved by planting into soil from which perennial weeds have been eliminated. The following plants are particularly useful because of their dense foliage.

- *Arabis alpina* subsp. *caucasica* 'Variegata'
- *Aubrieta* 'Doctor Mules'
- *Bergenia* 'Schneekönigen'
- *Bergenia* 'Sunningdale'
- *Erica* (all)
- *Hedera colchica* 'Dentata Variegata'
- *Mahonia aquifolium* 'Apollo'
- *Omphalodes verna*
- *Petasites fragrans*
- *Pachyphragma macrophyllum*
- *Pulmonaria* (all)

trees for small gardens

None of the following is suitable for very small gardens, where climbers on structures such as arches are a better way of creating height and shade. Some are more commonly grown as large shrubs rather than as trees.

- *Azara microphylla*
- *Magnolia* x *loebneri* 'Leonard Messel'
- *Prunus* x *blireana*
- *Prunus cerasifera* 'Pissardii'
- *Prunus dulcis*
- *Prunus mume* 'Beni-chidori'
- *Prunus* 'Pandora'
- *Pyrus calleryana* 'Chanticleer'
- *Salix caprea* 'Kilmarnock'

Prunus mume 'Beni-chidori'

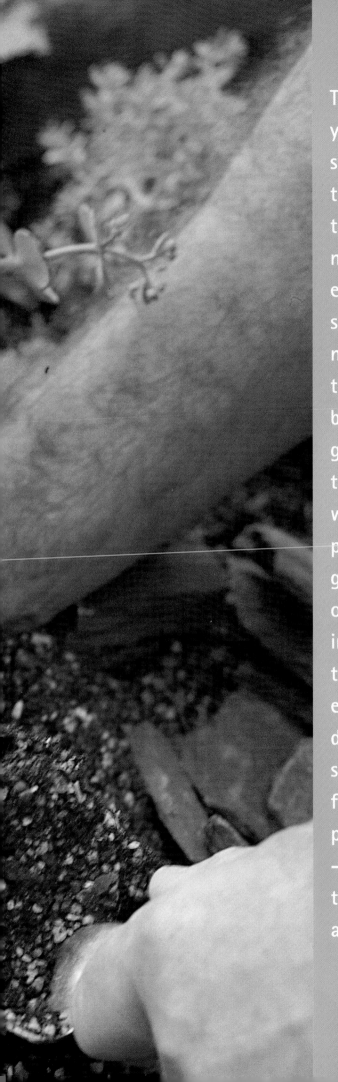

The start of the gardening year is a good time to take stock and make decisions for the future. An inventory of tools and equipment taken now will save time later, especially if some need sharpening or replacing, while new gardeners should equip themselves with quality tools before the season shifts up a gear. Garden features planned this season might include a wildflower meadow: allow previously mown grass to grow long in selected areas, or go one step farther and introduce special wildflowers to suit the habitat and environment. Why not add a deck, and look forward to sitting in a sea of grasses and flowers? On a smaller scale, plan and plant a window box – even try making your own – to look good through spring and the rest of the year.

garden projects

tools & equipment

Looking after a garden is easier and more pleasurable when you have the right tools for the job you are doing. A bewildering range is available, but all you need to get started is a simple kit of a few good-quality tools.

essential tools

A few basic tools will enable you to accomplish most garden tasks, but some extra items designed for particular jobs will add versatility to your tool kit. You may also want to try out a few more specialised items of equipment, some of which you may eventually find indispensable. A fertiliser spreader, for instance, could prove a worthwhile investment (see page 131) if you have a large lawn to feed but little spare time. And if you want to grow plants from seed or take cuttings, you will need propagation tools and equipment (see pages 132–3).

Cultivation tools are described on pages 126–7, pruning tools on pages 128–9 and lawn tools on pages 130–1.

the basic kit

The equipment shown here is described in detail on the following pages:

- spade (see page 126)
- fork (see page 126)
- trowel (see page 127)
- secateurs (see page 128)
- lawnmower (see page 130)
- watering can (see page 129)
- pocket knife (see page 129)
- gardening gloves (see opposite)

useful extras

The following additional tools and equipment will almost certainly be useful:

- rake (see page 126)
- hoe (see page 126)
- shears (see page 129)
- hand fork (see page 127)
- hand cultivator (see page 127)
- bucket (see page 129)
- hosepipe (see page 131)

buying tools

Durable, well-made tools are a pleasure to handle and can make light work of gardening tasks, so always buy the best you can afford. Anything less will prove a false economy, especially for the tools you rely on most, such as your spade.

Make sure the tool is right for the job and ask for advice if you are in doubt. Before buying, test it for comfort, balance, size and weight; a tool that is too heavy will be tiring to use over a long period of time, while a handle that is too short or long for you can cause wrist or back injury.

Compare the relative merits of the different materials the tool may be made of. For example, wooden handles are more shock-absorbent than metal ones. Stainless steel or teflon-coated blades, although more expensive, are easier to use and to clean, especially if you garden on clay.

gardening gloves

Often overlooked, these are invaluable for messy work and essential when handling prickly plants or applying garden chemicals. Two pairs are ideal: one of suede or supple leather for general use, and a thicker pair for rough work.

caring for tools

Tools that are regularly cleaned and neatly stored are always ready for use.
● **allocate storage space** for each tool where it is easily accessible and cannot be damaged. Suspend large items with cutting edges, such as spades and hoes, from hooks or clips on a wall or door and keep smaller tools together in a drawer or a box.
● **clean all tools after use.** Scrape or brush off soil and plant debris, especially from the handles, where hardened soil can cause discomfort during use. Wipe metal blades with an oily rag to prevent rust.
● **keep cutting tools sharp.** Pruning equipment needs regular honing to keep it sharp so that it cuts without damaging the plant, and without undue effort (see Winter). Spade and hoe blades are easier to use if you hammer out any dents that may form and occasionally file the edge sharp.

Regular use of a sharpening stone will keep blades sharp, making spades and hoes easier to use (top).

Fix purpose-made hooks or brackets to make the most of hanging space around the walls and doors of a shed (above).

● **clean, sharpen and oil or grease** all metal parts.
● **at the end of the growing season,** inspect tools before storing them over winter. Clean them all thoroughly. Check and repair or replace damaged handles, and wipe those made of wood with linseed oil.

hiring tools

Gardening equipment, especially larger or occasionally used items such as rotavators, hedgetrimmers and powered lawn rakes can be hired, saving you the cost and trouble of purchase and maintenance, as well as storage space. Book equipment in advance, particularly at busy times of year, and check if the hire firm can arrange delivery and collection if necessary. Inspect the tool's condition before accepting delivery or signing a hiring contract. Make sure you are shown how to use it safely if it is unfamiliar, and check whether any protective clothing is advisable.

Keep frequently used small tools and items of equipment, such as secateurs, trowel and sharpening stones, readily to hand (above).

tools & equipment/2

cultivation tools

Several versatile tools are designed for soil preparation, planting and weeding tasks. Stainless steel models, especially of spades and forks, are more expensive but easier to use and to clean.

spades, forks and rakes

● **spade** Used primarily for digging, making planting holes and moving or mixing soil, a spade is also useful for skimming off weeds, tidying border edges and mixing compost. The blade – of stainless, forged or coated steel – is attached to a wooden or metal shaft fitted with a plastic or wooden D or T-shaped handle. In a good-quality spade, the blade and tubular neck are forged from a single piece of metal for strength, and the blade has a tread for comfort.

Standard spades have a 28 x 20cm (11 x 8in) blade and a 70cm–1m (2ft 4in–3ft) shaft, but a border spade has a smaller blade for working in small spaces or where a lighter model is better.

● **fork** A garden fork is used for general cultivation work, such as breaking down soil after digging, pricking over and loosening the surface. It can also be used for moving or lifting crops, plants and bulky manure. Most forks have four metal prongs, or tines, forged from a single piece of metal, and are fitted with the same kinds of shafts and handles as spades. On a standard fork, the head or tines are 30 x 20cm (12 x 8in) long, but a border fork has smaller tines.

TOOL TIP Gardeners who find digging and cultivating difficult may find a spade and fork with special cranked handles or a spade with a sprung blade useful.

● **rake** A soil rake is used for levelling and surface preparation, especially when making a seedbed. The long wooden or plastic-covered metal handle is attached to a steel head fitted with forged steel tines. As you move the head backwards and forwards over soil, the tines loosen the surface and break up lumps as you level the ground. Held in a more upright

Border fork (top) and rake (above).

position, a rake can be used to comb stones and weeds across the surface. Once you have prepared a seedbed, you can turn the rake over and use a corner to draw out a drill for sowing. Cover seeds by drawing soil over them with the back of the rake, then tamp the head along the row, holding the rake upright.

hoes

There are many kinds of hoe, but the most important are the dutch, or push, hoe and the draw, or swan-necked, hoe. These can be used for making sowing drills and covering seeds with soil, as well as for weeding. Choose one you can use without bending your back.

● **dutch hoe** The flat rectangular blade is attached to a long handle at a slight angle. To loosen soil and destroy weeds while still small, push the hoe to and fro, with the blade just below the surface, as you walk backwards.

using **a fork or spade**
● keep your back straight
● insert the full head vertically into the soil to its maximum depth
● when lifting soil or plants, steady the handle with one hand and move the other close to the head
● clean the head regularly during use by plunging it into a bucket of sand or scraping it with a flat piece of wood or a paint scraper

Dutch hoe (left) and draw hoe (right).

• **draw hoe** The rectangular or semi-circular head, joined to the handle at a right angle, is used to chop out weeds and break up the surface while moving forwards. It is also good for scraping off stones and earthing up potatoes.

other types of hoe

• **tined hoe** The curved prongs of this hoe are effective for deeper cultivation as well as for weeding.

• **onion hoe** This is a short-handled draw hoe to weed between close-spaced plants.

hand tools

• **trowel** This small tool is used for surface cultivation – planting, removing weeds, loosening the soil surface and marking out seed drills – as well as for measuring small amounts of soil,

compost or fertiliser. The rounded, tapering blade, sometimes with cranked neck, is fitted with a 10–15cm (4–6in) wooden or plastic handle. Make sure that the head is forged from a single piece of steel and fitted to the handle with a separate ring or ferrule.

• **hand fork** Of similar construction and size to a trowel, this has three or four flattened tines and is used for weeding in confined spaces, lifting young plants and lightly cultivating small areas such as pots, window boxes and growing bags.

• **hand cultivator** This tined tool is used to loosen and aerate soil between plants and in spaces where a hoe cannot reach.

• **bulb planter** Used to bore holes in soil or a lawn when planting bulbs, this can save time when transplanting small pot-grown plants, which often neatly fit the 8cm (3in) wide holes, or even planting potatoes. It is a tapering steel cylinder attached to a short or long handle at one end, with cutting teeth at the other.

garden line

A garden line is simply two canes or spikes joined by a length of plastic twine, sometimes sold knotted at intervals to help identify distances.

cultivating a large area

Petrol-powered rotavators or cultivators are excellent for tilling a larger garden, turning in weeds and mixing in manure or compost. Attachments are available for earthing up, making seedbeds and tilling between crops. Most machines can be set to work at different depths and some have adjustable handles, allowing you to walk to one side on uncultivated soil. Buy a sturdy, easily managed model, suited to the size of the garden, and maintain it regularly, or hire an appropriate type and cultivate as much ground as possible in one go.

When working the soil, you will need a rake and hoe as well as a garden spade and fork. A garden line, used to mark out seed drills and areas of soil for digging, can be made from two spikes and some brightly coloured nylon string.

Hand **trowel** and fork (left), hand cultivator (above) and bulb planter (right).

Clockwise from left: tree pruners on fixed pole; pruning saw; bow saw; garden shears; one-handed shears; anvil loppers; bypass loppers; folding pruning saw; bypass secateurs.

Select the best secateurs you can afford (inset); if you have a lot of woody shrubs, anvil types (right) may be a better choice than bypass (left).

pruning and maintenance

Having the right tools for routine jobs like pruning, watering and tidying will make them seem less of a chore.

secateurs and loppers

The two main types of secateurs are for use on stems up to 1cm (½in) thick. Ratchet types can make cutting easier, as does a rubber stop fitted between the handles. Before buying, check that hand grips are comfortable and fit the span of your hand when open. Avoid cheap models, which are suitable only for light work. Left-handed models are available. (For maintenance, see Winter.)

● **bypass secateurs** Operating with a scissors action, these are used for most kinds of pruning, deadheading and trimming plants to size and shape.

● **anvil secateurs** A single sharp blade cuts against a flat surface, making these ideal for cutting hard, woody stems.

● **loppers** These are long-handled pruners for cutting stems up to about 2.5cm (1in) in diameter. They are fitted with anvil or bypass secateur heads, often with a ratchet to reduce the effort needed to cut hard, thick stems. Test for balance and weight before buying.

● **tree loppers or long-arm pruners** The cutting heads are on the end of fixed or extending poles up to 5m (15ft) long.

saws

● **pruning saw** A fixed or folding pruning saw will cut branches thicker than 2.5cm (1in) in diameter. The straight or curved handle and blade are designed for easy access in confined places between branches. Unlike wood-working saws, the large toughened teeth often cut only on the pulling stroke.

● **bow saw** This consists of a disposable blade tensioned between the ends of a bent tubular handle. It is used for the largest tree branches.

powered hedgetrimmers

An electric or petrol-powered hedge-trimmer can save time and effort if you have a large hedge to clip. They are available to buy or hire. Fitted with either single or double-sided reciprocating blades, these powerful machines require great care during use. Always keep power cables safely out of the way, and use a circuit breaker. Wear thick gloves, goggles or a face guard, and ear defenders.

shears

● **garden shears** Lightweight and heavy-duty models are available for trimming hedges, shrubs and small areas of grass. Straight-edged kinds are easy to sharpen and maintain, while those with wavy cutting edges are effective for cutting thicker stems, but need care with sharpening. Some shears have long or extending handles for greater reach. Test a pair for weight and balance before buying.

● **one-handed shears** Sprung to open automatically, these are useful for light trimming, deadheading and for cutting small areas of grass. They may be fitted with swivelling blades to adjust the angle of cut.

garden knives

● **pruning knife** This has a curved, folding blade and is used for trimming off thin sideshoots, cleaning up the edges of pruning wounds and taking cuttings.

● **pocket knife** A sharp pocket knife has a multitude of uses, from cutting string and opening bags of fertiliser to trimming and pruning plants (see page 133). Most models have a blade that folds away.

Pruning knife and pocket knife.

Good-quality carrying equipment will make gardening less tiring. Shown here is a pneumatic-tyred wheelbarrow with galvanised watering can and bucket, plastic carrying sheet and bags, and an all-purpose black carrier made of recycled materials.

carrying equipment

● **bucket** This indispensable and versatile item can be used for carrying materials, storing water and soaking plants, and can even double up as improvised seating. Plastic buckets are cheaper than metal ones, but have a shorter life.

● **carrying sheets and bags** Made of tear-proof woven plastic, carrying sheets and bags are useful for tidying the garden and for carrying prunings, trimmings and soft weeds. They are light and easily stored.

● **watering can** Made of plastic or metal, watering cans come in several sizes, often with volume levels marked on the side. For general use, choose one that holds 9 litres (2 gallons), but for the greenhouse choose a lighter 4.5 litre (1 gallon) model with a long spout. You will need two roses (sprinkler heads): fine for watering seeds and seedlings, and coarse for general watering. Buy the largest you can carry comfortably when full. Make sure it has a large enough opening for easy filling.

● **wheelbarrow** Useful for transporting heavy materials such as soil, compost and larger tools, wheelbarrows are made of plastic or metal. They are usually fitted with a single wheel; for frequent use over long distances, a pneumatic tyre is more comfortable than a solid one. Two-wheeled barrows are more stable on uneven ground. Some models can be fitted with side extensions for carrying leaves, and collapsible models are also available for use where storage space is limited.

● **trug** An elegant, lightweight container, a trug is useful for carrying garden tools as well as for transporting cut flowers and freshly harvested produce. Treat wooden trugs annually with preservative or linseed oil to keep them in good condition.

Watering can roses and a wooden garden trug.

tools & equipment/4

Edging shears (top) and strimmer (above).

caring for lawns

A range of specialised lawn-care tools is available to help keep a lawn looking good throughout the growing season. A lawnmower and other cutting tools are essential for keeping grass under control, while additional tools are designed to keep it healthy.

lawnmowers

The type and size of lawnmower you need will depend on the size of your lawn, your budget and how much effort you want to put into mowing. Mowers are generally defined by their cutting action and how they are powered.

cutting action

● **cylinder mowers** These have a number of blades arranged in a spiral to form a rotating cylinder. Cutting occurs as the blades pass close to a fixed blade set just below the cylinder, rather like the action of scissor blades. The quality of the cut depends on the rotation speed of the cylinder, how closely the rotating blades are passing the fixed blade and the number of blades on the cylinder – the more blades, the finer the cut.

Mains electricity-powered cylinder mower.

● **rotary mowers** A single blade or several blades, made from toughened metal or a hardened plastic, rotate horizontally at high speed, slicing through the grass. The effectiveness of the cut depends on the speed of rotation and the blades' sharpness.

Both types of mower produce a good finish if used correctly, but only rotary mowers are able to cope with cutting down long grass. Both will also produce a striped effect if equipped with a roller behind the cutting blades – stripes result not from the cutting action but from the roller pressing down the grass.

means of power

The models discussed here are all walk-behind mowers; ride-on mowers are too large for the average garden.

● **non-powered cylinder mowers** are driven entirely by human energy. They have a restricted cutting width of 25–45cm (10–18in) and can be tiring to use, especially on a large lawn, but are useful for a small grassed area.

● **petrol or diesel-powered mowers** are fitted with a two or four-stroke engine. Models may be cylinder, rotary or rotary hover (which float just above the ground rather than rely on wheels).

● **mains electricity-powered mowers** have a heavy-duty electric motor, and cylinder, rotary and rotary hover types are all available. They can be light to use, but there must be a handy power socket and the working area is restricted by the length of cable. It is important to follow a cutting pattern to avoid accidental damage to the cable, which can get in the way; always use a residual circuit breaker (RCB) in case of accidents.

● **battery-operated cylinder mowers** incorporate a motor and a heavy-duty battery, with a charger. The weight of the battery tends to make this type of mower heavier than others.

other cutting tools

An assortment of cutting implements has been designed for specific trimming jobs around lawn edges and for awkward places where lawnmowers cannot be used.

● **strimmers** These light, hand-held machines are useful for trimming long grass around trees or in difficult corners. Powered by a two-stroke petrol engine or mains electricity, they cut through grass using a length of nylon cord rotating horizontally at high speed.

● **shears** With straight handles set as an extension of the cutting blades, garden shears (see page 129) cut like scissors. They are useful for grass where the mower cannot reach. Edging shears have long handles set at right angles to the cutting blades and are used from a standing position to trim grass growing over the lawn edge.

● **half-moon edger** With a curved metal blade mounted onto a spade shaft and handle, the half-moon edging tool is used to trim lawn edges and cut turf.

Clockwise from top left: hollow-tined aerator; lawn scarifier; fertiliser spreader; lawn rake; leaf blower.

Seep hose

lawn health

To stay green and healthy, grass needs more attention than simply mowing. Debris in the form of moss or dead grass builds up over time and needs to be removed, as do fallen leaves in the autumn. Lawns also benefit from being aerated.

● **aerator** This introduces air into the soil and aerates grass roots. It consists of a set of tines or blades held in a frame; these are simply pushed into the ground all over the lawn. Some have hollow tines, which remove tiny cores of soil that can be replaced with a top-dressing or sand, if required.

● **scarifier** A scarifier will remove surface debris and dead grass. It is pushed over the lawn, rotating a series of tines or blades that rake through the grass.

● **fertiliser spreader** To feed a large area of lawn, this drum on wheels is a great asset. When it is pushed along, rotating blades below the drum spray out the granular fertiliser for up to 1m (3ft) on either side.

● **lawn rake** With spring tines arranged in a fan shape, this tool is ideal for raking out moss, collecting leaves and removing surface debris.

● **leaf blower or vacuum** This hand-held machine incorporates a strong fan powered by a two-stroke petrol engine or mains electricity. It blows leaves and debris into one area or sucks them into a chamber or bag within the machine. A push-along leaf sweeper is available too, whose rotating stiff bristles are driven by the land wheels. It collects leaves, debris and dead grass but is not very effective if leaves and grass are wet.

lawn watering equipment

Watering a lawn in dry weather is essential to keep it looking green throughout the summer.

hosepipes

● **hosepipe** For larger gardens, a hosepipe will prove invaluable. The best kind is reinforced with nylon, which prevents kinking and increases its life; make sure it will reach to the end of the garden. You need an appropriate connector to attach it to a tap and possibly a spray nozzle for the other end. A wall-mounted reel is convenient for storing and a freestanding reel on wheels for storing and moving the hose around.

● **leaky pipe and seep hose** These perforated hosepipes can be laid on a lawn and moved around every so often to deliver a fine spray or a gentle trickle of water. They are less wasteful of water than sprinklers.

sprinklers

Attached to the end of a hosepipe, a sprinkler is convenient for watering a large area of grass.

● **static sprinklers** spray a circular area of the lawn.

● **oscillating sprinklers** revolve or swing from side to side and cover a large area; their reach can be adjusted.

● **travelling sprinklers** creep slowly across the lawn, powered by the water flow.

● **'pop up' sprinklers** are permanently installed below lawns and rock gardens; they remain out of sight until water pressure pushes them above ground.

tools & equipment/5

propagation equipment

When sowing seed and taking cuttings, the right compost (see page 134) and equipment, with a few specialised tools, will increase your chances of success.

containers

● **pots** Stock up with a selection of pots, ranging in size from 6–8cm (2½–3in) for individual seedlings and cuttings to 20–25cm (8–10in) for large plants and greenhouse shrubs. Square pots hold more compost than round ones and pack closer together on the greenhouse staging. Extra-deep pots (growing tubes or long toms) are for long-rooted seedlings such as sweet peas.

A selection of plastic seed trays, including modular trays and cellular inserts, are shown here, together with plastic pots, long paper tubes and degradable coir pots standing in a home-made wooden seed tray.

home-made **seed trays**
You can make your own sturdy seed trays from wooden slats. They need to be 4cm (1½in) deep for sowing, but for pricked out seedlings 7cm (2½in) deep trays will allow stronger root systems to develop.

Pots can be plastic or clay (see pages 135–6), but degradable pots made of peat, coir or paper are ideal for propagating plants that resent root disturbance, as they are planted out with their contents to gradually decompose in the soil.

● **trays** Full or half-size trays are usually shallow and made of thin plastic that lasts for only a few seasons.

Terracotta pans for raising alpines.

Most can be fitted with a clear lid for germinating seeds and rooting cuttings. Some are divided into 6, 12 or more cells for growing plants separately, or can be fitted with cellular inserts (modules) for sowing large seeds or pricking out individual seedlings.

● **pans** Like pots but only a third or half as deep, pans are useful for sowing seeds and raising shallow-rooted, slow-growing plants like alpines and dwarf bulbs.

A metal compost tidy separates off an area of staging for potting up. Also useful are rooting hormone, diluted copper fungicide, long-spouted small watering can, mister, sieve and scoop.

other items

● **rooting hormone** The lower tips of cuttings are dipped in this liquid or powdered hormone suspension to aid rooting. Do not contaminate, store in a refrigerator and discard after a year.

● **copper fungicide** This powdered or liquid concentrate is diluted, then watered onto seedlings and freshly sown seeds as protection against damping-off and other fungal diseases.

● **scoop** A compost scoop is handy for decanting compost from large bags.

● **sieve** A meshed sieve, or riddle, is used to separate coarse compost or soil from finer particles, especially when covering seeds and preparing a seedbed. Buy sieves with different meshes or buy one with a selection of graded inserts. Wire mesh is more durable than plastic.

● **knife** A folding pocket knife, or craft knife with disposable blades, is essential for cuttings. Keep it dry and very sharp, and sterilise the blade after use.

● **dibber** This slim, tapered tool is used when transplanting seedlings to make holes in compost. Some kinds have a two-pronged fork at the other end for separating and lifting seedlings. Larger dibbers, sheathed with a metal nose, are for planting and transplanting outdoors. Improvise with a pencil under glass and sharpened broken spade handle outdoors.

● **widger** Shaped like a narrow, fluted spatula, this is useful for lifting out seedlings and rooted cuttings without disturbing their neighbours.

● **labels** You will need a supply of plastic labels and a soft lead pencil to identify seeds and seedlings. Brightly coloured ones are useful if you wish to distinguish between batches of plants. Labels used outdoors must be weather-resistant and conspicuous; use a waterproof marker.

● **thermometers** Temperature levels are important under glass, especially in a propagator, where the right amount of heat can be critical for germination. Use a maximum-minimum thermometer to record the daily range of temperatures, and a soil thermometer to test composts, cuttings beds in propagating cases and outdoor seedbeds.

● **propagator** For a controlled environment in which to root cuttings and germinate seedlings, a propagator is almost essential. The simplest type is a clear plastic-covered box that takes a few seed trays. Electrically heated propagating trays are available for use on windowsills. The most sophisticated type is a large frame for staging, fitted with a hinged lid, soil heating cable and thermostat, and automatic misting unit.

● **glass** Small panes of clear glass are useful for covering pots and trays of seeds to prevent them from drying out.

● **plastic bags** Keep a stock of new or used clear bags to enclose pots and trays of cuttings to keep humidity levels high.

Capillary matting is laid over plastic sheeting on the staging (right). It absorbs water from a reservoir at the side so that the pots and trays standing on it can take up moisture as required.

Thermometers, plant labels and pocket knife are invaluable for sowing and propagating under glass.

watering equipment

● **water trays** These are useful for pots and trays that need watering from below. You can buy purpose-made shallow plastic trays or use an old roasting tin.

● **long-spouted watering can** A small watering can with a long spout fitted with a very fine rose is ideal for gently watering seed trays and seedlings and for reaching over the staging.

● **mister** Several 500ml (1 pint) hand sprays will be useful for misting cuttings and young plants. Keep one filled with water and others, labelled, for copper fungicide solution or diluted liquid feed.

● **capillary matting** This reduces the need to water and is useful if you are away for any length of time.

containers & compost

Containers come in a vast range of designs and materials and offer tremendous scope for planting, but choosing the right compost for the plants is all-important, as their rooting area is more limited than in the ground.

types of potting compost

Potting compost is designed to retain water while remaining well aerated, ensuring that plant roots are never short of oxygen. Buy compost little and often to ensure it is fresh, store it in a shed or greenhouse where it will stay at indoor temperatures, and keep open bags covered to prevent them from drying out.

soil-less compost

Usually sold as 'multi-purpose', soil-less compost is light and clean to use. It is excellent for short-lived seasonal displays and where weight is an issue, such as in hanging baskets. However, its structure breaks down rapidly, rendering it unsuitable for long-lived container plants. Regular watering is vital as this type of compost dries out quickly and is hard to moisten again. Waterlogging can also be a problem during very wet weather, or if plants are over-watered. Fertiliser levels are short-lived, so plants will need feeding about six weeks after potting.

Traditionally, soil-less composts were peat based, which today has serious ecological implications, but many alternatives are available (see right).

soil-based compost

Compost that contains soil, also referred to as loam, has much more 'body' than soil-less types and is excellent for permanent plants that will remain in containers for more than a few months. The loam provides a good buffer against drought and is also less liable than soil-less types to suffer from waterlogging. This category includes composts made to the John Innes formulae, which are numbered according to the amount of fertiliser contained. John Innes No. 1 is suitable for propagation, while Nos. 2 and 3 are for established plants.

Always use potting compost in containers. Different types have been devised for a range of purposes, so success will often depend on making the correct choice for the plant's needs.

alternatives to peat

Many potting composts are based on peat harvested from bogs, which are valuable wildlife habitats. Home gardeners use about two-thirds of all the peat sold in Britain, so buying alternative composts based on recycled waste materials will make a real contribution towards protecting wildlife. The chief ones are coir (ground coconut husk fibres); wood waste from forestry and sawmills; and recycled 'green' household waste. If you do not want to change from peat, at least look for compost that is based on 'reclaimed' peat that has been filtered out of streams that feed into reservoirs.

When planting bulbs that need sharp drainage, such as lilies, add a third by volume of coarse grit to the compost.

ericaceous compost

Plants that dislike lime, such as azaleas, rhododendrons and pieris, need to be grown in ericaceous (lime-free) compost.

seed and cuttings composts

While multi-purpose compost can be used for seeds and cuttings, better results are achieved using compost designed for propagation. Fertiliser levels in both types are low, as high nutrient levels can damage delicate new roots. It is important to pot on or prick out young plants once cuttings are rooted or seedlings are large enough to handle, as they will be in need of more nutrients as well as more space.

• **seed compost** is fine textured to ensure good contact with the seed, especially small seeds, and developing roots; it retains moisture well.

• **cuttings compost** is free draining to avoid waterlogging, as cuttings are kept in a humid environment.

perlite and vermiculite

These lightweight, granular materials can be mixed into different composts to improve aeration and control drainage, especially for cuttings where a half-and-half mixture gives very good rooting.

Fine perlite retains moisture while still letting light through, so it is useful for covering seeds that need light in order to germinate.

Pot 'feet' raise containers off the ground to improve drainage.

choosing your containers

There is a seemingly limitless variety of container size and shape, and a choice to suit all budgets, including pots, planters, troughs, barrels and urns as well as hanging baskets and window boxes.

To achieve a sense of harmony on a patio, it is best to limit the choice of materials to one or two different types and rely on a variety of shapes and sizes to create interest. Make sure that design, materials and colour are in keeping with the style of your house and garden.

terracotta containers

Terracotta pots are a traditional choice; they look good almost anywhere and suit most plants. Unless your budget is large, a good compromise is to buy lots of inexpensive terracotta containers to create massed groupings of plants, and one or two substantial, decorative pots to catch the eye in high-profile locations.

Apart from being breakable, terracotta is also porous, so the compost in it dries out quickly, unless the sides of the pot are lined with polythene. Since not all terracotta is frost-proof, vulnerable pots must be taken under cover in winter.

gravel and broken crocks

All pots need a layer of coarse material before being filled with compost. Coarse and medium-size gravel are ideal for drainage and broken pieces of clay pot prevent compost from being washed out.

Plain manufactured pots in classic shapes are the cheapest of all, while those with decorative designs cost a little more (right above). Most expensive of all are lovely hand-thrown pots and olive oil jars (right below).

containers & compost/2

other containers

While terracotta pots suit almost all garden styles, you may need to match containers in other materials more closely to the character of the garden. (The range of troughs and window boxes is covered on pages 138–9.)

● **wood** is natural and long lasting, and looks good in almost any setting. Styles vary from smart Versailles tubs, often placed in pairs, to rustic half-barrels. Barrels are useful for growing large permanent plants, such as shrubs or small trees. Check that the metal bands of a barrel are sound and secure; you may need to drill drainage holes through the base.

● **galvanised metal containers** are usually made in simple designs such as troughs and florists' buckets, and best suit modern and minimal garden styles. However, as the thinness of the metal leaves the root area subject to wide fluctuations in temperature, they are unsuitable for outdoor winter use in most areas. Lining the container with a thick layer of newspaper will prevent the roots becoming too hot in summer.

● **glazed pots** are useful for introducing colour into fairly sophisticated gardens,

A **natural stone planter** is heavy but ages well.

but the designs and shades do not suit all gardens and bright colours can date quickly. As with terracotta, not all pots are frost-proof, but the glazing does prevent water loss through the sides.

● **stone containers,** whether natural or reconstituted (terrazzo), are at the top end of the price range. Except for simple stone troughs, most are made to classic designs, such as urns, best suited to grand or fairly formal gardens. They look best used singly, usually as a focal point in the garden, rather than rubbing shoulders with other pots on a patio. They are heavy and difficult to move.

● **containers in man-made materials** such as plastic and glass fibre are often a successful imitation of more expensive stone, terracotta and lead. In addition to

Wooden Versailles tubs and half barrel (top); glass fibre 'lead' and galvanised metal pots (above); glazed containers (right); plastic oil jar, reconstituted stone urn and terrazzo containers (far right).

being far easier on the wallet than the real thing, they are also lighter in weight and therefore more mobile. It is the passing of time that really shows up the difference: whereas genuine materials take on a patina of age and develop an attractive weathered look, fake materials will simply degenerate.

hanging baskets

Containers can be used to add colour above ground level. Hanging baskets are designed to be suspended singly from a stout bracket screwed to a fence post or wall, or from freestanding devices made to take several baskets. The main choice is between open-mesh and solid baskets.

● **open-mesh baskets** can be planted through the sides as well as the top to create a mass of colour, but they need to be lined and they dry out quickly. Plastic-coated wire baskets are cheap and widely available, while decorative designs with exposed wire are much more costly.

● **solid baskets** are made of either plastic, which may include 'self-watering' designs with a built-in reservoir, or natural pliable materials such as rattan. When planting, aim to completely conceal plastic models but show off attractive natural baskets.

● **liners for open mesh** hanging baskets are made from a number of different materials. The traditional one is sphagnum moss. As this is often gathered from the wild, many people prefer to use a recycled material: wool-based liners have good water retention, and coir comes in its natural brown colour as well as a dyed-green 'moss'.

compost for hanging baskets

Because the entire rootball is exposed to the dehydrating effects of sun and wind, hanging baskets benefit from a soil-less compost with water-retaining gel added. But this is inappropriate for winter containers, as good drainage is crucial to avoid frost damage to plant roots.

A collection of summer herbs growing in a rustic hanging basket (above). It will need watering daily and feeding weekly.

Open-mesh baskets come in different designs (below left). They will need to be lined with moss or a recycled liner (below right).

troughs & window boxes

Planting up a window box or two means that plants and flowers can be enjoyed close-up, inside as well as outside. Include some scented flowers, and fragrance will drift indoors through the open windows.

window box styles

Window boxes add personality and colour to the outside of the house and allow a cascade of flowers and foliage to soften the straight lines of a facade. Where garden space is limited or non-existent, window boxes can allow you to grow a wide selection of plants.

Style is important: in both design and material, a box should complement your house and windows. Plastic boxes, for instance, might suit a modern home but look out of place against an elegant Georgian town house, where terracotta or stone would be better suited. Equally, an ornate stone container might not suit a very simple house.

Design becomes less important once the container is packed with trailing plants that conceal its outlines and material. If the site permits, choose a container that is at least 20cm (8in) deep, to allow plenty of compost for good root growth and to prevent the compost from drying out too quickly.

safe fixings

Because a window sill, like a balcony or roof garden, is exposed to the elements, it is essential to secure all containers and boxes that could otherwise be dislodged by strong wind, or knocked off accidentally by someone cleaning or decorating. Security for window boxes above ground-floor level is even more essential, for a falling container might cause serious injury.

A guard rail or strong wires secured across the front of the sill is the best solution. If your window sills are not sufficiently wide, boxes can be secured beneath them on stout brackets.

If a windowsill is sloping, or not deep enough, you can fix the box to the wall below it, using sturdy brackets (above). Some sills have a built-in guard rail, such as this wrought iron support in which the window box sits (top).

materials

Depending on the size and site of the sill, weight may be a real consideration. Boxes made of thin materials, such as plastic or plywood, have poor insulating qualities and are best lined with newspaper to protect plant roots from extremes of temperature. (For general property of materials, see pages 136–7.)

- **plastic** is both inexpensive and lightweight, but is a poor insulator and does not look attractive. Over time it can turn brittle and crack, especially when exposed to frost or hot sun.
- **reconstituted stone** can look effective, particularly against an older building or a town house. However, a stone box is extremely heavy and must be placed where there is no danger of it falling, such as on a ground-floor window sill with a guard rail in front – or, even better, on the ground.

using a plastic liner

For a seamless succession of colour, use a liner with drainage holes that fits inside the window box and can be swapped several times a year. The next liner can be planted up and grown on elsewhere, so that the planting is well established by the start of its given season. The liner containing last season's plants is simply lifted out and replaced with the new one.

● **glass fibre,** often used to imitate stone or lead, is lightweight, strong and long-lasting; it is more expensive than plastic and makes a good imitation material.

● **terracotta** looks good on most buildings, and many decorative designs are available. However, it is fairly heavy and needs to be secured. Terracotta is porous, so it dries out quickly – an important consideration with window boxes as they already need frequent watering – but this can be remedied by lining the inside with plastic sheeting, without covering the drainage holes.

● **wooden boxes** are made in a wide range of styles, from hollowed rustic logs to stylish and decorative troughs. You can make your own quite easily (see page 140). Wood should be treated with wood stain, or painted, every year or two so that it lasts longer.

● **galvanised metal** window boxes have the drawbacks of other metal containers (see page 136); use a plastic insert. WINDOW BOX TIP For a wide window with a long sill, two boxes will be more stable, and easier to plant and to handle, than a single long window box.

A short-term spring planting of daffodils, yellow-eyed primulas and golden thyme has been assembled in this galvanised trough standing on the ground (above left). A longer-lived summer scheme can be started in a plastic insert.

Wooden window boxes may be left natural and treated with preservative (above right). Here, white autumn cyclamen, evergreen euonymus and trailing ivies make a simple but charming planting to last through winter.

The colour of the painted window box (below) is echoed in the choice of plants, with purple-blue hyacinths and bright blue muscari backed by red tulips and *Narcissus* 'Bridal Crown'; dainty forget-me-nots edge the display.

troughs & window boxes/2

building and planting up a simple window box

YOU WILL NEED • wood suitable for outdoor use, such as exterior grade plywood or old floorboards, at least 1.2cm (½in) thick • 4cm (1½in) square planed softwood for corner posts/legs • saw • measuring tape • wood glue • drill • drill bits • brass screws • screwdriver • 4 angle brackets • paint or wood preservative • paintbrush • crocks • kitchen cloth • compost • plants

3 Screw angle brackets inside the box to keep it true and square.

6 Before filling, place a layer of crocks or polystyrene chips in the base of the box to aid drainage. Cover the drainage layer with a piece of disposable kitchen cloth, which will allow water to drain but prevent compost seeping through and soiling your sills and wall.

1 Cut two matching pieces of wood 20cm (8in) deep and a little less than the length of the sill, for the box front and back. Cut two smaller matching pieces, 20cm (8in) deep and slightly less wide than the sill for the sides. Cut four corner posts 2.5cm (1in) taller than the depth of the box.

4 Cut a piece of wood for the base, the length of the front and as wide as the side. Mark and cut out a square recess to fit round each corner post, and glue and screw the base to the box.

5 Using a large drill bit, drill several 1cm (½in) holes near the corners and sides of the base for drainage. Apply two or three coats of paint or preservative. Coat the inside with preservative even if you paint only the visible top edges.

2 Form each corner by glueing then screwing a corner post to the outer edges of one long and one short panel, lining it up with the top and keeping it flush with their inside faces. On one exposed side of the post, drill pilot holes 5cm (2in) from top and bottom; countersink the screws. Repeat on the other side with a 1cm (½in) difference so that the screws do not clash. Screw all four panels together in this way.

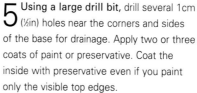

7 Half-fill the box with compost. Place the plants on this while still in their pots, so they can be moved around until you are happy with the arrangement. Keep in mind that a window box will be seen from indoors as well as out, so position the plants accordingly. Take them out of their pots and plant them, then fill the spaces in between with more compost. Leave a gap of about 2.5cm (1in) between the top of the compost and the rim of the box, which allows room for watering.

planting up a window box

Window boxes are enjoying a popularity not seen since their Victorian heyday, when displays would be changed four or five times a year. Nowadays, few people want to go to such lengths, and it pays to consider how much work you want to put in before choosing your plants. For example, the permanent plants with attractive foliage, listed right, can be left in the box all year, while flowers for seasonal colour would need to be changed at the end of the season.

colour schemes

Choose plants in colours to complement your house and window, and therefore show off the plants to their best. Pale flowers and foliage make a handsome contrast with red brick, while light-coloured walls provide a superb backdrop to bright, richly coloured flowers and dark leaves. The simplest schemes are the most effective: red with white; blue with yellow or white; orange with red or yellow; pink with blue. Add foliage plants in complementary shades to act as a buffer between the flowers, such as lime-green foliage with yellow flowers, or silver foliage with blue.
EDGING TIP At the edges of a wide window box, plant annual climbers such as morning glory (*Ipomoea tricolor*) and canary creeper (*Tropaeolum peregrinum*) to train up and around the window.

window box plant care

Frequent watering is vital, as window boxes tend to be sited in sheltered spots that receive little or no rainfall. When in doubt, just stick your finger into the compost to see how dry it is.

As a rough guide, water up to twice a day in summer, every day or two in spring and autumn, and weekly in winter. Pour water on the compost, not the plants, and avoid watering in hot sun if possible,

as splashed flowers and foliage are liable to become scorched. Regular feeding is also essential during the growing season. Either insert controlled-release fertiliser pellets in spring and summer, or feed weekly with a liquid fertiliser.

Deadheading, or the removal of faded flowers before they set seed, not only keeps the window box looking tidy but

also encourages the production of more flowers over a longer period, ensuring that your display will last longer.

Permanent plants such as shrubs will need topdressing each year in early spring, which means replacing the upper few centimetres of compost with some fresh potting compost mixed with controlled-release fertiliser.

window box plants for year-round interest
PERMANENT PLANTS WITH ATTRACTIVE FOLIAGE • bugle (*Ajuga reptans* varieties) • *Berberis thunbergii* 'Atropurpurea Nana' • dwarf box (*Buxus sempervirens* 'Suffruticosa') • *Convolvulus cneorum* • *Cordyline australis* varieties • *Euonymus fortunei* varieties • *Euonymus japonicus* 'Aureus' • variegated ground ivy (*Glechoma hederacea* 'Variegata') • dwarf hebes such as *Hebe pinguifolia* 'Pagei' • ivy (*Hedera helix* varieties) • *Heuchera* varieties • golden creeping jenny (*Lysimachia nummularia* 'Aurea') • lesser periwinkle varieties (*Vinca minor*) with variegated foliage • evergreen ornamental grasses such as *Carex oshimensis* 'Evergold' and *Festuca glauca* 'Elijah Blue'
DECIDUOUS FROST-TENDER PLANTS FOR FOLIAGE INTEREST • *Helichrysum petiolare* • *Plectranthus forsteri* 'Marginatus' • *Senecio cineraria*

flowering plants for seasonal colour
SPRING • double daisies (*Bellis perennis*) • lily-of-the-valley (*Convallaria majalis*) • crocuses • hyacinth (*Hyacinthus orientalis* varieties) • grape hyacinths (*Muscari armeniacum*) • forget-me-nots (*Myosotis sylvatica* varieties) • *Narcissus* • polyanthus • *Primula* 'Wanda' • tulips (compact varieties such as 'Red Riding Hood') • *Viola* Sorbet Series and *V. sororia* 'Freckles'
SUMMER • blue pimpernel (*Anagallis monellii*) • *Begonia semperflorens* • *Bidens ferulifolia* • *Brachyscome iberidifolia* • diascias • *Felicia amelloides* • fuchsias • busy lizzies (*Impatiens*) • *Isotoma axillaris* • *Lobelia erinus* • *Lobularia maritima* • *Lotus berthelotii* • *Mimulus* x *hybridus* 'Calypso' • nemesias • pelargoniums • petunias • salvias • *Scaevola aemula* • bacopa (*Sutera*) • verbenas • pansies (*Viola*)
AUTUMN • *Cyclamen persicum*, especially dwarf Miracle Series • *Erica gracilis* • *Solanum capsicastrum* (Most summer-flowering plants continue to give a good display of blooms well into autumn if deadheaded.)
WINTER • snowdrops (*Galanthus*) • winter-flowering pansies (*Viola*)

A summer window box relies on salvias for height, with a cascade of trailing lobelias round the sides.

displaying alpines

These compact perennials and shrubs have a jewel-like quality and thrive in well-drained conditions. They can be displayed in a number of ways, as long as their basic growing requirements are met.

suitable environments

True alpines are high-altitude plants under 15cm (6in) high, but any plant small enough to look good planted with them, including dwarf conifers, can be loosely described as an alpine or rock plant and many thrive in a fast-draining medium. In addition to traditional rock gardens and alpine beds, raised beds, containers, paving and even walls can provide the right kind of environment.

Plants that are especially susceptible to damp will benefit from a collar of grit beneath their foliage. Covering all

the compost with coarse grit or fine gravel creates an attractive mulch that will control weeds, improve surface drainage and discourage slugs. When planting, consider the growth habit of each plant and allow sufficient room for it to spread. Plants that are prone to rotting off at soil level, such as sempervivums, are best planted into vertical pockets between rocks, where drainage will be especially sharp.

rock gardens

The traditional method of displaying a wide range of alpines and rock plants outdoors is a purpose-built bed that re-creates their natural habitat. Ideally, it should be constructed to imitate a rocky outcrop or scree, combining variously sized rocks with free-draining soil, and plants positioned both in the soil and between the rocks.

A rock garden, especially a large one, can be challenging to construct because of the weight of rocks, but it can be the ideal solution for awkward slopes, where mowing, digging or other forms of cultivation are difficult.

dry stone walls

As well as providing a perfect haven for some rock plants, a dry stone wall will also display them to advantage, allowing them to be appreciated at close quarters. Plants with succulent leaves that require excellent drainage to survive winter wet, such as sedums and sempervivums, thrive especially well in the dry, almost soil-free conditions.

In a colourful rock garden created near a stream, dwarf primulas and centaureas thrive alongside vivid green cushions of saxifrage, the whole bed covered with a mulch of fine gravel.

paving

A large number of low spreading plants enjoy having their leaves and stems exposed to dry, bright conditions as long as the roots are cool and shaded, with moisture always available. Paved areas provide exactly these conditions, as plants in the cracks between slabs can spread their roots under them. Not only do plants in paving look attractive and soften hard edges, but their foliage blocks out sunlight and prevents weed seeds germinating.

containers

Troughs and sinks or similar-shaped containers are ideal for displaying plants in a restricted area, and many of the slower growing alpines thrive in these conditions for years. Make sure the container has good drainage and is filled with a free-draining compost.

raised beds

A raised bed is an excellent way to display a larger selection of alpines. Dwarf shrubs and conifers can be used to add height, and low-growing or mat-forming alpine or rock species will cover the surface. Position trailing plants so that their foliage cascades over the edge of the bed. Railway sleepers make a particularly effective retaining material for a raised bed (see opposite), as their natural colouring will not overshadow the plants, especially when young and tiny.

RAILWAY SLEEPER TIP If using second-hand sleepers for your raised bed, check with your supplier that they were not treated with creosote before 2003, as this type of creosote has since been banned by the EU.

making a raised alpine bed

YOU WILL NEED • pegs and string • treated railway sleepers • spirit level • hammer • 15cm (6in) nails • spade • pea shingle • woven geotextile membrane • free-draining compost (see page 47) • large stones or rocks • fine gravel • trowel • plants

1 **Mark out the area** of the raised bed using pegs and string, and remove any surface vegetation from within it. Lay sleepers around the marked area to create a low retaining wall, leaving a 2–3cm (1in) gap at the end of each sleeper to let water drain through. Check for level.

2 **Lay a second tier** of railway sleepers above the first.

3 **Secure the top layer** by driving a long nail at an angle through each corner joint.

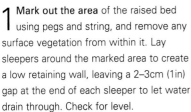

4 **Pour in enough pea shingle** over the base of the bed to create a layer at least 8cm (3in) deep. Cover with a geotextile sheet to keep the compost separate from the drainage material (inset). Fill the bed to within 5cm (2in) of the rim with free-draining compost. Alpines grow best in loam-based compost – a mix of equal parts John Innes No. 1 and crushed gravel is ideal (see page 47).

5 **Place a few large stones** or rocks on top of the bed and try out an arrangement of plants around them.

6 **Plant up the bed,** making sure the new alpines are firmly planted, but leaving the top of the rootballs slightly high. Spread a layer of gravel 2–3cm (1in) thick over the entire surface of the compost.

alpines **for raised beds**
• *Arenaria montana* • *Aubrieta* hybrids • *Erodium* 'County Park' • *Gentiana septemfida* • *Raoulia australis* • *Salix reticulata* • *Sedum* 'Bertram Anderson' • *Sedum spathulifolium* and *S. spathulifolium* 'Purpureum'

bedding schemes

Annual bedding is a traditional celebration of a season, in which a bed or border is planted up with a variety of easy-care flowers that bloom simultaneously over a long period to create a choreographed riot of colour.

seasonal schemes

Plants for bedding may be hardy or half-hardy annuals, biennials, bulbs or tender perennials, according to the season in which they flower. Spring bedding is normally composed of bulbs such as daffodils, tulips and hyacinths, planted in autumn together with biennials like wallflowers, pansies and forget-me-nots, and dug up when flowering ceases. Summer bedding uses hardy and half-hardy annuals, often blended with tender perennials such as pelargoniums and fuchsias, and carries the display from the end of the spring bedding season through to the autumn, when the cleared plants are replaced once more with spring bedding plants.

bedding styles

Formal bedding depends on symmetry: the plants are set out in a geometrical pattern, with taller varieties ('dot' plants) at the back, or in the centre of island beds, and the smallest plants along the edges. The space in between is filled with intermediate-height plants, grouped in a mosaic of repeated shapes (see opposite).

Informal bedding dispenses with the geometry of straight lines and patterns, instead setting out the plants in relaxed groups that may overlap and even flower at different times to produce a more natural effect. A version of the herbaceous border (see Winter), this often uses hardy and native annuals rather than tender bedding plants.

long-flowering **annuals and tender perennials**

FOR SUMMER BEDDING SCHEMES • *Ageratum houstonianum* • *Begonia semperflorens* • gazania • heliotrope • busy lizzie (*Impatiens*) • *Lobelia erinus* • alyssum (*Lobularia maritima*) • *Nemesia strumosa* • pelargonium • petunia • *Phlox drummondii* • *Solenostemon* • *Tagetes*
FOR HARDY ANNUAL BEDS • *Antirrhinum* • *Calendula* • cornflower (*Centaurea cyanus*) • *Convolvulus minor* • cosmos • love-in-a-mist (*Gypsophila*) • *Salvia viridis*

sowing a hardy annual bed

Short-lived but inexpensive, hardy annuals are great summer bed or border fillers. Of all seasonal flowers, they are the easiest to grow, as seed is sown directly in the soil where they are to flower. In a new garden or cleared patch, they can be sown in spring to cover an entire area by summer, creating a colourful blaze. In an established border, you can use annuals as gap-fillers for extra bursts of colour. In the right conditions many will self-seed freely, which means virtually no work apart from thinning out congested clumps of seedlings.

1 **Weed and rake** the soil to a fine tilth, then mark out an informal shape for each variety by trickling sand onto the ground.

2 **Within each outlined shape,** draw out shallow lines or drills with a trowel, using a stick as a guide.

3 **Sow seed thinly** in each drill. Cover with a little soil, and firm down using the back of a rake. After a few weeks, remove weed seedlings by hand and thin annual seedlings as needed (see page 27).

Hardy annuals look best in informal groups. Here, purple, pink and white *Salvia viridis* and pink lavatera form colourful drifts in a border (above).

formal bedding scheme

This example of a symmetrical summer bed is filled with half-hardy annuals and tender perennials. It will provide three months of vibrant colour, starting around midsummer.

1 *Canna* 'Assaut'
2 *Heliotropium arborescens* 'Marine', as half-standards
3 *Abutilon* 'Souvenir de Bonn'
4 *Fuchsia* 'Lady Thumb'
5 *Cosmos sulphureus* 'Sunset'
6 *Senecio cineraria* 'Silver Dust'

---

formal bedding guidelines

- **choose an open sunny site,** sheltered from strong winds, especially if you include tall central 'dot' plants over 60cm (2ft) high, such as cordylines, cannas or standard plants.
- **keep the design bold and simple.** In large beds, use large blocks of plants – smaller ones can look too fussy.
- **make sure plants** are acclimatised, and water before planting.

- **begin in the centre** with the dot plants, spacing them 1m (3ft) apart; support with canes if needed.
- **frame the bed with edging plants,** 15cm (6in) from the sides and 10–15cm (4–6in) apart, according to size and vigour.
- **finally, fill in the spaces** with flowers of medium height, spaced 23–30cm (9–12in) apart.

---

colour schemes

For the best results, plan out the scheme before planting. There are no firm rules about colour combinations; you could blend a few complementary shades in a gentle or subtle design, or mix a whole rainbow of contrasting colours. Reds and oranges have a hot impact, while blue, mauve and white are tranquil. Remember that leaves can be as colourful as flowers, and many foliage plants such as coleus, silver senecio and golden helichrysum make a real contribution to a scheme.

raising the plants

Even a small flower bed can absorb a surprisingly large number of plants. You need to decide whether to buy them as young plants, which can be expensive but is less demanding on time and care, or to grow them from seed, a much cheaper option but dependent on having a greenhouse and lots of attention while the seedlings grow to flowering size.

Popular annuals and tender perennials are usually offered by garden centres as seedlings or plug plants early in the season, or as larger plants in bud or flower a few weeks later. A much wider range is available if you grow them from seed, starting 12–16 weeks before you need to plant out – spring bedding in mid-autumn and summer bedding after the last spring frosts. Remember that half-hardy annuals like begonias and impatiens need heat for germination and early growth. The most successful are F_1 hybrids, which produce uniform plants with large, bright flowers.

maintaining a scheme

Thoroughly water the bed immediately after planting, and repeat every seven days if there is no substantial rainfall. Keep the ground bare of weeds, at first by hoeing and later, when the bedding plants have filled out, by hand weeding. A mulch of lawn garden compost will help suppress weeds as well as keep the soil moist. Give plants a high-potash feed at midsummer and repeat monthly to keep them in peak condition; prolong flowering by deadheading.

At the end of the season, clear the exhausted plants en masse and prepare the ground for the next display. After the spring bedding, dig up and dry bulbs, and discard herbaceous flowers; remove weeds, tidy the edges, spread a dressing of general fertiliser and rake the surface level or into a gentle mound ready for the summer plants. When these have finished in mid-autumn, clear the bed; compost the annuals after saving any seed, and transfer tender perennials to a greenhouse. Fork in a 5cm (2in) layer of garden compost all over the bed and level, ready for the next season.

wildflower meadows

Visualise an enchanting carpet of wildflowers or a richly coloured tapestry of prairie planting in place of a labour-intensive lawn, and it is easy to see why these informal gardening styles are now firmly in favour.

seasonal meadows

The chief benefits of meadow plantings are masses of beautiful flowers for months, far less time spent mowing, and a haven for insects and other creatures, which are losing their habitats to intensive farming and development. If your garden is large you could create more than one type of meadow, with colour from spring to autumn.

spring meadows

The freshness of spring flowers is enchanting set against a backdrop of vivid green, just-opening leaves. Wild daffodils and pools of azure bluebells spangled with gleaming white greater stitchwort (*Stellaria holostea*) bring a shimmering beauty to partly shaded areas; clumps of golden cowslips (*Primula veris*) and blue self-heal (*Prunella vulgaris*) thrive in sun; and for damp soil there are the chequered flowers of snake's head fritillaries (*Fritillaria meleagris*), deep pink ragged robin (*Lychnis flos-cuculi*) and paler lady's smock (*Cardamine pratensis*).

A spring meadow is mown from around late June to mid-July onwards, once the flowers have set seed, which makes it ideal if you want a generous-sized area of grass that is usable in summer and where children can play.

summer meadows

The tangled abundance of a summer meadow is alive with butterflies and insects during the day, but takes on an ethereal beauty in the morning and evening when lit by the low rays of the sun. Flowering grasses look lovely and provide a perfect foil for field scabious (*Knautia arvensis*), purple knapweed (*Centaurea scabiosa*), lady's bedstraw (*Galium verum*), musk mallow (*Malva moschata*), yarrow (*Achillea millefolium*)

native wildflowers

You can plant your meadow with different types of bulb and annual and perennial flowers, so long as they are in keeping with their surroundings. For the greatest benefit to wildlife, use a high percentage of native plants, such as those mentioned (left), on which local insects have evolved to feed and breed. The flickering beauty of butterflies and the soothing hum of bees will add to your enjoyment of the meadow, where even less welcome insects like aphids have their uses by attracting birds in search of food.

Paths through a spring meadow studded with buttercups provide an attractive contrast between short and long turf (below). Mow paths regularly from late June.

and ox-eye daisy (*Leucanthemum vulgare*). Mow a summer meadow occasionally in spring until late May or early June, then leave until flowering has finished and the plants have set seed in late September before you cut again.

mowing a meadow

Consider how you use the garden and try to retain a close-cut lawn near the house for sitting out. Mown grass paths that meander through the flowers allow visitors to wander through a meadow; these are best kept regularly cut to create a sharp and attractive contrast between long and short grass.

Make a note of the mowing regime your meadow requires, as cutting at the right time is crucial to success; allowing the plants to bloom unhindered is important so that they set seed for next year. After cutting, rake up and remove clippings to avoid raising nutrient levels in the soil and overwhelming the plants.

prairie planting

This concept unites the naturalistic style of planting popular in countries such as Germany with the prairies of North America, to create a stunning kaleidoscope of summer and autumn colour. Tough, easily grown perennials and ornamental grasses are planted to look as natural as possible by repeating the same varieties in informal groups or drifts. This style of gardening, also described as a modern meadow or a natural herbaceous border, is ideal for a sunny site and well-drained soil.

For the first two years, you must keep down the weeds until your plants have established, but after that little upkeep is required. The chief job is the mass cutting-down of all the plants during the dormant season, in late winter to early spring. Leaving the plants until

Tall cow parsley and buttercups have colonised the long grass in an orchard (left).

In an unusual summer meadow, yellow rattle, ox-eye daisies and lesser spotted orchids create a gentle tapestry of colour (below). The meadow should not be mown until the flowers have set seed.

plants **for prairie gardens**

ORNAMENTAL GRASSES • *Calamagrostis* x *acutiflora* • *Deschampsia* x *cespitosa* • *Helictotrichon sempervirens* • *Miscanthus sinensis* • *Stipa tenuissima*

PERENNIALS • *Achillea* • *Aster lateriflorus* • *Echinacea purpurea* • *Helenium* • *Helianthus* • *Salvia* x *sylvestris* • *Solidago*

then allows you to enjoy the effects of frost on dead flowerheads and foliage, and provides places for beneficial insects to hibernate. Use a strimmer to make light work of cutting a large area, and rake out the dead foliage of ornamental grasses. Later in spring, you can hoe out any unwanted self-sown seedlings to avoid the more vigorous plants becoming too dominant.

A wide range of perennials and grasses are suitable for prairie gardens (see above). You can include bulbs and hardy annuals for colour in spring and early summer, but you must cut down and clear the border in late winter so as not to damage their new growth. Plants should look natural and thrive with minimal attention, so ornate double flowers are out, as are high-maintenance plants like delphiniums, which need staking and slug protection.

wildflower meadows/2

creating a meadow

An established meadow is low on maintenance once you have made preparations for long-term success. Most wildflowers are raised and planted in a similar way to garden plants, but they need poorer conditions to thrive.

converting an existing lawn

Changing your lawn to a meadow needs to be done over a couple of years if the soil is rich and the grass has been fed. In such a situation the grasses grow so vigorously that they would out-perform all but the strongest of wildflowers such as cow parsley (*Anthriscus sylvestris*), which is why this plant turns roadside verges into a froth of white in early summer. It is vital to reduce the soil's fertility, so stop using fertilisers, cut the lawn regularly and remove clippings so they do not return nutrients to the soil.

A quicker but more laborious way to reduce fertility is to skim off the turf along with the top 5–8cm (2–3in) of soil. You can do the job by hand, which is very hard work, or hire a turf-stripping machine that cuts and lifts turf. (Leave the turf, stacked grass-side down, for a year – it makes lovely crumbly topsoil.)

On poorer soil, where clippings have been removed and the grass has not been fed, wildflower planting can begin much sooner. Leave the lawn uncut for a few months to see what plants are growing but have been unable to flower.

preparing the ground

You also need to lower fertility when preparing bare soil, unless it is already poor, stony or sandy. You can do this by growing a crop of hungry vegetables such as potatoes or cabbages (but not beans or peas, which add nitrogen to the soil). Then get rid of existing weeds using a systemic weedkiller while they are in active growth and lightly dig the ground several weeks later, once they are dead. Alternatively, dig the ground and remove all the roots of perennial weeds by hand. Rake the soil to break down lumps and level it, ready for sowing. Leave for several weeks so that weed seeds can germinate and you can hoe them off before you sow.

meadows from seed

Most meadow seed mixtures are a blend of grasses, quick-growing annual flowers such as field poppy (*Papaver rhoeas*), corn marigold (*Chrysanthemum segatum*) and corncockle (*Agrostemma githago*), and perennials such as those mentioned under summer meadows on page 146. The best time to sow is late summer to early autumn, preferably after rain when the soil is still moist. Choice plants like cowslips are better raised in pots and planted out individually (see opposite).

Classic cornfield flowers – poppies, ox-eye daisies and blue cornflowers – bring shimmering dots of colour to this summer wildflower meadow.

Buy seed from a seed merchant who produces native-grown stock if you can. Sow seed either direct (see right) or in pots or trays of moist soil-based seed compost such as John Innes No.1. Sow seeds thinly and cover with a fine layer of compost. Stand the containers in a coldframe or a sheltered spot outside, in which case cover the compost with a thin layer of horticultural grit. When the seedlings appear next spring, prick them out into trays; some seed may not germinate in its first year, so be patient.

raising wildflowers in pots

To increase the chances of success with perennial wildflowers, raise plants in pots of soil-based potting compost and do not plant them out until well established. Raising your plants from seed is the cheapest option, particularly for a large area, or you can buy plug plants and grow them on in containers for a couple of months. Established pot-grown plants can also be bought, ready to plant out straight away, but the larger the plant, the greater the cost.

Another way to get a wide selection of plants on a limited budget is to buy a couple of pot-grown specimens of each of your chosen wildflower variety and plant each one in a circle of bare soil. There is a good chance they will self-seed, in which case you can pot up the seedlings and grow them on for planting out in your meadow the following year.

Plant out established pot-grown plants in a meadow in autumn or

spring, when the growing conditions are likely to be ideal for quick establishment and there is little need for artificial watering. A bulb planter is the best tool for the job; short-handled models are fine for a small area, but a long-handled one is worth the extra money if you are planting on a large scale. You will also need some buckets of good garden soil for backfilling.

sowing a meadow direct

1 **Mix the fine seeds** with four times their volume of dry horticultural sand, to ensure accurate application and even distribution.

2 **Scatter the seeds evenly** on prepared ground. Then rake the earth very lightly to cover seeds with a thin layer of soil. Water during dry spells until the seeds germinate.

planting pot-grown wildflowers

1 **Using a bulb planter,** take out and discard a core of grass and soil.

2 **Knock the plant** out of its pot and place it in the hole so that the top of the rootball is level with the ground.

3 **Back-fill around the rootball** with garden soil, and water in thoroughly. Continue to water plants during dry weather.

building a deck

For outdoor sitting areas and walkways, timber decking has certain advantages over traditional paving materials – it is warmer underfoot, often looks more natural in an outdoor setting and is easier to tailor to your needs.

decking over paving

YOU WILL NEED • measuring tape
• pencil • panel or circular saw
• 7.5 x 5cm (3 x 2in) timber joists
• clear wood preservative • paintbrush
• cordless drill with twist drill bits
and screwdriver bits • 7.5cm (3in) and
6.3cm (2½in) zinc-plated countersunk
screws (decking screws can be bought)
• spirit level • 10cm (4in) masonry bolts
• packing materials, such as pieces of
wood or slate • string line • decking
boards (see Measuring up) • mitre saw
jig (optional) • decking sealer or stain
(optional)

2 **If you need** to secure the frame to a house wall, use 10cm (4in) masonry bolts.

1 **Cut the timber** into lengths to create the supporting framework. Brush cuts with preservative and butt together in position. Drill pilot holes, then secure each butt joint using two 7.5cm (3in) screws. Fix joists and any transverse bracing timbers in place. Check that the framework is square and level, with a slight fall for drainage.

3 **Fix the transverse joists** in position (see Measuring up box, opposite, for how to space them). Wedge packing material underneath any part of the frame that is unsupported due to unevenness in the existing paving.

TREATING CUT ENDS TIP Any cuts made in pressure-treated wood will expose untreated wood, so coat liberally with clear wood preservative before assembling.

4 **Cut the first decking board** to length and lay it in place across the supporting framework and transverse joists, aligning it with one long edge. To improve drainage and ensure even spacing between the boards, use nails or pieces of card to leave a 1–2mm (¹⁄₁₆in) gap between boards, removing and re-using them as you fix each board in place.

5 **Drill two pilot holes** through the board over every joist and every section of the outer framework. Use a string line to help you align the screws across the deck's width. Screw the board to the joists and frame using 6.3cm (2½in) screws. Cut the remaining boards, varying the lengths if you wish to stagger the ends, and fix in place in the same way.

You may have to cut the final board down in width to fit it in position. Set a circular saw to match the width required. If sawing by hand, clamp the board to your workbench and tackle a metre at a time. Get a helper to support the end of the board as you work your way along it. Fix to the frame in the usual way. Seal or stain the deck if desired.

measuring up

To work out the timber needed, measure the width and length of the paved area to be covered and plan the layout of the supporting framework on paper. You need to form a straight-sided frame round the perimeter and fix transverse joists across it – every 40cm (16in) if using 2.5cm (1in) thick decking boards, or every 60cm (2ft) for thicker boards. For joists over 3m (10ft) long, fix transverse braces every 2m (6ft) to prevent warping. Work out the number of joists you need to cover the area, and calculate the amount of timber you will need for the whole framework. For the decking boards, find out the width and length of the decking boards you are using, then calculate the number of boards you require.

decking basics

Decking is simply a suspended timber floor constructed outdoors (see Summer). It consists of a framework of load-bearing timber joists to which boards are fixed. The framework must be strong enough to support any load that is likely to be placed on the decking, including garden furniture and plant containers – as well as people.

The simplest type of deck is built directly on top of an existing area of paving – concrete, paving slabs or pavers – as long as this is flat and mainly level, with a very slight drainage slope away from the house. On sloping or uneven sites, the framework can be supported by vertical posts set into the ground, secured either with an in-ground concrete collar, like a fence post (see Autumn), or using a metal fence post spike. Separate sections of decking can be built in this way to create a terraced effect.

Raised decks higher than 1m (3ft) can provide a superb vantage point over the garden, but they need a more substantial supporting framework and have to be fitted with guard rails.

choosing materials

Hardwood is the most durable material for decking (see Summer), but it is very expensive for anything more than a small area. Softwood is cheaper, but must be treated with preservative to resist rot and insect attack. Pressure-treated timber, which has had the preservative forced deep into the wood, will last many years.

Decking boards in the form of planks are the most economical surface; use planed timber to avoid splinters. Many boards are available with a grooved profile, which improves rainwater drainage and provides a non-slip surface. Economy decking boards are machined from 10 x 2.5cm (4 x 1in) timber, but wider and/or thicker boards often look

You will need to conceal the edges of a deck's supporting framework. Measure and cut boards to fit, then fix them at 1m (3ft) intervals so the top edge is flush with the top of the decking. Lights are set into the edge of this deck (above).

better. These require fewer fixings and a less substantial supporting framework, so their higher price may be offset by savings on installation time and number of joists required. Prefabricated decking tiles and panels can also be bought.

Rustproof screws should be used throughout; nails will rust and spoil the look of the decking, and do not resist the natural warping that occurs with timber that is alternately drenched in rain and dried out by hot sun. A cordless drill or cordless screwdriver will drive the screws and countersink them in one operation. Otherwise you will need a countersink bit to ensure that the screw heads do not protrude. Lining up the screws across the width of the deck gives a neater finish; use a string line as a guide. Decking boards can be cut to make a pattern or varied in length, but cut ends must meet over a timber joist.

Timber for the framework should always be sawn, rather than planed, and treated with preservative. Use 7.5 x 5cm (3 x 2in) timber joists for a framework resting on solid ground. For a suspended structure, use 10 x 5cm (4 x 2in) or 15 x 5cm (6 x 2in) joists. Secure them to 7.5cm or 10cm (3 or 4in) square posts, using 13cm (5in) coach bolts.

dividers & windbreaks

Screens divide up a garden and are useful for hiding all those essential but unlovely items, such as sheds and compost bins. In exposed gardens they provide shelter for people and plants, creating permanent windbreaks around a seating area or a temporary shelter while plants establish.

garden screening

While boundary screens are usually chosen for privacy and security (see Autumn), this is rarely the case for screens within the garden. This means that a much wider choice of materials is available, from open trellis work to a temporary living screen for summer only, of sunflowers or jerusalem artichokes.

dividing up a larger garden

Large gardens always gain from being broken up in some way, to create a sense of perspective. Dividing a good-sized plot into separate areas, and at the same time creating some vistas, means that you can then design and plant each section to a different theme. Generally, the areas with a formal design should be close to the house, allowing the style to become more natural farther away. Screen informal areas with a palisade, simply made of wooden uprights cut to the same (or even varying) height, and set a few centimetres apart. Wide timber boards can be used in the same way, set either face on, or angled to give greater privacy from one direction. Remember that any timber screen can be treated with coloured wood stain to create a more decorative effect.

trellis dividers

Wooden trellis comes in styles and sizes to match virtually every garden and budget, from economical square trellis made of sawn softwood to stylish, much costlier diamond and lattice designs. Use one of the stains now available to colour-match the wood to planting schemes, or other garden woodwork. Trellis also comes in other materials such as wire, metal, bamboo and willow.

Consider first how much actual screening you require, as some types of trellis are much more open and 'see-through' than others. Choose a style that matches the overall design of your garden, such as a wirework or good-quality lattice timber trellis in a formal garden and woven willow or plain square trellis for a cottage-style plot.

windbreaks and screens

Garden dividers serve an important role as permanent windbreaks in an exposed garden, to create shelter for people and plants, perhaps around a patio or seating area. The best option is a permeable screen, which will filter the wind and create shelter more effectively than a solid barrier, such as a wall or dense hedge, where wind turbulence may build up on the lee side.

Versatile and quick to erect, trellis makes a good screen, here separating off a vegetable area planted with sweetcorn (above).

A living 'trellis' created from willow stems makes an open, see-through screen that suits an informal garden. Planted while dormant, the rods will sprout in spring, eventually fusing together at the top (right). It needs trimming several times a year.

For an immediate result, choose close-woven willow hurdles or trellis made using broad, closely spaced wood panels. But if you can wait a couple of years, choose standard trellis and cover it with climbing plants. (Take care not to choose over-vigorous climbers – they might eventually form such a top-heavy mass of foliage that the wind brings them down, together with the support.)

Hedges can be an excellent solution for the longer term in larger gardens. A hedge 1.5–2m (5–6ft) tall makes the best divider and windbreak. Keep the sides trimmed as well as the top, or it may occupy too much space. Suitable evergreen shrubs include golden privet (*Ligustrum ovalifolium* 'Aureum'), shrubby honeysuckle (*Lonicera nitida*), holly (*Ilex aquifolium*), yew (*Taxus baccata*) and western red cedar (*Thuja plicata* 'Atrovirens').

This evergreen hedge of *Lonicera nitida* creates a year-round divider, which also acts as a backdrop for plants (below). It needs clipping at least twice a year to keep its crisp outline.

creating a temporary windbreak

1 **After planting** an evergreen shrub in an exposed site, use a mallet or sledgehammer to drive in several strong stakes on the windward side, arranging them roughly in a semi-circle.

2 **Stretch woven plastic mesh** or special windbreak netting from one end to the other, round the outside of the stakes, and staple or tie it in place.

temporary windbreaks

Where a screen is required for only a short time, such as the duration of the summer, or until a hedge or border becomes established, you can opt for a cheaper and easier temporary divider. Rolls of single-thickness bamboo, willow stems or peeled reed make a quick, effective screen, or you can buy purpose-made plastic mesh (see above). These windbreaks are easily put up against a support of spaced fence posts, stapled to the posts themselves or attached to stout galvanised wire running between the posts. Screens like this may last three to five years, or possibly longer, before they start to deteriorate.

plants for summer screening

Tall, fast-growing annual or perennial plants can make a superb summer-only visual screen. Jerusalem artichoke (*Helianthus tuberosus*) is a tough, hardy perennial that grows to 3m (10ft) and can itself be used as a windbreak. Sunflowers (*Helianthus annuus*) are annuals that rapidly grow to well over 2m (6ft) from a spring sowing. Plume poppy (*Macleaya cordata*) may need staking; it grows to 2.1m (7ft), as does the grass *Miscanthus sacchariflorus*, but this is unsuitable for cold areas.

Summer screen of sunflowers (*Helianthus annuus*)

all-season index

This index covers all six seasonal volumes in the *All-Season Guide to Gardening*. It will help you to track a specific plant or subject through the year, as well as to locate specific information when you are unsure which volume to refer to. The page references are preceded by the volume title, according to the abbreviations in the following key:

ESp Early Spring
LSp Late Spring
Su Summer
LSu Late Summer
A Autumn
W Winter

For easy reference, the abbreviations are repeated at the top of each page. Throughout the index, page numbers in *italics* refer to illustrations and captions.

ALL-SEASON INDEX

ALL-SEASON INDEX

ALL-SEASON INDEX

acknowledgments

Photographs were supplied by the following people and organisations. Where relevant, the number of a picture as it appears on a page is given. Abbreviations are used as follows: t top, c centre, b bottom, l left, r right. MB Mark Bolton, CB Chris Burrows, HSC Harry Smith Collection, SC Sarah Cuttle, JD Jacqui Dracup, CF C Fairweather, GPL Garden Picture Library, JG John Glover, JH Jerry Harpur, MH Marcus Harpur, SH Sunniva Harte, NH Neil Holmes, AL Andrew Lawson, S&OM S & O Mathews, CN Clive Nichols, MN Mike Newton, PH Photos Horticultural, RD Reader's Digest, HR Howard Rice, MLS Mayer le Scanff, BT Brigitte Thomas, MT Maddie Thornhill, SSP Sea Spring Photos, JS J Sira, JW Jo Whitworth, MW Mark Winwood

Front cover Flowerphotos, photographer Carol Sharp Back cover tl SC, cl JW, tcr, tr & bl MW, bl JD 1 SC 2-3 GPL/HR 4-5 MB 8-9 RD 10 t GPL/MLS, bl GPL/HR, br GPL/JG 11 tl MH, tc GPL/JS, tr GPL/JG, b MH (Chiff Chaffs, Dorset) 12 r GPL/HR 13 t JH, bl MB, bc GPL/MB, bl CN 14 tl MB, tr GPL/BT, b MH 15 tl GPL/MB, tr GPL/SH, bl GPL/HR, br GPL/J Wade 16 tr GPL/M Howes, r GPL/BT, bl GPL/JG 17 tl GPL/R Hyam, tr JH, c CN, b JH 18 l CN, r GPL/MLS 19 tl GPL/JG, tr GPL/J Wade, bl GPL/M Howes, bc CN, br MB 20 tl MB, tr HSC, b MW 21 l AL, tr CN, br JH 22 M Brigdale 24 l SC, r MW 25 tl, tc & tr MW, b SC 26 MW 27 tl & b MW, tr GPL/D Cavagnaro 28 SC 29 MW 30 l SC, c & r MW 31 t MW, cl, cr, bl & br SC 32 t & c MW, b SC, 33 tl & c SC, tr & b MW 34 l MW, r SC 35 SC 36 tl SC, tr MW, b JW 37 MW 38 l SC, r RD 39 tl MW, tr HSC, bl & br MW 40 tl, tr & c MW, b JW 41 t MW, b SC 42 l JW, r S&OM 43 t MW, cl, cr, c inset & br SC, bl RD 44 tl SC, bl, bcl, bcl inset & bcr MW, br MB 45 tl, tc, bl & bc SC, tr & br MW 46 t MW, c SC, b HSC 47 SC 48 MW 49 tl & tr SC, bl, bc & br MW 50 l & r SC, bc SC 51 l SC, r MB (Design: Bob Purnell) 52-3 MW 54 MT 55-58 MW 59 tl, tc, bl, bc & br MW, tr SSP 60 l SC, tr MT, bl MW, br SC 61 tl MW, tc MW, tr SC, c MW, b SC 62 l MT, c & r MW 63-64 MW 65 tl, tr, bl & bc MW, br SC 66-7 MW 68-9 all SC except bl & br MW 70 t SC, bl & br MW 71 MW 72 tl & b SC, tr MW 73 tl, tr & cl SC, c, cr & br MW 74-5 HSC 76-7 (1) GPL/MLS, (2, 10, 11) RD, (3) AL, (4 & 5) JW, (6) GPL/MLS, (7) S&OM, (8) GPL/NH, (9) GPL/R Butcher 78-9 (1) GPL/JG, (2) GPL/HR, (3) GPL/MLS, (4, 7, 11) JW, (5) GPL/NH, (6) HSC, (8) RD, (9) GPL/SH, (10) PH 80 (1) JW, (2, 4, 5, 8) S&OM, (3) RD, (6) HSC, (7) SC 81 (1) Colegrave Seeds Ltd, (2) HSC, (3) A-Z Botanical, (4) GPL/HR, (5) GPL/JG 82-3 (1, 5) HSC, (2) GPL/JS, (3, 7, 9) RD, (4) MB, (6) MB, (8) S&OM, (10) GPL/JS, (11) GPL/SH 84-5 (1, 2, 3, 8, 11, 12) RD, (4) MB, (5) GPL/A l Lord, (6) GPL/B Carter, (7) S&OM, (9) GPL/JG, (10) HSC 86-7 (1,10) GPL/CB, (2, 4, 6, 9) RD, (3) GPL/NH, (5) HSC, (7) GPL/JG,

(8) GPL/SH, (11) SC 88-9 (1) RD, (2, 3, 4, 9,12) MB, (5) GPL/P Bonduell, (7) GPL/NH, (6, 8, 10) HSC, (11) GPL/CB 90 (1) GPL/J Beedle, (2, 6) PH, (3) GPL/JG, (4) RD, (5) GPL/CB, (7) GPL/B Challinor, (8) GPL/E Rooney 91 (1) PH, (2) HSC, (3) GPL/E Crichton, (4) GPL/JG, (5) AL, (6) MW 92-3 (1) GPL/JG, (2) GPL/S Wooster, (3) HSC, (4) GPL/R White, (5, 9) GPL/CF, (6) GPL/JG, (7, 8, 10, 11) JW, (12) HSC 94-5 (1) GPL/Lamontagne, (2, 5, 7) HSC, (3) GPL/HR, (4, 6, 9, 10) JW, (8) GPL/NH, (11) RD, (12) JD 96-7 (1) HSC, (2, 7) JW, (3) GPL/D Willery, (4, 5, 8, 9) RD, (6) S&OM, (10, 11) GPL/JS 98-9 (1, 9, 10) JW, (2, 11) HSC, (3, 4, 5) RD, (6) S&OM, (7) GPL/HR, (8) PH, (12) JD 100-101 (1, 3, 6) RD, (2, 4, 5, 7, 10) JD, (8, 11) HSC, (9, 12) GPL/JG 102-103 (1) GPL/D England, (2, 3, 4, 12) JD, (5) GPL/J Hurst, (6) GPL/R Butcher, (7, 8) RD, (9) A-Z Botanical, (10) HSC, (11) GPL/BT 104 (1, 2, 3, 7, 8) JD, (4) S&OM, (5) JD, (6) HSC 105 (1, 2) RD, (3, 5) GPL/JG, (4) GPL/R Hyam, (6) HSC 106-107 (1) MB, (2) HSC, (3, 6) GPL/JG, (4) RD, (5, 10) HSC, (7, 11, 12) JD, (8) GPL/NH, (9) GPL/HR 108 (1) JD, (2, 5) HSC, (3) GPL/HR, (4) GPL/J Pavia, (6) RD 109 (1) GPL/JG, (2) GPL/P Bonduel, (3) A-Z Botanical, (4, 5) S&OM 110-111 (1, 2, 4, 6, 7, 8, 9, 10) MT, (3) GPL/J Pavia, (5) MW 112-113 (1, 11) SSP, (2, 3, 6, 7, 8, 9, 10) MT, (4, 5, 12) MN 114-15 (1) GPL/JP, (2, 5, 11) HSC, (3, 10) GPL/CF, (4) S&OM, (6) GPL/HR, (7, 8) RD, (9) GPL/JS 116-117 (1, 2, 9) JD, (3) GPL/JG, (4, 11) HSC, (5, 8, 10) RD, (6) PH, (7) GPL/JP 118 l SC, c MB, r GPL/JG 119 l RD, r GPL/JG 120 l RD, r GPL/NH 121 l JW, r GPL/HR 122-3 MW 124 SC 125 t & br MW, bl SC 126 all MW 127 tl, tr, bl & bcl MW, bcr & br SC 128 SC 129 t, bc & br SC, bl MN 130 t MW, c & b SC 131 MW 132 SC 133 tl & tr SC, br MW 134 t SC, b MW 135 SC 136-7 SC 138 tl AL, bl CN, br SC 139 tl MB, tr CN (Welbeck), b GPL/F Strauss 140-1 SC 142 MB (Chelsea Flower Show 2000 – Alpine Garden Society) 143 MW 144 bl, bcl & bcr MW, br AL 146 MB (Design: A Swithinbank) 147 l MB (Design: M Martin, St.Dominics, Cornwall), r AL 148 GPL/G Dann 149 SC 150 SC 151 tl SC, tr CN (Design: S Layton) 152 bl MB, br CN 153 tc & tr SC, bl GPL/JG, br CN

Illustration on page 145 by Ian Sidaway.
Front cover: Narcissus. Back cover, clockwise from top left: an assortment of vegetable seeds; Primula vulgaris; thinning out seedlings; aerating a lawn; Chaenomeles speciosa 'Nivalis'; emerging blue hyacinths

Amazon Publishing would like to thank Adrian Hall Garden Centres and, for supplying tools shown on pages 124–129, Bulldog Tools and Burgon & Ball Ltd. Thanks also to the following, who allowed us to use their gardens for photography: Andi and Meg Clevely, Bridget Heal, Alison Shackleton and Capel Manor Limited. We are grateful to David Murphy for help with the projects.

Early Spring is part of a series of gardening books called the All-Season Guide to Gardening. It was created for Reader's Digest by Amazon Publishing Limited.

Series Editor Carole McGlynn
Art Director Ruth Prentice

Editors Barbara Haynes, Jackie Matthews, Alison Freegard; also Norma MacMillan
Design Jo Grey
Photographic art direction Ruth Prentice
Special photography Sarah Cuttle, Mark Winwood
Writers Steve Bradley, Andi Clevely, Sue Fisher, David Joyce, Mike Lawrence, Anne Swithinbank
Picture research Clare Limpus, Mel Watson, Sarah Wilson
Consultants Jonathan Edwards, Mike Lawrence
DTP Felix Gannon
Editorial Assistant Elizabeth Woodland
Indexer Hilary Bird

FOR READER'S DIGEST
Project Editor Christine Noble
Pre-press Accounts Manager Penny Grose

READER'S DIGEST GENERAL BOOKS
Editorial Director Cortina Butler
Art Director Nick Clark

First Edition Copyright © 2003
The Reader's Digest Association Limited,
11 Westferry Circus, Canary Wharf,
London E14 4HE
www.readersdigest.co.uk
Reprinted with amendments 2003

Copyright © 2003 Reader's Digest Association Far East Limited
Philippines copyright © 2003 Reader's Digest Association Far East Limited

We are committed to both the quality of our products and the service we provide to our customers. We value your comments, so please feel free to contact us on 08705 113366, or via our website at www.readersdigest.co.uk If you have any comments about the content of our books, you can email us at gbeditorial@readersdigest.co.uk

Origination Colour Systems Limited, London
Printed and bound in Europe by Arvato Iberia

ISBN 0 276 42713 0
BOOK CODE 621-006-2
CONCEPT CODE UK0087